Lecture Notes in Computer Science   2545
Edited by G. Goos, J. Hartmanis, and J. van Leeuwen

T0233038

Springer
Berlin
Heidelberg
New York
Barcelona
Hong Kong
London
Milan
Paris
Tokyo

Peter Forbrig   Quentin Limbourg
Bodo Urban   Jean Vanderdonckt (Eds.)

Interactive Systems

Design, Specification, and Verification

9th International Workshop, DSV-IS 2002
Rostock, Germany, June 12-14, 2002
Revised Papers

 Springer

Series Editors

Volume Editors

Peter Forbrig
Universität Rostock
Fachbereich Informatik
Albert-Einstein-Str. 21, 18051 Rostock, Germany
E-mail: Peter.Forbrig@informatik.uni-rostock.de

Quentin Limbourg
Jean Vanderdonckt
Université catholique de Louvain (UCL)
Faculty of Economical, Social and Political Sciences (ESPO)
School of Management (IAG), Information Systems Unit (ISYS)
Place des Doyens, 1, 1348 Louvain-La-Neuve, Belgium
E-mail: {vanderdonckt/limbourg}@isys.ucl.ac.be

Bodo Urban
Fraunhofer-Institut für Graphische Datenverarbeitung
Joachim-Jungius-Str. 11, 18059 Rostock, Germany
E-mail: Bodo.Urban@rostock.igd.fhg.de

Cataloging-in-Publication Data applied for

A catalog record for this book is available from the Library of Congress.

Bibliographic information published by Die Deutsche Bibliothek
Die Deutsche Bibliothek lists this publication in the Deutsche Nationalbibliografie;
detailed bibliographic data is available in the Internet at http://dnb.ddb.de

CR Subject Classification (1998): H.5.2, H.5, I.3, D.2, F.3

ISSN 0302-9743
ISBN 3-540-00266-9 Springer-Verlag Berlin Heidelberg New York

This work is subject to copyright. All rights are reserved, whether the whole or part of the material is
concerned, specifically the rights of translation, reprinting, re-use of illustrations, recitation, broadcasting,
reproduction on microfilms or in any other way, and storage in data banks. Duplication of this publication
or parts thereof is permitted only under the provisions of the German Copyright Law of September 9, 1965,
in its current version, and permission for use must always be obtained from Springer-Verlag. Violations are
liable for prosecution under the German Copyright Law.

Springer-Verlag Berlin Heidelberg New York
a member of BertelsmannSpringer Science+Business Media GmbH

http://www.springer.de

© Springer-Verlag Berlin Heidelberg 2002
Printed in Germany

Typesetting: Camera-ready by author, data conversion by PTP Berlin, Stefan Sossna e. K.
Printed on acid-free paper   SPIN 10871649   06/3142   5 4 3 2 1 0

Preface

Design, Specification, and Verification of Interactive Systems (DSV-IS) is the annual meeting of the human-computer interaction community interested in all aspects of the design, specification, and verification of interactive systems. It serves as the principal international forum for reporting outstanding research, development, and industrial experience in this area. The 9th DSV-IS workshop will provide a forum for the exchange of ideas on diverse approaches to the design and implementation of interactive systems. The particular focus of this year's event is on models and their role in supporting the design and development of interactive systems for ubiquitous computing. Usability of interactive systems for ubiquitous computing is a key factor of future software developments. The challenge in user interface development is no longer to implement a single (stationary) user interface from specification but rather to enable user interfaces for a wide variety of devices (e.g., mobile devices, cellular phones, PDAs, pocket PCs, handheld PCs, ...) and multimodal input channels. In addition, deploying the same user interface across a wide variety of devices, appliances, and platforms raises the question of how to factor out common interaction components and patterns across the different instances of the user interface, while preserving (some) consistency. Rather than reproducing the same parts on different platforms, common bricks and blocks might be used. Some platforms are well suited for certain interactive tasks, while others are not at all able to support them. This edition is dedicated to all forms of patterns involved in human-computer interaction: cross platform, design, globalization, mobility, ubiquity, and usability.

June 2002

Peter Forbrig,
Quentin Limbourg,
Jean Vanderdonckt,
Bodo Urban
DSV-IS 2002 Proceedings co-editors

Organization

DSV-IS 2002 is jointly organized by the Department of Computer Science, University of Rostock (Germany) and the School of Management (IAG), Université catholique de Louvain (Belgium).

Program Committee

Conference Chair: Peter Forbrig (University of Rostock, Germany)
Conference Co-chair: Bodo Urban (Fraunhofer Institute for Computer Graphics, Germany)
Program Chair: Jean Vanderdonckt (Université catholique de Louvain, Belgium)
Organizing Chair: Peter Forbrig (University of Rostock, Germany)
Proceedings Coordinator: Quentin Limbourg (Université catholique de Louvain, Belgium)

Scientific Committee

Ghassan Al-Qaimari, Royal Melbourne Institute of Technology, Australia
Gilbert Cockton, University of Sunderland, United Kingdom
Joëlle Coutaz, University Joseph Fourier, CLIPS-IMAG Lab., Grenoble, France
Alan Dix, Lancaster University, United Kingdom
David Duce, Oxford Brookes University, United Kingdom
Ulrich Eisenecker, University of Applied Sciences, Kaiserslautern, Germany
Giorgio Faconti, CNUCE-CNR, Italy
Peter Forbrig, University of Rostock, Germany
Nick Graham, Queen's University, Canada
Richard Griffiths, University of Brighton, United Kingdom
Phil Gray, University of Glasgow, Scotland
Jan Gulliksen, University of Uppsala, Sweden
Michael Harrison, University of York, United Kingdom
Michael Herczeg, University of Lübeck, Germany
Michael Holloway, NASA Langley Research Center, USA
Chris Johnson, University of Glasgow, Scotland
Peter Johnson, University of Bath, United Kingdom
Thomas Kirste, Fraunhofer Institute for Computer Graphics, Rostock, Germany
Panos Markopoulos, Technische Universiteit Eindhoven, The Netherlands
Christian Märtin, Augsburg University of Applied Sciences, Germany
Miguel Gea Megías, University of Granada, Spain
Erik G. Nilsson, SINTEF, Norway
Dan Olsen, Brigham Young University, USA

Philippe Palanque, LIIHS-IRIT, Université Paul Sabatier (Toulouse 3), France
Fabio Paternò, CNUCE-CNR, Italy
Angel Puerta, RedWhale Software Corp., USA
Matthias Rauterberg, Technical University of Eindhoven, The Netherlands
Kevin Schneider, University of Saskatchewan, Canada
Ahmed Seffah, Concordia University, Montreal, Canada
Pavel Slavik, Czech Technical University, Prague, Czech Republic
Chris Stary, University of Linz, Austria
Gerd Szwillus, University of Paderborn, Germany
Michael Tauber, University of Paderborn, Germany
Manfred Tsheligi, Center for Usability Research and Engineering, Austria
Bodo Urban, Fraunhofer Institute for Computer Graphics, Rostock, Germany
Martijn van Welie, Satama Interactive, Amsterdam, The Netherlands
Jean Vanderdonckt, Université catholique de Louvain, Belgium

Sponsoring Institutions

Eurographics, Geneva, Switzerland
Gesellschaft für Informatik, Rostock, Germany
INI-GraphicsNet, Germany
Institut d'Administration et de Gestion, Louvain-la-Neuve, Belgium
Institut Graphische Datenverarbeitung, Germany
Université catholique de Louvain, Louvain-la-Neuve, Belgium
University of Rostock, Rostock, Germany

Table of Contents

From a Formal User Model to Design Rules

Paul Curzon[1] and Ann Blandford[2]

[1] Middlesex University, Interaction Design Centre, Bramley Road, London N14 4YZ
[2] University College London Interaction Centre, 26 Bedford Way,
London WC1H 0AP
p.curzon@mdx.ac.uk, a.blandford@ucl.ac.uk

Abstract. Design rules sometimes seem to contradict. We examine how a formal description of user behaviour can help explain the context when such rules are, or are not, applicable. We describe how they can be justified from a formally specified generic user model. This model was developed by formalising cognitively plausible behaviour, based on results from cognitive psychology. We examine how various classes of erroneous actions emerge from the underlying model. Our lightweight semi-formal reasoning from the user model makes predictions that could be used as the basis for further usability studies. Although the user model is very simple, a range of error patterns and design principles emerge.

1 Introduction

With the increasing ubiquity of interactive computer systems, usability becomes increasingly important. Minor usability problems can scale to having major economic and social consequences. Usability of interactive designs has many aspects. In this paper, we focus on design principles that reduce the potential for "user error" occurring. We examine how, from the behaviour specified by a simple formal model of cognition, various potential erroneous actions emerge with poorly designed systems. Furthermore, we derive well-known design rules from the model. We use the fact that the rules are grounded in a formal model of cognition to explore the scope of application of the rules. Formal specification allows precision about the meaning of that which is formalised. Providing such precision to ensure different people have the same understanding of a concept has been suggested as the major benefit of formal models in interaction design [1]. One approach would be to formalise the design rules themselves (see [1,14]). Here, we semi-formally derive design rules from a formal model rather than just asserting them. In principle, formal derivations could also be done. By "semi-formal" we mean that we use informal high-level argument (about a fully formal model), as opposed to the explicit application of inference rules of the underlying logic.

We first define simple **principles of cognition**. These are principles that generalise the way humans act in terms of the mental attributes of knowledge, tasks and goals. The principles considered do not cover the full range of human cognition. Rather they focus on particular aspects of cognitive behaviour. They are each backed up by evidence from HCI and psychology studies. Those presented are not intended to be complete but to demonstrate the approach.

P. Forbrig et al. (Eds.): DSV-IS 2002, LNCS 2545, pp. 1–15, 2002.
© Springer-Verlag Berlin Heidelberg 2002

We have developed a **formal model** of these principles written in higher-order logic. This description is a generic formal user model. By "generic" we mean that it can be targeted to different tasks and interactive systems. The underlying principles of cognition are formalised once in the model, rather than having to be re-formalised for each new task or system of interest. Whilst higher-order logic is not essential for this, its use makes the formal specifications simpler and more natural than the use of a first-order logic would. Here we use it to make precise the general principles considered, to allow us to then reason about their consequences with respect to user error. Combining the principles of cognition into a single model rather than formalising them separately allows reasoning about their interaction, and about how multiple minor errors might interact.

The principles, and more formally the user model, specify **cognitively plausible behaviour** (see [5]). That is, they specify possible traces of user actions that can be justified in terms of the specific principles. Of course users might also act outside this behaviour, about which situations the model says nothing. Its predictive power is bounded by the situations where people act according to the principles specified. That does not preclude useful results from being obtained, provided their scope is remembered. The model allows us to investigate what happens if a person does act in such plausible ways. The behaviour defined is neither "correct" nor "incorrect". It could be either depending on the environment and task in question. It is, rather, "likely" behaviour.

We show how cognitively plausible behaviour can in specific circumstances be considered as resulting in **erroneous actions**. We discuss the circumstances in which such erroneous actions can result, reasoning from the formal model. In particular, we relate them to Hollnagel's error phenotypes [11]. In doing so, we identify cognitively plausible ways in which the erroneous actions could arise. We show that a wide variety are covered from even a minimal formal definition of cognitively plausible behaviour, demonstrating the generality of the approach.

Finally, we semi-formally derive **design rules** from the formal model that, if followed, ensure that the erroneous actions identified will not be made for the specific cognitive reasons embodied by the principles of cognition. Even though the user model is capable of making the errors, the rules ensure that the environments in which they would emerge do not occur. Other errors are, of course, still possible. The design rules are well known and our contribution is not the rules themselves, but rather the demonstration that they can be justified from a formalisation of a small set of principles. Because the design rules are derived, we can be precise about their scope of applicability, for example unpacking the situations where different design rules appear at first sight to be contradictory.

We use railway ticket vending machines to illustrate the points. They are ubiquitous and are increasingly replacing manned ticket offices. However, existing designs continue to exhibit design problems that encourage user error [16]. Previous work explored how the user model considered here could be used to analyse interactive system designs by treating it as a component of that system with a fixed design [7,8], proving that a specific task will always be completed eventually. This was done using an interactive proof system, HOL [10]. Here we use the user model as the basis of reasoning about interactive systems in general. The process of doing so also acts, in part, to validate the model for formal verification. Our approach is similar to that of [2] in that we are working from a (albeit different and more formal) model of user behaviour to high level guidance. There the emphasis is on a semi-formal basis underpinning the craft skill in spotting when a design has usability problems. In contrast, we are concerned with guidance for a designer rather than for a usability analyst.

2   Formalising Cognitively Plausible Behaviour

Our user model was developed by formally modelling principles of cognitively plausible behaviour. We do not model erroneous actions explicitly (as is done for example in [9]). Instead, they emerge from an abstract description of cognitively plausible behaviour. The behaviour described could correspond to correct or incorrect actions being taken depending on the circumstances. The principles considered are: non-determinism; goal-based termination; task-based termination; reactive behaviour; communication goals; mental triggers; no-option-based termination; and relevance. This list is not intended to be exhaustive, but to cover a variety of classes of cognitive principles, based on the motor system, simple knowledge based cognition, goal-based cognition, etc. Also, some of the principles are formalised in a simple way, our intention at this stage being to test the approach, rather than modelling the full richness of the principles. In future work we will increase the richness of the descriptions. In subsequent sections we refer to cognitively plausible behaviour when strictly meaning the subset of cognitively plausible behaviour embedded in the current version of our model.

By modelling the principles we are giving a knowledge level description in the terms of Newell [12]. We do not attempt to model underlying neural architecture nor the higher level cognitive architecture such as working memory units. Instead our model is that of an abstract specification, intended for ease of reasoning. The focus of the description is in terms of internal goals and knowledge of a user. This contrasts with a description of a user's actions as, say, a finite state machine that makes no mention of such cognitive attributes.

The user model is based on a series of non-deterministic temporally guarded action rules. Each describes an action that a user could rationally make. The rules are grouped corresponding to the user performing actions for specific cognitively related reasons. Each such group then has a single generic description. Each rule has a guard-action form. They state that if the guard holds at some point then the NEXT action taken by the user is that given. By next in this context we mean the first action of interest taken by the user after the current point in time. The rules each have the form: guard t AND NEXT actions action t, stating that a guard is true at time t and the NEXT action performed from the list of actions relevant to the interaction (given by the list actions) is action. The action is identified by its position in the list of all actions. Here we give an overview; the formalisation is given in more detail in [8].

Non-determinism: In any situation, any one of several behaviours that are plausible might be taken. The separate behaviours are specified as rules. Each rule is formalised in the user model non-deterministically. That is, it is one of a series of options, any of which could be taken. The model does not assert that a rule will be followed, just that it may be followed. Below, we present the formalisation of several such rules. They form the core of the user model. By combining them, the model asserts that the behaviour of any rule whose guards are true at a point in time is cognitively plausible at that time. It cannot be assumed that any specific rule will be the one that the person will follow.

Goal-based termination behaviour: Cognitive psychology studies have shown that users intermittently, but persistently, terminate interactions as soon as their goal has been achieved [6]. It is formalised as a guarded rule as described above. We must supply a relation to the user model that indicates over time whether the goal is achieved or not. This is referred to as a special signal, goalachieved, in the formal definitions. We also use a special signal, finished, to indicate whether the user considers the interaction to be over. With a ticket machine this may correspond to the person walking away, starting a new interaction (perhaps by hitting a reset button), etc. Both goalachieved and finished are signals that, given a time, return a boolean value indicating whether the goal is achieved or the interaction terminated (respectively) at that time. If the goal is achieved at a time then the user model terminates the interaction next: goalachieved t AND NEXT actions finished t. Note that goalachieved is a higher-order function and can as such represent an arbitrarily complex condition. It might, for example, be that the user has a particular object, that the count of some series of objects is greater than some number or a combination of such atomic conditions. In specifying the user model we just state that it is a boolean function whose value may vary over time. This makes use of the higher-order nature of the specification language.

Task-based termination behaviour: For the purposes of analysis, the model specifies that a user will terminate an interaction when their whole task is achieved. In achieving a goal, subsidiary tasks are often generated. For the user to complete the task associated with their goal they must also complete all subsidiary tasks. Examples of such tasks with respect to a ticket machine include taking back a credit card or taking change [6]. One way to specify these tasks would be to explicitly describe each such task. Instead we use the more general concept of an interaction invariant [8]. The underlying reason why these tasks must be performed is that in interacting with the system some part of the state must be temporarily perturbed in order to achieve the desired task. Before the interaction is completed such perturbations must be undone. For example, to pay at a ticket machine using a credit card requires the card being inserted and later returned. A condition on the state that holds at the start of the interaction – that the user has the card – must be restored by the end. We specify the need to perform these completion tasks indirectly by supplying the interaction invariant as a higher-order argument to the user model. The interaction invariant is an invariant in a similar sense to a loop invariant in program verification. It is an invariant at the level of abstraction of whole interactions. Full task completion involves not only completing the user's goal, but also restoring the invariant by completing all the subsidiary tasks generated in the process. For a ticket machine the invariant might specify that the value of a person's possessions at the end is at least as high as it was at the start of the interaction.

We assume that on completing the task in this sense of goal achieved and invariant restored, the interaction will be considered terminated by the user, irrespective of any other possible actions apart from actions already mentally triggered (discussed below). This is modelled using an if construct rather than disjunction to give it priority. If both the goal has been achieved and the invariant restored then the user will terminate the interaction, irrespective of what other non-deterministic rules may potentially be active. Otherwise one of the non-deterministic rules will be fired.

```
IF (invariant t) AND (goalachieved t) THEN NEXT actions finished t
                                    ELSE non-deterministic rules
```

Reactive behaviour: A user may react to a stimulus or message from a device, doing the action suggested by the stimulus. For example, if a flashing light comes on next to the coin slot of a ticket vending machine, a user might, if the light is noticed, react by inserting coins if it appears to help the user achieve their goal. Reactive behaviour is specified as a general class of behaviour: in a given interaction there may be many different stimuli to react to. Rather than specify this class of behaviour for each, we define the behaviour generically. REACT gives the rule defining what it means to react to a given stimulus.

```
REACT as stimulus action t = stimulus t AND NEXT as action t
```

If at time t, the specified **stimulus** is active, the NEXT action taken by the user out of the possible actions, **actions**, at an unspecified later time, may be **action**. As there may be a range of signals designed to be reactive, the user model is supplied with a list of stimulus-action pairs: $[(s1, a1); \ldots (sn, an)]$. A list recursive relation, given a list of such pairs, extracts the components and asserts the above rule about them. They are combined using disjunction in the recursive definition, so are non-deterministic choices, and this definition is combined with the other non-deterministic rules. Grd and Act extract a pair's components. "s :: st" refers to the list with first element s and remainder of list st.

```
(REACTS as [] t = FALSE) AND
(REACTS as (s :: st) t =
   ((REACTS as st t) OR (REACT as (Grd s) (Act s) t)))
```

Communication goal behaviour: A user enters an interaction with knowledge of task dependent sub-goals that must be discharged. Given the opportunity, they may attempt to discharge any such communication goals [3]. The precise nature of the action associated with the communication goal may not be known in advance. A communication goal specification is a task level partial plan. It is a pre-determined plan that has arisen from knowledge of the task in hand independent of the environment in which that task will be accomplished. It is not a fully specified plan, in that no order of the corresponding actions may be specified. In the sense of [3] a communication goal is purely about information communication. Here we use the idea more generally to include other actions that are known to be necessary to complete a task. For example, when purchasing a ticket, in some way the destination and ticket type must be specified as well as payment made. The way that these must be done and their order may not be known in advance. However, a person enters an interaction with the aim of purchasing a ticket primed for these communication goals to be addressed. If the person sees an apparent opportunity to discharge a communication goal they may do so. Once they have done so they will not expect to need to do so again. No fixed order is assumed over how communication goals will be discharged if their discharge is apparently possible. For example, if a "return ticket" button is visible then the person may press that first if that is what they see first. If a button with their destination is visible then they may press it first. Communication goals are a reason why people do not just follow instructions.

Communication goals are modelled as guard-action pairs as for reactive signals. The guard describes the situation under which the discharge of the communication goal appears possible. It will include a label signal indicating that the input exists and that it corresponds to the desired action. In the current version of the model, the use of a special label signal is not built into the generic model but is included as part of the guard by convention. As for reactive behaviour, a list of (guard, action) pairs is supplied to correspond to each communication goal. A similar recursive definition to REACTIVE above is defined and included as a disjunct with the non-deterministic rules. This determines when a communication goal may be discharged. However, unlike the reactive signal list that does not change through an interaction, communication goals are discharged. This corresponds to them disappearing from the user's mental list of intentions. We model this by removing them from the communication goal list when done. A daemon, separate from the non-deterministic rules, does this. It monitors the actions taken by the user on each cycle, removing any from the list used for the subsequent cycle. The action removed may be taken for some reason other than it being a communication goal, such as due to reactive behaviour. All that matters to the daemon is that it is taken. The communication goal list that a user enters the interaction with initially is provided as an argument to the user model.

Mental triggers: A user commits to taking an action in a way that cannot be revoked after a certain point. Once a signal has been sent from the brain to the motor system to take an action, the signal cannot be stopped even if the person becomes aware that it is wrong before the action is taken. Rather than associate an external stimulus directly with an external action using the disjunctive rules, we associate them with mental "actions" that trigger the process of taking the actual action. Thus the actions in each of the rules described so far will not be externally visible actions, but internal mental actions. For example, on deciding to press a button labelled with the destination "Liverpool", at the point when the decision is made the mental trigger action takes place and after a very short delay, the actual action takes place. A further category of trigger rules is then introduced that links the mental decision to the actual action. If one of the mental actions is taken on a cycle then the next action will be the externally visible action it triggers. There is always at least a one-cycle delay between the trigger and external action. A recursive function combines a list of triggers into a series of choices as with the reactive rules. The user model must be supplied with a guard-action pair list linking mental triggers with external actions. As with task-based termination, mental triggers are given a higher priority than the non-deterministic rules. If a trigger is fired then it will be the next action taken. Only if no fired trigger is outstanding do the other rules come into play, including task-based termination.

No-option-based termination behaviour: A user may terminate an interaction when there is no apparent action they can take that would help complete the task. For example, if on a touch screen ticket machine, the user wishes to buy a weekly season ticket, but the options presented include nothing about season tickets, then the person might give up, assuming their goal is not achievable. The model includes a final default non-deterministic rule that models this case. The guard to this rule is constructed automatically in the model from the information supplied to create the other rules. In practice, in this situation, people could behave in a range of ways including pressing buttons at random. Our model treats a situation where no "rational" action is available as resulting in the interaction terminating – even if a possible action may become possible in the future. Note that a possible action that a person could take is to wait. However, they will only do so given some reason – that is, it must be an action in an explicit reactive rule. For example, a ticket machine might display a message "Please Wait". If they see it, the person reacts by waiting.

Relevance: A user will only take an action if there is something to suggest it corresponds to the desired effect. We do not currently model this explicitly: however, it is implicit in most of the rules. For example, communication goals and the termination rules are by definition only fired when relevant. In particular, the "label" signals referred to above are intended to address aspects of relevance. A button for the destination "Liverpool" is modelled by one signal representing whether the button is visible/relevant at a given time and a second about whether the button is pressed at each time instance.

Putting it together: The core rules are combined with other house keeping rules (most notably, the communication goal filtering daemon) and a model of possessions that specifies, for example, that a user ceases to have a possession if it is given up. We omit the details here due to space constraints. A further clause added to the model is the initial conditions – notably the initial communication goal list. These are all combined using conjunction into a single relation USER that models the full user model. It takes as arguments the various pieces of information such as the goal, interaction invariant, list of actions, etc. referred to in the description above.

3   The Erroneous Actions That Emerge

Erroneous actions are the proximate cause of failure attributed to human error in the sense that it was a particular action (or inaction) that immediately caused the problem: users pressing a button at the wrong time, for example. However, to understand the problem, and so ensure it does not happen again, approaches that consider the proximate causes alone are insufficient. It is important to consider why the person took that action. The ultimate causes can have many sources. Here we consider situations where the ultimate causes of an error are that limitations of human cognition have not been addressed in the design. An example might be that the person pressed the button at that moment because their knowledge of the task suggested it sensible. Hollnagel [11] distinguishes between human error **phenotypes** (classes of erroneous actions) and **genotypes** (the underlying psychological cause). He identifies a range of simple phenotypes: repetition of an action, reversing the order of actions, omission of actions, late actions, early actions, replacement of one action by another, insertion of an additional action from elsewhere in the task, and intrusion of an additional action unrelated to the task. These are single deviations from required behaviour.

In practical designs it is generally infeasible to make erroneous actions impossible. Fields [9] uses model-checking to identify errors by introducing the above problems explicitly into task specifications. A problem with this approach is that it gives many false negatives: few tasks are possible if such errors are arbitrarily made. The verifier must determine which are real problems. A definition of what is cognitively plausible is one way to make this judgement. A more appropriate aim is therefore to ensure that cognitively plausible erroneous actions are not made. To ensure this, it is necessary to consider the genotypes of the possible erroneous actions. We examine how our simple user model can exhibit behaviour corresponding to these errors. We thus show, based on reasoning about the formal model, that, from the minimal principles we started with, a wide range of classes of erroneous actions in the form of phenotypes occur.

We now look at each simple phenotype and at the situations where they are cognitively plausible. We do not claim to model all cognitively plausible phenotypical actions. There are other ways each could occur for reasons we do not consider. However, not all errors that result from the model were explicitly considered when the principles were defined. The scope of the model in terms of erroneous actions is wider than those it was originally expected to encompass.

Repetition of actions: The first class of erroneous action is to repeat an action already performed. There are situations where this is cognitively plausible according to our user model. The current user model will repeat actions if guided to do so by the device in a reactive manner. If the guards of an action remain true then the user model may follow those instructions a second time since there is nothing in the model to prevent this. If the guidance is erroneous then the user model will make an erroneous action. Occasions where an interactive device asks erroneously for an action that has already been performed are perhaps rare (and it might be argued that in this situation the action was correct but the device incorrect). However, one way it could occur is due to a lack of feedback to indicate the action was performed successfully. The current user model would do this if reactive signals guided the action and continued to do so after the action had been completed. In particular, with a ticket machine, if a light next to a coin slot continued to flash for a period after the correct money had been inserted a person might assume they had not inserted enough and start to insert more. An action originally performed as a communication goal could be repeated if a reactive prompt to do so later appeared (though not the other way round since once performed reactively the action is removed as a communication goal). For example, if a person pressed the button for "Liverpool" and was later presented with a screen asking them to select a destination they might do so again.

Reversing the order of actions: A second class of error is to reverse the order of two actions. This pattern of behaviour can arise from our model as a result of the way communication goals are modelled. In particular, communication goals can be discharged by the user model in any order. Therefore, if an interactive system requires a particular sequence, then the order may be erroneously reversed by the user model if the actions correspond to communication goals. A person might insert money and then press the destination button when a particular ticket machine requires the money to be inserted second. This does not apply to non-communication goal actions, however. For example, two actions that are device dependent (pressing a confirmation button and one to release change, for example) will not be reversed by the user model.

Omission of actions: The user model may omit actions at the end of a sequence. In particular, it may terminate the interaction at any point once the goal has been achieved. For example, once the person is holding the ticket they intended to buy, they may walk away from the machine, leaving their change, credit card or even return portion of their ticket. Whatever other rules are active, once the goal is achieved, the completion rule is active, so could be fired. The user model may also omit trailing actions if there is no apparent action possible. If at any time instance the guard of no other rule is active, then the guard of the termination rule becomes active and so the user model terminates. There must always be some action possible. This could be to pause but only if given reactive guidance to do so. For example, if there is a period when the ticket machine prints the ticket, where the person must do nothing, then with no feedback they may abort. In this respect the user model does not quite reflect the way people behave. If there is no action possible the user model is guaranteed to terminate, whereas in reality a person might pause before giving up. However, if the concern is user error, this is not critical as either way termination is possible so task completion is not guaranteed. If the user model took an action early due to it corresponding to a communication goal (e.g. selecting a destination first instead of ticket type) then the model would assume that the action had had the desired effect. The action (selecting a destination) would be removed from the communication goal list: the model "believes" it has been performed. It then would not be done at the appropriate point in the interaction i.e., a second (omission) error would occur. In this situation the correct action would be a repetition of the earlier action – repetition is not an error in this situation.

Late actions: The user model does not put any time bounds on actions. All rules simply assert that once an action is selected then it will eventually occur. If any action must be done in a time critical manner, then the user model will be capable of failing to do so. In practice this is too restrictive – it means the current user model will always be able to fail with a device that resets after some time interval, for example, as would be normal for a ticket machine. Where such time criticality is inherent in a design, extra assumptions that deadlines are met would need to be added explicitly.

Early actions: If there are periods when an action can apparently be performed, but if performed is ignored by the computer system, then in some circumstances the user model would take the next action early. In particular, if the user has outstanding communication goals then the corresponding actions may be taken early. This will potentially occur even if the device gives explicit guidance that the user must wait. This corresponds to the situation where a person does not notice the guidance but takes the action because they know they have to and have seen the opportunity. Similarly, if the device is presenting an apparent opportunity for reactive behaviour before it is ready to accept that action then the user model could react to it.

Replacement of one action by another: Replacement can occur due to communication goals if the device requires a specific action to be taken but its interface suggests that a communication goal can be discharged. For example, if the coin slot is visible but a destination selection required first, the person may insert money as discussed earlier. The user model may make the communication goal action rather than the required one, even if instructions are being displayed. Similarly, if reactive signals give incorrect guidance that suggests an action should be taken then that guidance may be followed. It can also occur due to trigger rules and environmental changes. In particular, if a change of state in the computer system can occur, not in response to a user action, then if the user model has already committed to some action (such as pressing a button), but its effect changes between the commitment being made and the action actually being taken, then the wrong effect will occur. This can lead to a person doing something they know is wrong. The change could occur due to a machine time-out or an environmental change (e.g. the time changing to off-peak travel).

Insertion of actions from elsewhere in the task: Insertion of an action can occur with communication goals. They can be attempted by the user model at any point in the interaction where the opportunity to discharge them apparently presents itself. With reactive tasks, it will occur only if the device gives a reactive signal to suggest it can be done when it cannot.

Intrusion of actions unrelated to the task: Actions unrelated to the task can intrude with the user model as a result of reactive signals on the device. If a device supports multiple tasks and uses reactive signals that signal an action to be performed that is not part of the task, such an action may be taken.

In summary, the principles of cognition implemented in the model generate behaviours that account for Hollnagel's various phenotypes. Similarly, those same principles of cognition can be used to derive and reason about design principles.

4   Design Rules

We now examine some usability design rules and how they solve the problems identified. Ad-hoc lists of design rules can easily appear to be contradictory or only apply in certain situations. By basing them on cognitively plausible principles, we can reason about their scope and make this scope more precise. For example, should systems always be permissive [15], allowing any action to be taken, or only under certain circumstances? Permissiveness appears to contradict forcing functions [13] when only certain actions are made possible. By reasoning from cognitive principles we can untangle these surface contradictions.

Completion actions: The user model contains a rule to terminate if the goal is achieved. Whatever other rules are active, this one could be activated due to the non-deterministic nature of the rules. The user model can therefore terminate the moment its goal is achieved. Furthermore, no output from the device can prevent this as it would just result in additional rules being active which cannot preclude some other action being taken. For the user model to guarantee to not terminate early for this reason it must only be possible for a user to terminate once the task is completed. Thus for our user model the task must be completed no later than the goal. Any design that requires the user model to perform extra completion tasks must ensure they are done before the goal is achieved. The rule will then only be active precisely when the task termination rule will be active, so that termination does not occur before the task rule is achieved. In practice (e.g. when termination involves logging out from a system) it may not always be possible to satisfy this design rule; in such situations, another means of restoring the invariant needs to be found. An attempted verification of a design that did not follow this design rule would fail because there would be a path where the goal was achieved and so termination would occur on that path, when the task was not achieved. In particular, as noted above, providing extra information is not sufficient. For a ticket machine, taking the ticket must be the last action of the user. They must by then have taken change or hold their credit card, or these must be returned in the same place and at the same time as the ticket. Multiple ticket parts (e.g. the return ticket) must also be dispensed together.

Provide information about what to do: Actions that are not communication goals can only be triggered in the model if they are a response to reactive signals – information indicating that the given rule is the next to be performed to achieve the given task. Therefore, if an action must be performed that does not correspond to a communication goal then information in the form of clear reactive guidance needs to be provided to tell the user to take the action. In the case of a ticket machine, if a button must be pressed to confirm the ticket selected is the one required, then instructions to do this must be provided. For communication goal actions, reactive information is not needed, though information linking the communication goal to the specific action is needed: something (such as the presence of a visible coin slot for inserting money) must make it clear that the communication goal can be discharged.

Providing information is not enough: The above design rule concerned always providing information. This one is that that is not good enough – so might appear to be contradictory. However, it depends on the situation. A simple design rule might be to clearly indicate the order that actions should be taken. This approach is often used where, for example, a panel gives instructions or lights flash to indicate the next button to press. However, the user model is non-deterministic. There may be several rules active and therefore several possible actions that could be taken. Reactive signals are not modelled as having higher priority than any other signal. Other possible actions are, for example, to terminate the interaction (if the goal is achieved), or discharge a communication goal. If the guards of such rules are active then they are possible actions. Making other signals true cannot make such a guard false; it can only make false guards true, so increasing the range of possible actions. Therefore, just providing flashing lights or beeps or other reactive signals is not enough to ensure correct operation. An attempted verification of such a design would fail because it would not be possible to prove that the correct action was taken. Some other action would be possible which could ultimately lead to the user aborting the interaction. If any possible path leads to abortion before the goal is achieved then the correctness statement will be unprovable as it states that the goal is achieved on all paths. Is providing information ever enough? According to the model – yes. It is sufficient if the user has nothing else to do and the action clearly takes them towards their goal. Thus (for our principles) if all communication goals are discharged (the ticket has been specified and money inserted) and the goal is not achieved (no ticket is held) then providing information is useful and necessary.

Forcing functions: The fact that the user model is capable of taking several different options and that giving reactive signals and messages is not enough means that some other way is needed to ensure the options are narrowed down to only the correct ones. As Norman [13] suggests, in good design, only correct actions for the range of tasks supported at a point should be possible. This suggests the use of forcing functions. Somehow the design must ensure that the only cognitively plausible actions are correct ones. This does not mean there must only be one button to press at any time, but only one button that can possibly be of use. Within the limits of the model, this means that if communication goals are not yet discharged, and should not yet be discharged, then there should be no apparent opportunity to discharge them. For example, a soft screen might be used so that the only buttons pressable correspond to ones that can now correctly be pressed. If money cannot be inserted then the coin slot should be closed. Similarly, the solution to post-completion errors is to not allow the goal to be achieved until the task is completed – forcing the user to complete other completion tasks first (where possible), as discussed above.

Permissiveness: Forcing functions follow the design principle that the options available to the user should be reduced. An alternative way of solving the same problem is to do the opposite and make the design permissive [15]: that is, it does not force a particular ordering of events. In this case, the design should be such that each of the actions that can be taken by the user model are accepted by the design and lead to the task being achieved. With our user model, permissiveness cannot be used universally, however. For example, it is not sufficient with completion tasks to allow them to be done in any order. As we have seen, if the goal is achieved before the task is completed then the user model leaves open the possibility of termination. There is no way the design can recover – once the user model terminates it does not re-start the task. Therefore, in this situation, being permissive does not work. The ticket must be released last. That action corresponds to the goal so cannot be permissive. At times in an interaction when communication goals are outstanding, the user model could discharge them if the opportunity is present. Thus permissiveness is a useful design rule to apply to communication goals. In particular, permissiveness should be applied if forcing functions are not used when communication goals are active. A communication goal that appears dischargable should be dischargable. For example, a ticket machine could allow destination and ticket type to be chosen in any order.

Visibility: The user model provides for both reactive behaviour and directly goal-based behaviour. All user model actions are guarded by a signal indicating the presence of information suggesting it is an appropriate action. If a control is not labelled then the user model will not take the action. Thus all controls must be labelled if the user model is to use them. This does not mean that labels must be written. The form of a control may be considered sufficient to warrant the signal being asserted. For example, a coin slot advertises by its form that it is for the insertion of coins. This would need to be decided by a usability expert using complementary techniques. Also, it only needs to be visible at the point where the user model must take the action. Thus visibility need not be universal.

Give immediate feedback: If there is no possible action apparent to the model then it will abort. If a user must wait while a ticket is printed, then feedback to wait should appear immediately with nothing else apparently possible (e.g. no other buttons visible). One possible reactive action can always be to pause provided it is guarded by the existence of a "please wait" message.

Do not change the interface under the user's feet: The existence of trigger behaviour, where there is a delay between the user making a decision and acting on it, but after which they cannot stop themselves, leads to a design rule that the interface should not change except in response to user action. More specifically, a possible design rule is that no input to the computer system should change its meaning spontaneously. This is quite restrictive, however. Less restrictive design possibilities are available to overcome the problems. For example, most ticket machines have timeouts – if no action is made in some period then the machine resets to some initial state. The user model does not strictly support such behaviour at present. However, one possibility with the current limited user model, and as used by some cash points, is to ask the user if they want more time after some delay. However, this means the buttons change their meanings. What did mean "I want to go to Liverpool" suddenly means "I do not want more time", for example. Such problems can be overcome, provided the old buttons all mean "I want more time", and the one that means no more time previously was not linked to any action – or with a soft-button interface did not exist at all. Such a design would only work with the user model if reactive signals were being used, as if the action were taken as a result of a communication goal, then that communication goal would have been discharged. The user model would only take the action again if prompted reactively to.

Where possible, determine the user's task early: The user model can take reactive actions intended for other tasks. This can be overcome if multiple task devices determine the task to be performed at the first point of divergence between the tasks. For example, a ticket machine that can also be used as a cash point may have a common initial sequence inserting a credit card. However, once the tasks diverge, the next device action should be to determine the task the user is engaged in, in a way that makes no other actions (specifically communication goals for any of the tasks) apparently possible. From then on actions from other tasks will not need to intrude in the design. This is important since a communication goal can be discharged at any point where apparently possible. In complex situations this will be difficult to achieve.

5   Conclusions and Further Work

We have outlined a formal description of a very simple user model. The user model describes fallible behaviour. However, rather than explicitly describing erroneous behaviour, it is based on cognitively plausible behaviour. Despite this we show that a wide variety of erroneous actions can occur from the behaviour described in appropriate circumstances. We have considered how devices (software, hardware or even everyday objects) must be designed if a person acting as specified by the user model would be able to successfully use the device. We have shown how well-known design rules, if followed, would allow this to occur. Each of these rules removes potential sources of user error that would prevent the verification of a design against the user model using the techniques described in [7]. We thus provide a theoretically based set of design rules, built upon a formal model. This model has very precise semantics that are open to inspection. Of course our reasoning is about what the user model might do rather than about any real person. As such, the results should be treated with care. However, errors that the user model could make are cognitively plausible and so worth attention.

One of our aims was to demonstrate a lightweight use of formal methods. As such, we have started with a formal description of user behaviour and used it as the basis for semi-formal reasoning about what erroneous behaviours emerge, and the design principles that would prevent behaviours emerging. Such semi-formal reasoning could contain errors. We also intend to explore the formal, machine-checked derivation of the design principles. Using HOL (the proof system the user model is defined within), this would involve giving formal descriptions of design rules and proving that – under the assumptions of the user model – particular erroneous situations would not occur.

Our model is intended to demonstrate the principles of the approach and covers only a small subset of cognitively plausible behaviour. As we develop it, it will give a more accurate description of what is cognitively plausible. We intend to extend it in a variety of ways. As this is done, more erroneous behaviour will be possible. For example, habitual behaviour is currently not modelled. Also many aspects of an interactive systems are parameters of the user model. However, generally a user actually determines this information by observation of the machine's interface. The model could be modified so that such information is an input in the model (i.e. collected as part of the interaction) rather than supplied by the verifier. We have essentially made predictions about the effects of following design rules. In broad scope these are well known and based on usability experiments. However, one of our arguments is that more detailed predictions can be made about the scope of the design rules, relating them back to concepts such as communication goals. The predictions resulting from the model could be used as the basis for designing further experiments to validate the model, or further refine it. We have also suggested there are tasks where it might be very difficult or even impossible to produce a design that satisfies all the underlying principles, so that some may need to be sacrificed in particular situations. We intend to explore this issue further.

References

1. A.E. Blandford, P.J. Barnard and M.D. Harrison. Using Interaction Framework to guide the design of interactive systems. *International Journal of Human Computer Studies*, 43:101-130, Academic Press 1995.
2. A. Blandford, R. Butterworth and P. Curzon, Puma Footprints: Linking Theory and Craft Skill in Usability Evaluation. *Proc. Interact 2001*, pp 577-584, IOS 2001.
3. A. Blandford and R. Young, The role of communication goals in interaction. In *Adjunct Proceedings of HCI'98*, 1998.
4. R. Butterworth, A. Blandford and D. Duke. Using formal models to explore display based usability issues. *J. of Visual Languages and Computing*, 10:455–479, 1999.
5. R. Butterworth, A. Blandford and D. Duke. Demonstrating the cognitive plausibility of interactive system specifications, *FACS*, 12:237–259 2000.
6. M. Byrne and S. Bovair. A working memory model of a common procedural error. *Cognitive Science*, 21 (1):31–61, 1997.
7. P. Curzon and A. Blandford, Detecting Multiple Classes of User Errors, *Eng. for Human-Computer Interaction*, M. Little and L. Nigay (Eds) pp 57–71, LNCS 2254, Springer 2001.
8. P. Curzon and A. Blandford, A User Model for Avoiding Design Induced Errors in Soft-Key Interactive Systems, *TPHOLs 2001: Supplementary Procs.*, R.J. Bolton and P.B. Jackson (eds), U. of Edinburgh, ED-INF-RR-0046, pp 33–48, 2001.
9. R.E. Fields. *Analysis of erroneous actions in the design of critical systems.* PhD Thesis. U. of York, Dept. of Computer Science, Tech. Report YCST 2001/09. 2001.
10. M.J.C. Gordon and T.F. Melham. *Introduction to HOL: A Theorem Proving Environment for Higher-Order Logic.* Cambridge University Press, U.K., 1993.
11. E. Hollnagel. *Cognitive Reliability & Error Analysis Method.* Elsevier 1998.
12. A. Newell. *Unified Theories of Cognition.* Harvard University Press, 1990.
13. D.A. Norman. *The Design of Everyday Things.* MIT Press 1998.
14. C.R. Roast. Modelling Unwanted Commitment in Information Artifacts, S. Chatty and P. Dewan (eds) *Eng. for Human-Computer Interaction*, pp 77–90, Kluwer, 1998.
15. H. Thimbleby. Permissive User Interfaces, *International Journal of Human-Computer Studies*, (54)3:333–350, 2001.
16. H. Thimbleby, A. Blandford, P. Cairns, P. Curzon and M. Jones. User Interface Design as Systems Design. To appear in *the Proceedings of HCI 2002*, Sept. 2002.

A Coloured Petri Net Formalisation for a UML-Based Notation Applied to Cooperative System Modelling

José Luis Garrido and Miguel Gea

Dpt. Lenguajes y Sistemas Informáticos, University of Granada,
E.T.S.I. Informática, C/Daniel Saucedo Aranda s/n, 18071 Granada, Spain
http://giig.ugr.es
{jgarrido,mgea}@ugr.es

Abstract. New approaches are currently being adopted to address the development of cooperative systems, although not many standards exist that can be used to develop this type of interactive system. We apply the standard Unified Modelling Language (UML) notation within a methodology aimed at the analysis and design of such systems, and present a semantic formalisation of the UML notation used to model cooperative systems. The semantics and its application are described on the basis of translation schemes to Coloured Petri Nets and the benefits of formalisation are shown.

1 Introduction

To date, Computer-Supported Cooperative Work (CSCW) [15] has comprehended various systems: Workflow Management Systems (MfMS), computer-mediated communication (CMC) (e.g. e-mail), decision support systems, shared artefacts and applications (e.g. shared whiteboards, collaborative writing systems), meeting systems, etc. These can be categorised in several ways. One of these is by the function that the system performs, and another interesting one is based on two dimensions: time (synchronous or asynchronous) and space (co-located or remote). The outcome matrix is very useful to refer to the particular circumstances that a groupware application aims to address. Groupware [6,3] has been defined as a computer-based system that supports groups of people engaged in a common task (or goal) and that provides an interface to a shared environment. We note that in the set of fields and systems embraced by CSCW there are many explicit and implicit related concepts. These tend to either logical or technological aspects, such as interaction, communication, coordination, information, group, behaviour, distribution, control, etc. An additional difficulty is that the same term is frequently used in two or more fields but with different meanings and implications. For instance, human-computer interaction (HCI) particularly addresses psychological and computer issues; on the other hand, in human-human interaction within group activities, social issues acquire more relevance. An introductory study of the concepts involved in specifying the general principles and properties of CSCW systems is presented in [7].

P. Forbrig et al. (Eds.): DSV-IS 2002, LNCS 2545, pp. 16–28, 2002.
© Springer-Verlag Berlin Heidelberg 2002

The development of groupware applications is more difficult than that of a single-user application, because social protocols and group activities must be taken into account for a successful design [12], and so techniques aimed at enhancing group interaction activities should be applied. The inherent complexity of any interactive system requires a great deal of effort in the formulation of specifications, and formal methods may be used to achieve this goal [2,13]. At the modelling stage, support should be provided to study the system being developed.

The work presented in this paper is part of a new methodology called AMENITIES [9] (acronym for A MEthodology for aNalysis and desIgn of cooperaTIve systEmS). This methodology is based on behaviour and task models for the analysis and design of generic cooperative systems. The set of behaviour and task models (called Cooperative Model of AMENITIES) is a conceptual model which comprises the foundation of the methodology. The paper shows how to formalise the semantics for the Cooperative Model, which uses a UML-based notation, by describing translation schemes to Coloured Petri Net (CPN) formalism [14]. The paper is organised as follows. Section 2 reviews related work. Sect. 3 justifies the use of CPN formalism to define UML semantics. The conceptual framework for the Cooperative Model is introduced in Sect. 4 and an application example of this model is presented in Sect. 5. Then, on the basis of the example provided, the question is addressed of how, formally, to represent the model to be studied (Sect. 6). Finally, Sect. 7 summarises the main conclusions.

2 Related Work

Several approaches have been proposed to specify cooperative systems, focused on representing user tasks [19]. Thus, the system specification is a collection of user goals each of which is defined by the sequence of tasks that allow us to achieve a desired objective. Several notations have been proposed, such as GTA (Groupware Task Analysis) [29] and CTT (ConcurTaskTrees) [22]. GTA proposes an ontology-based system study for task world models, that is, a framework in which participants (agents and users' roles), artefacts (objects) and situations (goals, events) take place. Moreover, a set of relationships between these are clearly identified (uses, performed-by, play, etc). CTT provides a hierarchical graphical notation to describe concurrent tasks, and allows us to specify cooperation by adding a hierarchical specification with temporal constraints for each cooperative task. This extension and others aim to establish common tasks for several users and the relationships between them. An approach describing both task and system models by means of a dialect of Petri Nets (ICO formalism) is presented in [21], demonstrating how formal task models improve the design of interactive systems.

These task-based approaches study the system from the user's point of view, describing the cognitive skills required for correct use. However, most such techniques do not consider certain dynamic aspects in the problem domain [18]. For example, the user's role may change during real situations (e.g. the responsibilities in an office department), and the ways in which the objectives to be achieved may vary (e.g. a new commercial strategy, different work organisation). Thus, group organisation and evolution over time should be taken into account when social organisations are described.

On the other hand, our work is based on UML notation to describe cooperative systems by extending task-based approaches with ethnographic and cognitive issues. The advantage of this election is the use of a standard successfully adopted in software engineering. However, it is a semi-formal notation and various proposals have been made to formalise UML for different purposes, including:

- Stochastic Petri Nets, derived from UML statecharts and a collaboration diagram, for performance analysis [16].
- Validation of architectural software design with UML collaboration diagrams using CPN behavioural templates [23].
- Development of the CPN of a system by deriving Object Oriented Petri Nets Models from UML statecharts and connecting them using UML collaboration diagrams [26].
- Defining formal operational semantics by transforming UML state diagrams into graphs [11].
- Giving execution semantics for UML activity diagrams intended for workflow modelling [5].
- Definition of a semantics for collaboration and activity diagrams based on Place-Transition Petri Nets with informal inscriptions [10].

In general, these proposals focus on software analysis or toolkit construction for code generation, although some consider workflow modelling using activity diagrams.

3   UML Semantics versus CPN Semantics

The OMG Unified Modelling Language Specification [20] (in its current version 1.4) specifies syntax and informal semantics of the notations embraced by UML. This specification is clearly focused on software models. In particular, with respect to the behavioural UML notations that we use for the cooperative model of AMENITIES, the following text appearing in this reference should be highlighted:

1. Statecharts. "A statechart diagram can be used to describe the behaviour of instances of a model element such as an object or an interaction... The semantics and notation described are substantially those of David Harel's statecharts with modifications to make them object-oriented".
2. Activity diagrams. "An activity graph is a variation of a state machine in which the states represent the performance of actions or subactivities... It represents a state machine of a procedure itself".

A statechart (or activity diagram) is a graph that represents a state machine. The relationships between a state machine and its context have no special notation. The state machine also provides the semantic foundation for activity graphs. The specification document provides, for statecharts and activity diagrams, both a specification of the notation (graphic syntax) and an informal definition (in English) of their semantics.

The semantics of a UML state machine (i.e. the metamodel) is described in terms of the operations of a hypothetical machine that implements a state machine specification. Thus, this operational semantics is defined by the following key components:

- A queue of incoming event instances to be dispatched.
- The dispatcher mechanism for event processing.
- An event processor that processes dispatched event instances according to the general semantics and the specific form of the state machine in question.

Our main motivation in describing the semantics of UML notation applied to CSCW systems by using CPNs is that the existence of several variation points allows different semantic interpretations that might be required in different application domains. This is usually our case, and so high-level Petri Nets are used for the formal specification. This provides the following advantages:

- CPNs provide true concurrency semantics by means of the step concept, i.e. when at least two non-conflictive transitions may occur at the same time. It is the ideal situation for our application domain, as the model must be supported by a multithreaded state machine (several actors moving within the same space of states).
- The combination of states, activities, decisions, data, events and complex transitions (namely fork-join constructions) means that the UML state machine notation is very rich. CPNs allow us to express, in the same formalism, both the kind of system we are dealing with and its execution.
- Formal semantics is better in order to carry out a complete and highly automated analysis (i.e. validation and verification of properties) for the system being designed.

4   Framework

The cooperative model of AMENITIES, which is the core of the methodology, adopts an overall view of a system. Hence, the system embraces computer-based systems as well as the end-users themselves and related aspects such as organisation, communication, collaboration [27] and coordination [17]. This paper does not deal with the user's behaviour except that related to the interaction between different users. It is even possible to model interactions in which no computer-based system is involved [8]. The model allows us to carry out task analysis and modelling, as well as represent other related aspects such as roles, capabilities, constraints, etc. The notation used is basicly that of UML [25] only that instead of applying it to specify concrete classes for implementation, we consider other more abstract classes (group, role, ...) in the domain of cooperative systems. Because the emphasis is to study behaviour rather than structural aspects, class diagrams are not shown in this paper.

Several definitions of framework have been made, depending on the level where it is applied. In this context, a framework should give a higher common abstraction level between a family of related systems to be described in terms of general concepts. Thus, a framework is a pattern encompassing the principal common concepts of a kind of system and the relationships between them.

We define the basic terminology as follows. An action is a basic unit of work, executable atomically. A subactivity is a set of related subactivities and/or actions. A task is a set of subactivities intended to achieve certain goals. A role is a designator for a set of capabilities to carry out work, including tasks, skills, constraints and responsibilities/authorities. An actor is a user, program, or entity that can play a role in the execution of, or responsibility for, tasks. A cooperative task is one that must be carried out by more than one actor, playing either the same role or different ones. A group is a set of actors playing roles and organised around one or more cooperative tasks. A group may be composed, i.e. formed from related subgroups. A constraint (also called a law) is a limitation imposed by the system that allows it to adjust the set of possible behaviours dynamically. Finally, a capability is a constraint that directly affects an actor or group, enabling them to respond to new challenges offered by the system, as a result either of external events or of internal events produced by the interaction between participants (i.e. actors, groups or the system itself).

The method for building the cooperative model (as is shown in the next section) is based on two key concepts defined above: work and group. We use the notion of task to structure and describe the work that must be performed by the group. This provides the way to translate work, i.e. something that is tacit and implicit, into something that is concrete and explicit. Nonetheless, tasks are also considered at a very abstract level as noted above. A group, on the other hand, can be more or less explicit. Sometimes organisational aspects determine the way people work, but in other cases personal and/or operational aspects are the basis for organising people in order to perform an activity. The notion of role, in any case, allows us both to specify groups as needed and to establish dynamic relations between actors and tasks.

5   Example of Cooperative Model

As an example to introduce the syntax and semantics of statecharts and activity diagrams of UML according to the application domain (i.e. cooperative work), we have modelled the current system used in Emergency Coordination Centres in Sweden and the U.S.A. [1]. These systems were designed and implemented fulfilling the control requirements of extreme situations. The Centre distributes tasks and is responsible, in the case of large-scale accidents, for the coordination of the organisations involved (police, fire brigade and medical help), until all units have arrived at the scene of the accident. At that point, the fire brigade takes over responsibility for coordination. The main goal is to assign and manage resources as fast as possible, as well as to assess the particular conditions of each emergency. The sequence of steps to build the cooperative model is shown in the following subsections.

5.1   Organisation Group

The first step in the method is to specify groups by means of UML state-charts, as shown in Figure 1(a) . This is based on identifying the related roles, there is one state for each role. The concept of role allows us to state the dynamic connections between actors and tasks. Thus, the basic structure of the organisation is described: actors play the roles `Operator`, `AssistantOperator` and `ResourceResponsible`. In this case, capabilities (e.g. guard `[operator?]`) initially determine which role is played by each actor, depending on his/her professional category, specialisation and/or skills. It also specifies (e.g. guard `[FreeOperators=0]`) under which constraints dynamic behaviour changes must be produced, sometimes as a result of interactions between members of the group.

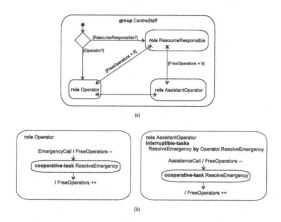

(a)

(b)

Fig. 1. (a) Group definition (b) Role definitions

5.2   Role Definition

Actors' knowledge of the system is determined by the functionality of the latter. In Fig. 1(b) the tasks that can or must be performed are identified. Thus, each role is actually a UML composed state including a submachine for each task that can/must be performed. Here, the defined roles collaborate on the single task `ResolveEmergency`. For the role `AssistantOperator`, the task being performed can be interrupted (section `interruptible-tasks`) if there is a new emergency.

In this situation, the actor will behave as `Operator` in order to respond to this new emergency.

5.3   Task Definition

The next step describes by means of UML activity diagrams the subactivities/actions needed to carry out each task (Fig. 2). By means of sequential (arrows) and concurrent (thick bars) constructions, temporal- ordered constraints of subactivities are specified. Diamonds may also be used to specify decision points involved in certain strategies during task performance. For each subactivity or action, the task definition includes specifying those responsible and the optional roles needed to accomplish it. Optional roles are shown between brackets and the symbol '|' specifies an inclusive-or relationship. This role specification is an extension to UML swimlanes for activity diagrams.

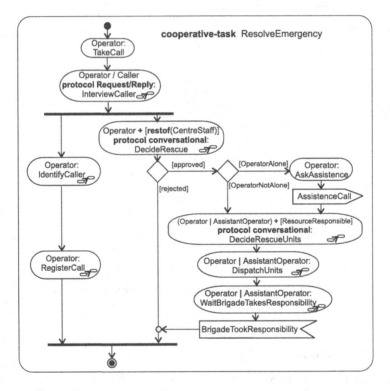

Fig. 2. Task Definition

5.4   Specification of Interactions between Actors

The above task definition includes several tasks to be carried out by means of interaction protocols. For instance, the subactivity `InterviewCaller` specifies the type of protocol `Request-Reply` that should be used to accomplish this, as well as the participants involved: `Operator` asks and `Caller` answers. On the order hand, the activity `DecideRescueUnits` specifies a conversational protocol, i.e. any participant can take part in this activity in any order and with the same degree of responsibility.

6   Semantics for the Cooperative Model

This section states the foundation of a specific semantics for the cooperative model. The idea is to be able to automate the behavioural analysis for the cooperative system by making explicit concurrency, non-determinism, synchronization and resource sharing. CPN can be sujected to various Petri Nets analysis techniques which aid in the validation of UML behavioural specification.

6.1   Translation Schemes from UML to CPN

In the following subsections, we discuss the key points in formally defining notation semantics according to the application domain. This is obtained by translating elements of the cooperative model to CPN components, as shown in Fig. 3, which is the corresponding CPN for the above modelling example. The subnet `ResolveEmergency` in Fig. 3(b) is for the transition with the same name in Fig. 3(a).

State/Activity Mapping. There exist two general alternatives to apply transformations from the cooperative model to the CPN model:

1. Identify subactivities with places in the CPN, allowing them to be interrupted (if necessary) in a direct way. In a cooperative system, there are both atomic and non-atomic activities, subactivities and actions respectively. Subactivities can be interrupted (if specified), such that the actors playing them may leave and return to the subactivity later. For example, the actor playing the role `AssistantOperator` in Fig. 2 can abandon the subactivity `DecideRescue` during its performance.
2. Conversely, the other possibility is to identify subactivities with transitions. At first glance, no activity could be interrupted since transition firing is considered instantaneous in Petri Nets.

We have chosen the second alternative, for several reasons. First, mapping subactivities into places poses the following problem: if a place represents a subactivity state, when the actor returns the subactivity will start again. Thus, to represent the leaving point where a subactivity continues would be impossible.

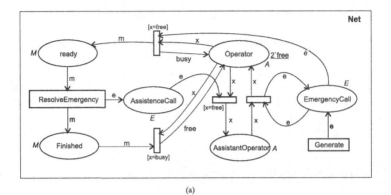

(a)

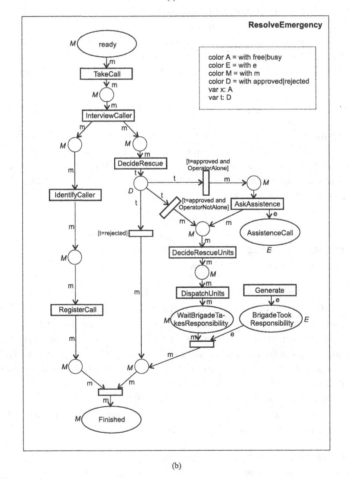

(b)

Fig. 3. CPN for the Emergency Coordination Centre

Secondly, the common Petri Net hierarchical modelling technique is by means of substitution transitions, and therefore if a transition represents a subactivity, there always remains the possibility of decomposing it into various actions (other transitions) and resting points (places) that enable interruptions and returns. This is also the ideal solution to the previous problem. Thirdly, modelling subactivities by transitions allows us to model data flow in the places of the subactivity flow more clearly (e.g. place of type D in Fig. 3(b)).

Actors and Resources. As shown in the CPN model in Fig 3(a), a role is considered equivalent to a type of resource, which is represented in a Petri Net as a place and a specific type associated (type A). Hence, there would be one token in the place for each actor playing this role. Each one of these places is labelled with the corresponding role name. For instance, there is a place labelled Operator with a token type A and, initially, two free value tokens (inscription 2'free). For the sake of simplicity, the net does not include the role ResourceResponsible, and hence does not include the transition to take the initial decision corresponding to the diamond in Fig 1(a). The arcs from role places to the subactivity transitions and vice versa, corresponding to the roles performing activities in Fig. 2(b), have also been omitted.

Guards. In CPN, transitions can have guards associated, which implies that the UML guards have a direct translation to CPN models, i.e. while the guard condition is not satisfied the transition cannot occur. Guards expressed in natural language must be interpreted. This is done in part (Fig. 3(b)) for the two consecutive decision points in Fig. 2. These are merged in the CPN, producing as many transitions as the total number of outgoing paths. The first condition (approved or rejected) in the guard is translated on the basis of a specific piece of information outgoing from the activity DecideRescue (type D token). With respect to the second condition (OperatorAlone or OperatorNotAlone), this is not interpreted in Fig. 3(b) in order to simplify type A as much as possible and to avoid additional arcs.

Events. Fig. 3 includes two types of event: one internal event (place AssistenceCall) and two external ones (EmergencyCall and BrigadeTookResponsibility places). Irrespective of the type of event, these are explicit signals translated into extra places receiving tokens from internal actions (AskAssistence) or the environment (Generate). These places send tokens to subactivities/actions (transitions) that require them. Thus, the net firing rule ensures that the transition receiving tokens cannot occur before the event has happened.

6.2   Validation and Property Verification

CPNs allow us to validate and evaluate the usability of a system by performing automatic and/or guided executions. These simulation techniques can also carry out performance analysis by calculating transaction throughputs, etc. Moreover, by applying other analysis techniques it is possible to verify static and dynamic properties in order to provide the complement to the simulation. Some of these properties are that:

- There are no activities in the system that cannot be realised (dead transitions). If initially dead transitions exist, then the system was bad designed.
- It is always possible to return to a subactivity if we wish (liveness). For instance, this might allow us to rectify previous mistakes.
- It is always possible to return to a state before (home properties). For instance, to compare the results of applying different strategies to solve the same problem.
- The system may stop before completion (deadlock). Thus, a work might never be finished, or it might be necessary to allocate more human resources to perform it.
- Certain tokens are never destroyed (conservation). Hence, resources are maintained in the system. This should be true for actors.

7   Conclusions

UML, with the nine notations embodied, is suggested as a general and standard notation for the analysis, design and development of object-oriented software systems. UML semantics is intended for the latter field; it is not a formal description. Neither does it define a standard process for its application, of which we are taking advantage, but is intended to be useful with iterative development processes.

In practice, the modelling power of UML is demonstrated by applying it to diverse types of systems. New approaches to address the analysis and design of cooperative systems must advance towards how to study and obtain interesting properties for systems. We argue that concepts should be correctly represented, at appropriate levels and that clear semantic links between them should be provided for useful integration, thereby resulting in a more powerful, useful and flexible system from all points of view.

Our main aim is to obtain the benefits of using an standard notation as UML:

- it allows us to model open, reactive systems [4], i.e., the main features of cooperative systems,
- there exist several UML-based tools to design and generate software (RationalRose, ArgoUML, ...), and
- new UML-based approaches are arising to model user interfaces [24,28].

On the other hand, it is necessary the application of formal methods to the engineering of cooperative systems in order to build CSCW systems correctly. For this purpose, CPNs have a graphical representation and well-defined semantics, which allows compact and manageable representations and therefore one more powerful analysis than that of UML.

References

1. Artman, H., Waern, Y.: Distributed Cognition in an Emergency Co-ordination Center. Cognition, Technology and Work, 1 (1999) 237–246
2. Dix, A.: "Formal Methods for Interactive Systems". Academic Press (1991)
3. Ehrlich, K.: Designing Groupware Applications: A Work-Centered Design Approach. In: Beaudouin-Lafon, M. (ed.): Computer Supported Cooperative Work. Wiley (1999) 1–28
4. Eshuis, R., Wieringa, R.: A Comparison of Petri Net and Activity Diagram Variants. In: Weber, Ehrig, Reisig (eds.): Proc. 2nd. International Colloquium on Petri Net Technologies for Modelling Communication Based Systems (September 2001) 93–104
5. Eshuis, R., Wieringa, R.: An Execution Algorithm for UML Activity Graphs. In Proc. UML'2001. LNCS 2185, Springer (October 2001)
6. Ellis, C.A., Gibbs, S.J., & Rein, G.L.: Groupware: some issues and experiences. Communications of the ACM, Vol. 34, No. 1 (January 1991) 38-58
7. Garrido, J.L., Gea, M., Gutiérrez, F.L., Padilla, N.: Designing Cooperative Systems for Human Collaboration. In: Dieng, R., Giboin, A., Karsenty, L., De Michelis, G. (eds.): Designing Cooperative Systems - The Use of Theories and Models. IOS Press-Ohmsha (2000) 399–412
8. Garrido, J.L., Gea, M.: Modelling Dynamic Group Behaviours. In: Johnson, C. (ed.): Interactive Systems – Design, Specification and Verification. LNCS 2220. Springer (2001) 128–143
9. Garrido, J.L., Gea, M., Padilla, N., Cañas, J.J., Waern, Y.: AMENITIES: Modelado de Entornos Cooperativos. In: Aedo, I., Díaz, P., Fernández, C. (eds.): Actas del III Congreso Internacional Interacción Persona-Ordenador 2002 (Interacción'02), Madrid, Spain (Mayo 2002) 97–104
10. Gehrke, T., Goltz, U., Wehrheim, H.: The dynamic models' of UML: Toward a semantics and its application in the development process. Hildesheimer Informatik-Bericht 11/98, Institut fur Informatik, Universitat Hildesheimer (1998)
11. Gogolla, M., Presicce, F.P.: State Diagrams in UML: A Formal Semantics using Graph Transformations. In Proceeding ICSE'98 - Workshop on Precise Semantics of Modeling Techniques (PSMT'98) 55–72
12. Grudin, J.: Groupware and Cooperative Work: Problems and Prospects. Reprinted in Baecker, R.M. (ed.) Readings in Groupware and Computer Supported Cooperative Work, San Mateo, CA, Morgan Kaufman Publishers (1993) 97–105
13. Harrison, M., Thimbleby, H. (eds.): Formal Methods in Human-Computer Interaction. Cambridge University Press (1990)
14. Jensen, K.: Coloured Petri Nets – Basic Concepts, Analysis Methods and Practical Use. Second Edition Springer(1996)
15. Jordan, B.: Ethnographic Workplace Studies and CSCW. In: Shapiro, D., Tauber, M.J., Traunmueller, R. (eds.): The Design of Computer Supported Cooperative Work and Groupware System. North-Holland, Amsterdam (1996) 17–42
16. King, P., Pooley, R.: Using UML to Derive Stochastic Petri Net Models. In N. Davies and J. Bradley, editors. UKPEW '99, Proceedings of the Fifteenth UK Performance Engineering Workshop, Department of Computer Science, The University of Bristol (July 1999) 45–56
17. Malone, T.W., Crowston, K.: What is Coordination Theory and How Can It Help Design Cooperative Work Systems. Proceedings of the Conference on Computer Supported Cooperative Work (CSCW'90). ACM Press, New York (1990) 357–370

18. McGrath, J.: Time, Interaction and Performance: a theory of groups. In Readings in Groupware and Computer-Supported Cooperative Work. R. Baecker (ed). Morgan Kauffman (1993)
19. Nardi, B. (ed): Context and Consciousness: Activity Theory and Human Computer Interaction. MIT Press, Cambridge MA (1995)
20. OMG: Unified Modelling Language Specification. http://www.omg.org (September 2001)
21. Palanque, P., Bastide, R.: Synergistic modelling of task, users and systems using formal specification techniques. Interacting with Computers 9 (1997) 129–153
22. Paternò, F.: Model-based Design and Evaluation of Interactive Applications. Springer-Verlag (2000)
23. Pettit, R.G., Gomaa, H.: Validation of Dynamic Behavior in UML Using Colored Petri Nets. UML'2000 WORKSHOP. Dynamic Behaviour in UML Models: Semantic Questions. On Line Proceedings (2000) http://www.disi.unige.it/person/ReggioG/UMLWORKSHOP/PROGRAM.html
24. Pinheiro da Silva, P., Paton, N.W.: User Interface Modelling with UML. In Information Modelling and Knowledge Bases XII. 10th European-Japanese Conference on Infomation Modelling and Knowledge Representation. Saariselka, Finland (May 2000). Kangassalo, H., Joakkola, H., Kawaguchi, E. (Eds.) Amsterdam, IOS Press (2001) 203–217
25. Rumbaugh, J., Jacobson, I., Booch, G.: The Unified Modeling Language – Reference Manual. Addison-Wesley (1999)
26. Saldhana, J.A., Shatz, S.M.: UML to Object Petri Net Models: An approach for Modeling and Analysis. In Procceding of Twelfth International Conference on Software Engineering and Knowledge Engineering (SEKE2000)
27. Terveen, L.G.: An Overview of Human-Computer Collaboration. In Knolowledge-Based Systems Journal, Special Issue on Human-Computer Collaboration (1995) 67–81
28. TUPIS'00: Towards a UML Profile for Interactive Systems Development. Workshop of UML'2000. http://math.uma.pt/tupis00/
29. van der Veer, G.C., van Welie, M.: Task Based Groupware Design: Putting theory into practice. In Proc. of Symposium on Designing Interactive Systems (DIS'2000) New York (August 2000) 326–337

Adaptive User Interface for Mobile Devices*

Nikola Mitrović and Eduardo Mena

IIS Department, University of Zaragoza, Maria de Luna 3,
50018 Zaragoza, Spain
mitrovic@prometeo.cps.unizar.es
emena@posta.unizar.es
http://www.cps.unizar.es/~mena

Abstract. Adapting a graphical user interface (GUI) to a variety of resources with different capabilities is one of the most interesting questions
of today's mobile computation. The GUI constructed for one application
should be usable on different interactive devices, e.g. WebTV terminals,
WAP phones or Java-enabled devices. In this paper, we discuss existing
solutions and present a solution based on mobile agents. Mobile agents
construct their GUI using third-party eXtensible User interface Language
(XUL), jXUL middleware and XSL transformations. Mobile agents move
to host computers and then build their GUI, or act as a proxy to devices
without sufficient processing capabilities (e.g., WAP devices). The result
is an adaptable GUI platform that can be run on multiple devices without modifications, supporting different resources and architectures. We
show the application of this approach by implementing a mobile currency
converter and survey.

1 Introduction

Constructing graphical user interfaces (GUIs) in mobile computing area faces
many challenges. Main problems are raised from the fact that various target
devices have different processing powers, GUI organization and capabilities.

Solutions in this area mainly focus on web applications with client-server
architecture, creating specialized and centralized services that transform one
type of user interface in another. Some solutions propose creating separate GUI
solutions for each device type, that are later dispatched according to the request
type (or request origin). Some authors propose XML-described user interfaces
that could be later presented as Java AWT [1] or Swing [1], or that can be
transformed with XSLT [2].

The idea of this work is to transparently adapt graphical user interface by
using mobile agent systems. Agents are highly mobile, and are often hosted
by platforms that support different models of user interface or have different
processing capabilities. Agents are autonomous, and can handle network errors
(unreachable hosts, etc.) autonomously; also, they can move to the target device

---

* This work was supported by the DGA project P084/2001.

P. Forbrig et al. (Eds.): DSV-IS 2002, LNCS 2545, pp. 29–43, 2002.
© Springer-Verlag Berlin Heidelberg 2002

instead of target device requesting service from a server. Agents can be sent to a home computer supporting Java and Swing. On the other side, an agent can play the role of a proxy server for a wireless device, such as mobile telephone or a Web terminal, and in that case it should produce WML [4] or HTML [3], respectively. In contrast, solutions not using mobile agents are client-server systems or use middleware programs that are installed on each user device. Therefore, new updates lead to reinstalling client programs on every user device, which does not happen when using mobile agents (only the mobile agent needs to be updated).

Our prototype adapts user interface using mobile agents [8] that process a user interface definition described in a language called Extensible User-interface Language (XUL) [5], [13]. This interface definition is later adapted using XSL transformations to other notations (HTML, WML, etc). The XUL interpretation on Java-enabled platforms is interpreted by jXUL platform. The jXUL is a third-party middleware that renders XUL using standard Swing interface. Agents automatically adapt the interface definition to the clients' interface, making multiple middleware implementations unnecessary.

This approach gives good results when deployment is needed not only as a web application, or only as a desktop application. This approach combines these approaches, and is truly mobile in its nature; agents can autonomously determine what kind of interface should be presented. One of the advantages of mobile agents approach is that the GUI goes mobile and can be constructed in function of autonomous operation of mobile agent. For example, we could have a user interface that is modified depending on information collected from the agent's trip on the network, and that can be later presented on any type of the device.

The rest of this paper is as follows. Section 2 gives an overview of state of the art and the related work. Section 3 introduces extensible user interface language (XUL) and gives an overview of its possibilities and limitations. Section 4 introduces mobile agent technology. Section 5 we introduce our motivating example and explain bound between mobile agents and GUI. Section 6 describes sample scenario that shows the presented technique. Section 7 concludes the paper and discusses the future work.

2   State of the Art and Related Work

Various approaches to adapting user interfaces to various devices are present. Basically the approaches are grouped into two categories: web applications and classic desktop applications. While the first category [11], [14] treats only web content and transformations of web content in order to be usable on other (mostly mobile) devices, the second category treats the problems of universally defining the user interface, so it can be later reproduced by various program implementations [9], [10], [12], [24], [25] (or middlewares) on various platforms.

2.1   Adaptable XML-Defined Interfaces

Several solutions for defining user interface are present at the moment of writing of this article. Without providing details, we mention some approaches: language-based, grammar-based, e.g., BNF, event-based, constraint-based, UAN (User Action Notation, in particular for direct manipulation) and widget-based. However, the XML-based efforts are most interesting for us, since they provide flexibility and easy manipulation. Some of such efforts include XUL [5], the extensible user interface language, UIML (User Interface Mark-up Language) [26], [10] and XIML [32].

Luyten, et al. [24] investigated the possibility of rendering their own XML-like mark-up languages to Java AWT and Swing, or converting the interface definition to other formats using XSL transformations or XPath. However, this approach is focused on creating different middleware (or transformation) for different platforms (that are not Java compatible), and not on transparent modification of user interface. Also, their prototyped solution do not run in a truly mobile environment (mobile agents), and is focused on rendering the user definition files on multiple platforms by using different middlewares. At the time being, this prototype also lack complete language definition.

Other approaches, such the one from Müeller, et al. [25], are more focused on defining the universal XML notation that can be used for platform independent interface generation.

2.2   Web Applications and Adaptable User Interfaces

Application servers are mostly oriented on how to transform web contents to various other formats that can be used on mobile devices (cHTML [30], WML [4], etc.). However, different approaches exist.

Microsoft, one of the industry leaders, in its next-generation technology ".NET" offers Mobile Web Forms [11]. These forms are based on restricted set of components that, to our knowledge, cannot be extended with additional widgets. Each component is intelligent component that transforms its appearance in function of available resources. The controls are highly bound with the .NET family of languages. Unfortunately, Microsoft's solutions are still available only on the Windows platforms, the number of widgets is limited, and the desktop applications are not taken into the consideration.

Other industry leaders, such as IBM, have slightly different approaches. IBM's Transcoding Publisher [14] actually transforms web contents to variety of other formats, giving the user possibility of customisation of the transformation parameters. Some interesting features such as JavaScript [7] transformation and automatic image format transformations are included. Users should be able to customize the transformations in order to maximize the quality the output, which can be a significant plus for complex web applications; another good side is IBM's commitment to Java, therefore multiple platforms are supported. However, the drawback of the approach is ability to transform only web contents, and in a centralized fashion.

Other "traditional" solutions in the web-area also exist, and consist on parsing the request information, and redirecting the petition to the appropriate content [15]. The content is created separately for each device type, and is stored separately. When the user accesses the server with a mobile device, the server will recognize the request type, and will redirect the user to the appropriate content. This solution has a significant overhead, because the content should be created multiple times in order to support different formats. Scalability of this solution can be also questioned.

All these approaches support different level of customisations, but however only web applications. The user interface generation is centralized – on the server.

3   Extensible User-Interface Language – XUL

Extensible User interface Language [5], [13] is designed for cross-platform user interface definition. This language is incorporated in Mozilla project [17], acting as a user interface definition language. Being part of Mozilla project, XUL is open and connectable to other Mozilla projects. The format is organized with modern user interface definition in mind, supporting variety of available controls.

XUL lacks the abstraction layer of interface definition, and is restricted to window-based user interface. It is capable of referencing Cascading Style Sheets (CSS) [18] to define the layout of elements. The user actions, property access and functionality can be stored in JavaScript (ECMAscript) [7] files. However, we found XUL as suitable open source solution for our purpose.

A simple XUL window in Fig. 1 could be defined as in Fig. 2.

Fig. 1. Window to be constructed

From this example, we can see that the interface definition is oriented to modern window-based interfaces. We are referencing a StyleSheet, JavaScript library, and using few labels, textbox and a button within the box tag. The box tag is main form of layout in XUL and is similar to Swing JPanel. This model allows you to divide a window into a series of boxes. Elements inside box will orient themselves horizontally or vertically. By combining a series of boxes,

```
<?xml version="1.0"?>
<window align="vertical" class="dialog" height="250" width="370" title="Currency
Converter">
 <link rel="stylesheet" href="html.css" type="text/css"/>
 <script language="JavaScript" src="eventHandlers.js"/>
 <box>
  <label control="lblTitle" value="Currency Converter"/>
 </box>
 <box>
  <label control="lblQty" value="Quantity:"/>
  <textbox value="0.00" id="txtQty"/>
 </box>
 <box>
  <button id="Convert" label="Convert!" oncommand="ccyConvert()"/>
 </box>
</window>
```

Fig. 2. Example XUL document

spacers and elements will flex, and you can control the layout of a window as can be seen in Fig. 1.

4   Mobile Agents and Agent Platforms

A mobile agent [8], [27] is a program that executes autonomously on a set of network hosts on behalf of an individual or organization. The agent visits the network hosts to execute parts of its program and may interact with other agents residing on that host or elsewhere, while working toward a goal. During their lifetime agents travel to different hosts, that can have distinct user interface possibilities. Agents typically posses several (or all) of the following characteristics; they are:

– Goal oriented: they are in charge of achieving a list of goals (*agenda*).
– Autonomous: they are independent entities that pursue certain objectives, and decide how and when to achieve them.
– Communicative/collaborative: to achieve their goal they can cooperate.
– Adaptive/learning: agents "learn" from their experience and modify their behavior respectively.
– Persistent: agent's state (should) persist until all the goals are achieved.
– Reactive: they react to their environment which also could change their behavior.
– They can stop their own execution, travel to another host and resume it once there.

They do not, by themselves, constitute a complete application. Instead, they form one by working in conjunction with an agent host and other agents. Many agents are meant to be used as intelligent electronic gophers – automated errand boys. Tell them what you want them to do – search the Internet for information on a topic, or assemble and order a computer according to your desired specifications – and they will do it and let you know when they have finished. Mobile

Agent Systems (MAS) are the middleware that allows creating and executing mobile agents. For this project, we choose Grasshopper [19] as the most intuitive and stable mobile agent platform, which supports standards such as FIPA [20], CORBA [21] and RMI [22]. In addition, the Grasshopper's feature Webhopper [19] that enables mobile agents for web is a significant plus comparing with other platforms, like Voyager and Aglets [31].

5   Using XUL with Mobile Agents in Multiple Platforms

The idea of this work was to use XUL together with the mobile agent paradigm [8], and to make a prototype that adapts XUL for hosting platform or for remote devices (e.g. a wireless device). By achieving this, one will have a truly mobile user interface that adapts to the platform on the fly.

5.1   A Motivating Example

We present these sample applications, meant to demonstrate the possible every day uses of a mobile agent that adapts its user interface to multiple devices.

The first example is a currency converter application that can be accessed from every point on the network. This application converts among three currencies (Euro, US Dollar, British Pound). We want this application to be accessible from various different devices (Java, WAP phone, web terminal). In all of these cases, the same application should be started, and the same (or equivalent) user interface should be used in order to reduce costs of application development.

The second example is a survey application. It should make a poll of the converter application users, calculate the stats, and return the data to the software company that built the converter application. Similarly to the converter application, we expect users that are taking a survey to have all sorts of devices, different connection types, and possibly problems with network coverage/links. The application ask users to rate the converter application with three possible answers (good, normal, bad), and calculate stats on the answers. All the answers are persisted so the statistics are made on all-times data. In case of loss of network coverage or broken network links, application should re-intent connection or try alternate route to the next host without prompting user.

In Section 6 we describe in detail these sample applications.

5.2   XUL Implementation – jXUL

jXUL [6] is a Open Source project that interprets XUL definition and renders it to Java Swing interface, similarly to [16]. Plans for jXUL are very ambitious, aiming to support very complex controls in future releases. Other open source projects that aim to rendering XUL with Java or to DHTML exist [28]; unfortunately, at the time of writing this paper, none of these has any public prototype available.

However, available jXUL implementation lacks basic functionality, such as assigning and getting values from components or ability to connect outer classes to the JavaScript engine that runs within jXUL. Therefore, we put significant effort into redesigning the existing components to support basic functionality, and extended the JavaScript engine functionality by adding connector classes that can be externally connected to jXUL middleware. Unfortunately, jXUL is built to render only to Java Swing, and not to other types of interfaces, so we had to develop for our prototype XSL transformations that transform XUL files to HTML and WML files.

5.3   Putting It All Together

The prototype built customizes mobile agents in such manner that programming a system that has adaptable user interface is almost completely transparent; programmers have only to extend the required class, connect the classes and to create interface definition files. This approach combines adaptivity with respect to alocating system functionality and adaptivity with respect to interface layout. However, level of plasticity [33] is basic and will be improved in the future work. The base classes will convert the XUL files to appropriate format and handle the communication.

Thus, we created a simple currency converter application that uses a few basic controls: labels, text boxes, radio buttons and classic buttons. In order to construct this application we need some XUL files (one for each window). The sample XUL file that we created for the sample currency converter is shown in Fig. 3.

After constructing the user interface definition, the worker class should be created. This class should carry all procedures that handle interface events, but the computation is not limited to this class. Because of Grasshopper limitations, we had to create this class as a connector class, to be used from jXUL's JavaScript, and therefore to be accessible from the user interface.

The structure of the sample method that we implemented for currency converter agent is shown in Fig. 4.

Code in Fig. 4 is used for any interpretation of XUL files; no modifications for any platforms should be made. As we can see, this method takes three parameters that are passed from the GUI and then process the request. While processing, the window is closed, and when the result is calculated it is opened again.

What we have created is a mobile agent that transforms itself into three forms: Java Swing, HTML or a WML application, depending on the user device capabilities. Also, the agent is acting both as a server and as an application at the same time - if the originator cannot accept mobile agents (e.g, wireless devices), the agent will act as a content server to that device. However, if mobile agents are accepted, the agent will act as standard application.

6   A Sample Scenario: Mobile Calculator and Survey

For our prototype we have set up the network consisting of five network nodes:

```
<?xml version="1.0" encoding="ISO-8859-1"?>
<!-- global window settings and JavaScript link -->
    <window align="vertical" height="255" width="410" title="Converter">
    <script language="JavaScript" src="Handler.js"/>
<!   title label -->
    <box> <label control="lblAll" value="Currency Converter"/> </box>

<!-- inserting the quantity edit box -->
    <vbox>
      <hbox>
        <label control="lblQty" value="Quantity:"/>
        <textbox value="0.00" id="Qty" size="20"/>
      </hbox>
    </vbox>
    <!-- inserting the From radio group -->
    <box>
        <label control="lblFrom" value="From:    "/>
        <radiogroup orient="vertical" id="From" selected="Usd">
          <radio id="Eur" label="Euros"/>
          <radio id="Usd" label="US Dollars"/>
          <radio id="Gbp" label="British Pounds"/>
        </radiogroup>

        <label control="lblTo" value="To:    "/>

<!-- inserting the To radio group -->
        <radiogroup orient="vertical" id="To" selected="Eur">
          <radio id="Eur" label="To Euros">
          <radio id="Usd" label="To US Dollars"/>
          <radio id="Gbp" label="To British Pounds"/>
        </radiogroup>
    </box>

<-- label that will be used for the Output -->
    <box>
        <label control="lblOutput" value="Result:  "/>
    </box>
    <box>
        <label id="Output" control="Output" value=""/>
    </box>

<!-- adding button -->
    <box>
        <button id="Convert" label="Convert" oncommand="convert()"/>
    </box>
  </window>
```

Fig. 3. XUL definition used in currency converter application

– The DesktopNode is a Java-enabled fixed computer that can render Swing; it is able to host mobile agents.
– The WebNode is a network terminal that can render only HTML. This node cannot host mobile agents.
– The WapNode is a mobile phone with Wap browser that can render WML; this node has a wireless connection to the network and cannot host mobile agents.
– The LaptopNode is a wireless laptop, it is Java-enabled, that can host mobile agents.
– The CorporateNode node is server computer, that hosts agents and can render Java Swing. Provides users with our sample applications implemented

```
public void convert(String From, String To, String Value) {
    // do the initialization
    \ldots
    //close the window
    _agent.closeWindow(_agent.Window);
    try
    {
      \ldots //do the computation
    }
    catch (Exception e)
    {
      \ldots //handle exception
    }
    //open the new window
    _agent.openWindow(_agent.Window.displayFile, this, "Output", result);
}
```

Fig. 4. Agent code attached to the currency converter interface

as mobile agents. This node also serves as a server for WebNode and WapNode, since these nodes were assumed not to have possibility of running Java. Of course, this is the worst-case scenario, since there is emerging number of mobile devices that run Java.

6.1   Currency Converter Application

The objective of the currency converter application (described in Section 5.1) was to demonstrate the adaptive interface concept. This application adapts its appearance to the originator of the request. As we can see in the Fig. 6, if DesktopNode or LaptopNode invoke the application, the mobile agent (application) moves there and then it will render the XUL files as Swing.

However, if the WapNode or WebNode invokes the application, a different action will occur. Since these nodes were cannot host agents the CorporateNode acting as server will process their requests.

As we can see in the Fig. 5, we have a mixed architecture. Clients that cannot support mobile agents (WebNode, WapNode) are using CorporateNode as server for their petitions, and therefore client-server architecture is present. However, our currency converter agent travels from CorporateNode to DesktopNode and LaptopNode, using mobile agent architecture.

In Fig. 6, Fig. 7 and Fig. 8, we show how the application looks if invoked from those three platforms. From the Fig. 6 and Fig. 7 we can see that the Swing and HTML outputs are not exactly the same. HTML output for this example could be improved by using tables, but we decided to use simple XSL transformations.

Fig. 8 shows the WML output on the M3Gate WAP browser simulator [29]. As we can see, the output differs significantly from the HTML and Swing outputs as device capabilities and rendering language are different and more limited. For

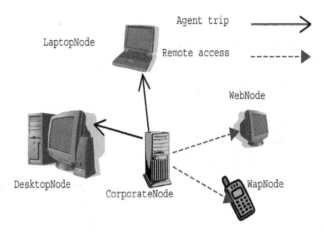

Fig. 5. Network topology and mobile agent trajectories for the currency converter application

Fig. 6. Currency converter agent rendered with Java Swing

example, as seen in Fig. 8, radio groups are initially presented as widgets (Fig. 8, on the left) that are later expanded to a full-screen selection (Fig. 8, on the right).

6.2   Survey Application

This application (explained in Section 5.1) shows benefits from mobile agent computing. Agents are autonomous, adaptive, learning, and mobile; survey application demonstrates these properties. The survey agent travels through the network, visiting the hosts that used our currency converter application. When it reaches the destination host, it transforms its appearance in the suitable form

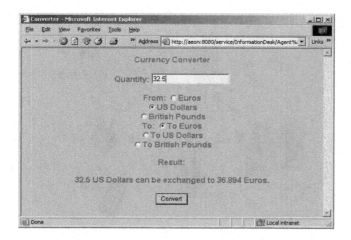

Fig. 7. Currency converter agent rendered as HTML

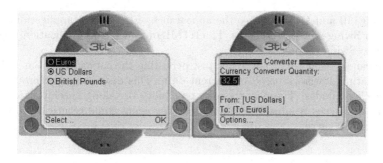

Fig. 8. Currency converter agent rendered as WML and the different output of Radio Group

to ask users for their opinion about the currency converter application. If the network host is unavailable or unreachable, the agent will autonomously decide what to do next. It could wait for host to be available, or continue with the other hosts and return later to the unavailable hosts. Statistics on collected data is calculated.

Fig. 9 shows the network topology that we established for this example. In this Figure we can see that survey application travels from CorporateNode to Desktop-Node and to the LaptopNode. Since the LaptopNode has wireless connection to the network, this link can be broken, and the agent will decide how to reach this node without reporting an error. WebNode and WapNode as we discussed have no processing power, therefore they are served from the CorporateNode. When these hosts complete the survey, the survey application returns to the CorporateNode to deliver results and statistics of the poll.

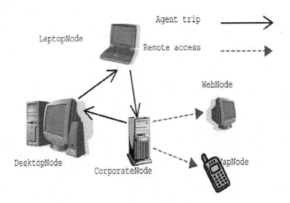

Fig. 9. Network topology and mobile agent trajectories for the survey application

In Fig. 10 and 11 we can see the appearance of the survey application, rendered for Swing and WML clients. The HTML output of this application is very similar to Swing output.

We can see that the agent is not just persisting the survey data, but in fact is calculating statistics based on current data. This distributes the processing among client nodes. There is an open possibility of taking special action depending on survey results. For example, survey agent could return home when it reaches 100 surveys.

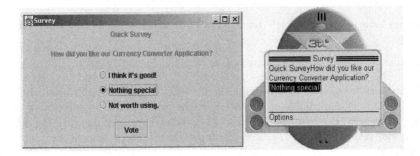

Fig. 10. Survey question, rendered as Swing and WML

Notice that the survey application is a "push" service. The user does not have to request a survey from some central host - agent will visit the client by its own initiative. This kind of service is possible when the user platform supports mobile agents. The users of currency converter application do not need to know about the existence of a survey about the converter application. As we can see from

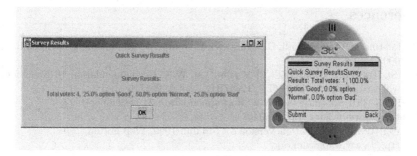

Fig. 11. Survey results, rendered as Swing and WML

the Fig. 9, when the survey is launched, the agent will visit their computer and will pop-up the survey.

Another example application for our approach would be an automated software update agent that could visit hosts, check present software versions and advise users on possible updates.

7 Conclusions and Future Work

In this paper we have presented an autonomous and mobile system, based on mobile agents, that transparently adapts GUI to the users. The main features of this approach are:

- We use and extend third-party middleware jXUL to render XUL to Swing.
- We have made simple XSL transformations in order to convert XUL to other mark-up languages, as HTML and WML.
- A Mobile GUI agent was prototyped, that transparently converts XUL-defined user interface to Java, Web and WAP devices.
- Our approach could be used for other mark-up languages similar to XUL.

This system is stable, gives required functionality, and because of it is mobile agent-based, it is very interested for its application to mobile environment.

However, this work has some limitations. Some platforms do not support elements that can occur in the user interface definition, such as image or sound. Design considerations should take place, and this is the area that should be investigated as a continuation of this work. Thus, our future work will be focused on:

- Transformations for more different outputs
- More efficient transformations, with back-end resource definitions
- Direct binding of XUL to Java without using JavaScript
- Data marshalling using XML metadata

References

1. Horstmann, C.S., Cornell, G.: Core Java 2, Volume 1: Fundamentals, Prentice Hall, 2000.
2. XSL Transformations (XSLT) Version 1.0, W3C Recommendation 16 November 1999, http://www.w3.org/TR/1999/REC-xslt-19991116
3. HTML 4.01 Specification, W3C Recommendation 24 December 1999, http://www.w3.org/TR/html401/
4. WAP-WML Specification Version 1.1, 16 Jun 1999, Wap Forum, http://www.wapforum.org/
5. XUL Tutorial, http://www.xulplanet.com/tutorials/xultu/
6. jXUL, http://jxul.sourceforge.net
7. ECMAScript Language Specification, 3rd Edition, December 1999, ECMA, http://www.ecma.ch/ecma1/stand/ecma-262.htm
8. Distributed Objects & Components: Mobile Agents, http://www.cetus-links.org/oo_mobile_agents.html
9. Mueller, A., Mundt, T., Lindner, W., Cap, C.H.: Platform Independent User Interface Generation with XML, ISAS-SCI (1) 2001: 299-304
10. Stöttner, H.: A Platform-Independent User Interface Description Language, Technical Report 16, Institute for Practical Computer Science, Johannes Kepler University Linz, Austria, March 2001.
11. Microsoft Corporation, Creating Mobile Web Applications with Mobile Web Forms in Visual Studio .NET,
    http://msdn.microsoft.com/vstudio/technical/articles/mobilewebforms.asp
12. XML-MT GUI Definition Language, http://www.mieterra.com/documentation/X-ML-MT.html
13. Cheng, T.: XUL – Creating Localizable XML GUI, Fifteenth Unicode Conference, 1999. http://www.mozilla.org/projects/intl/iuc15/paper/iuc15xul.html
14. IBM WebSphere Transcoding Publisher,
    http://www-3.ibm.com/software/webservers/transcoding/
15. Hild, S.G., Binding, C., Bourges-Waldegg, D., Steenkeste, C.: Application hosting for pervasive computing, IBM Research, 2000,
    http://www.research.ibm.com/journal/sj/401/hild.html
16. Olsen, D.R.Jr, Jefferies, S., Nielsen, T., Moyes, W., Fredrickson, P.: Cross-Modal Interaction using Xweb, UIST, 2000.
17. Mozilla project, http://www.mozilla.org
18. Meyer, E. A.: Cascading Style Sheets: The Definitive Guide, O'Reilly and Associates, 2000.
19. Grasshopper, IKV, http://www.grasshopper.de/
20. Foundation for Intelligent Physical Agents, http://www.fipa.org
21. Pope, A.: The CORBA Reference Guide: Understanding the Common Object Request Broker Architecture, Addison-Wesley Pub Co, 1998.
22. Java Remote Method Invocation, http://java.sun.com/products/jdk/rmi/
23. Resource Description Framework (RDF), W3C Specification,
    http://www.w3.org/RDF/
24. Lyten, K., Coninx, K.: An XML Runtime User Interface Description Language for Mobile Computing Devices, DSVIS, 2001.
25. Müller, A., Forbrig, P., Cap, C.: Model-Based User Interface Design Using Markup Concepts, DSVIS, 2001, 16–27.

26. Abrams, M., Phanouriou, C., Batongbacal, A.L., Williams, S.M., Shuster, J.E.: UIML: An Appliance-Independent XML User Interface Language. WWW8 / Computer Networks 31(11-16): 1695–1708 (1999)
27. Milojicic, D.S.: Trend Wars: Mobile agent applications. IEEE Concurrency 7(3): 80-90 (1999)
28. SourceForge Network, www.sourceforge.net
29. Numeric Algorithm Laboraties, www.m3gate.com, M3Gate WAP Simulator, 2001.
30. Compact HTML for Small Information Appliances, W3C Note 09-Feb-1998, http://www.w3.org/TR/1998/NOTE-compactHTML-19980209/
31. The Mobile Agent List, University of Stuttgart, http://mole.informatik.uni-stuttgart.de/mal/mal.html
32. XIML (eXtensible Interface Markup Language), http://www.ximl.org/
33. Thevenin, D. and Coutaz, J.: "Plasticity of User Interfaces: Frame-work and Research Agenda", Proc of IFIP TC 13 Int. Conf. on Human-Computer Interaction INTERACT'99, Edinburgh, August 1999, IOS Press, 1999.

Migratable User Interface Descriptions in Component-Based Development

Kris Luyten, Chris Vandervelpen, and Karin Coninx

Expertise Centre for Digital Media
Limburgs Universitair Centrum
Wetenschapspark 2
B-3590 Diepenbeek-Belgium
{kris.luyten, chris.vandervelpen, karin.coninx}@luc.ac.be

Abstract. In this paper we describe how a component-based approach can be combined with a user interface (UI) description language to get more flexible and adaptable UIs for embedded systems and mobile computing devices. We envision a new approach for building adaptable user interfaces for embedded systems, which can migrate from one device to another. Adaptability to the device constraints is especially important for adding reusability and extensibility to UIs for embedded systems: this way they are ready to keep pace with new technologies.

1 Introduction

The market of embedded systems and mobile computing devices is a fast evolving market. New technologies are introduced at a very high rate. One of the consequences of this evolution is the constant reinvention of user interfaces (UIs) for these devices. They lack the adaptability and flexibility to be deployed for new devices (possibly using new interaction techniques) without reprogramming them. One of the results of the SEESCOA[1] [13] project is a common software platform, using components for embedded systems on a Java Virtual Machine. Using this specific component-based approach for embedded systems, we can develop a framework for UIs adapting to the environment and device specific constraints as well as encourage reuse. The SEESCOA method is a component-based development approach combined with ideas of contract-based specification for software objects.

This paper presents our ongoing research on the possibility of creating a framework that will allow for runtime migratable UIs, which are independent of the target software platform, the target device and the interaction modalities. These UIs are merely considered as a presentation of a single service or of more functionally grouped services. We try to extend the work presented in [3,14,10] which all focus on how to abstract a UI for a platform- and device-independent

---

[1] Software Engineering for Embedded Systems using a Component-Oriented Approach,
http://www.cs.kuleuven.ac.be/cwis/research/distrinet/projects/SEESCOA/

P. Forbrig et al. (Eds.): DSV-IS 2002, LNCS 2545, pp. 44–58, 2002.
© Springer-Verlag Berlin Heidelberg 2002

usage. Like work presented in [9,6,1], we also use markup languages to describe UIs. However, our work goes a step further by allowing runtime generation of UIs using a markup language. These ideas are combined with a component-based approach allowing the designer to design UIs for particular components, which can be merged automatically at a later stage. This enables UI designers to concentrate on what is important for multi-device UIs: how to present the UI in a structured and logical manner. Unlike approaches like described in [10], we try to develop a truly distributed component-based approach, without relying on a client-server architecture.

Throughout the text we will use an example case study: a small camera surveillance system using 4 cameras. Each camera will be represented by a component. It will be possible to combine the four cameras by using a Mosaic component. This should make it possible to observe four cameras at the same time. Each camera has its own properties: some cameras can zoom in and out, other also allow to change the framerate,...

The next section, section 2, takes a look at how UIs for embedded systems or mobile computing devices can be described with a UI description language. An overview of related work is provided. Continuing with section 3, we show how these descriptions can be combined with software components in general, and SEESCOA components in particular. The case-study is presented in more detail to show the results of the approach proposed in this paper. In section 4, we consider how using markup languages and a component-based approach contributes to flexibility, adaptability and migratability of UIs. In particular attention is given to automatic layout management and multi-modal rendering possibilities. Finally conclusions with regard to the current work and possible extensions are formulated in section 6.

2   Describing User Interfaces for Embedded Systems

2.1   Abstracting the User Interface

When designing UIs for embedded systems, we should not take a widget-based approach, but an interaction- or task-based approach. We should be interested in how a user can interact with the offered service and how this can be instantiated afterwards using a concrete widget set. This kind of approach is thoroughly examined in [11] and is important in particular for embedded devices. Too much time is spent reinventing UIs for accessing the same services as technology evolves. One of the major enhancements we envision is the separation of UI design and low-level programming. Until now, embedded systems programmers have a dual task: implementing the actual embedded system and designing and implementing the UI for this system. The main reason for this way of working is the required technical knowledge and background of the system to provide a UI for it. Therefore we use a markup language to describe the UI for embedded systems and mobile computing devices.

2.2 An XML-Based User Interface Description

To describe a UI on a sufficiently abstract level the eXtensible Markup Language (XML)[5] is used. Listing 1.1 provides an example of how a UI can be described in XML. There are already several propositions and real world examples of the usage of XML to describe UIs: [10,2]. A list of advantages is given in [8]. One of the major advantages is that XML does not force any level of abstraction, so this level can be adapted to the requirements of the situation. Note that an XML document can be presented as a tree which turns out to be a great advantage in our approach. There are other approaches for describing User Interfaces, but we believe that an XML-based description offers the best solution in our component-based approach because of it heavily relies on hierarchical structures.

Listing 1.1. An example XML listing for a camera

```
<ui>
<title>Login</title>
<group name="videopanel">
  <interactor>
    <video name="video">
      <text>Camera 2 video stream</text>
      <mediasource>http://twiki.luc.ac.be/camera:8888</mediasource>
    </video>
  </interactor>
  <interactor>
    <range name="zoomrange">
      <text>Zoom</text>
      <min>-100</min>
      <max>100</max>
      <start>0</start>
      <tick>25</tick>
      <action>
        <func service="Mosaic.camera2">setZoom</func>
        <param name="zoomrange"/>
      </action>
    </range>
  </interactor>
  <interactor>
    <range name="focusrange">
      <text>Focus</text>
      ...
      <action>
      <func service="Mosaic.camera2">setFocus</func>
        <param name="focusrange"/>
      </action>
    </range>
  </interactor>
  <interactor>
    <button name="snapshot">
      <text>Take snapshot</text>
      <action><func service="Mosaic.camera2">saveImage</func></action>
```

```
    </button>
  </interactor>
</group>
</ui>
```

The example listing (listing 1.1) is *not* simplified: the UI description is meant to be human-readable and machine-processable at the same time. The description allows human users to specify the UI on a high level.

On the other hand, the structured and hierarchical approach by using XML as a notational language to describe the UI allows machines to process and use these descriptions without human intervention. Our notation uses a range of tags that are easy to read and understand for humans. In the current stage, a stable Document Type Definition or XML Schema is not available because we do not consider our specification to be complete. Nevertheless care has been taken to introduce no ambiguities in the specification and to enable easy migration to other specification languages, in case a certain XML-based notation for describing UIs will evolve into a standard.

The following interactors are currently supported by the system: range interactors, single and multiple choice interactors, a text interactor, push interactors (e.g. a button) and a canvas output interactor (e.g. a video stream). These can be composed to represent a new interactor with combined functionality. The available tags are still limited, but a lot of dialog-based UIs can already be implemented using these widgets (e.g. all kinds of web forms). There are two tag types which are of particular importance: **group** tags and **action** tags. The **group** tags allow to group objects which have no meaning when they are separated. An example of this is a "date interactor": the interactors involved for filling in a date should not be separated (listing 1.2). Groups can be nested: they can be hierarchically structured. This enables us to reuse groups of interactors, and make new composed groups. The **action** tags allow a user to specify which action to fire if the interactor (which is the parent node) is manipulated. The action tag specifies the target (this can be a class name, a server,...) and the functionality that has to be invoked from this target. It is also possible to specify parameters and use the names of the interactors or groups for these parameters. Our system will automatically extract the current content out of the interactor or group (to which these parameter identifiers point) and pass it to the invoked functionality. There is no need to indicate the type for the UI designer, the type checking will be done at runtime. This is advantageous for the level of abstraction, but demands a detailed exception handling algorithm, and allows little or no compile-time or design-time checks. Further implementation may be required to reveal more opportunities to check the validity of the description at design- or compile-time.

Listing 1.2. A date group

```
<group name="date">
 <interactor>
  <range name="day">...</range>
 </interactor>
 <interactor>
```

```
<range name="month">...</range>
</interactor>
<interactor>
 <range name="year">...</range>
</interactor>
</group>
```

3   User Interface Descriptions and Components

3.1   The SEESCOA Component Framework

Within the SEESCOA project a component frameworkfor embedded systems
is being developed. One of our involvements for this project is merging UI design and component-based development for embedded systems. The component
system is asynchronous and uses the Java programming language as a common
platform. Components communicate by sending asynchronous messages to each
other, and not by using traditional synchronous message calls.

A traditional approach, making a static UI as a layer on a service or a data
layer, has proven to lack flexibility. We consider components as units that contain
logically grouped functionality and data, each living in their own memory space.
They should offer an abstract description of how the service or data offered can
be presented. Think about components as software units offering a particular
service through their interface: their interface is actually a description of their
functionality. It is a natural extension to also allow components to describe what
they want to offer to a human user.

Each component can provide a description expressed in XML of the functionality it offers. Alternatively, they also could express in which way they could be
interacted with. This is not true for all components of course (some just offer basic functionality on a lower level for other components), so only the components
directly interested in human interaction should provide an abstract UI description. When building applications out of components a UI is automatically built:
each component has its UI in the form of an XML description. These XML descriptions can all be seen as subtrees of the final, composed UI description. I.e.
the UI will be automatically composed by connecting the UI descriptions of the
components in to a bigger UI description. Figure 3 shows how this works using
a small example: the Camera Mosaic component which is described in more detail the next section (section 3.3). Each component can contain a description of
their UI: a description of a Camera can be found in 1.3 and of the Mosaic in 1.4.
Figure 3 presents how the descriptions can be combined at runtime to create the
UI out of the components.

Listing 1.3. UI description of a single camera component

```
<group name="camera2">
  <interactor>
    <videowidget name="video">...</videowidget>
  </interactor>
  <interactor>
```

```
  <range name="zoomrange"><action>
    <func service="Surveillance.Controls">setFocus</func>
      <param name="camera2"/>
      <param name="zoomrange"/>
  </action></range>
</interactor>
<interactor><range name="focusrange">...</range></interactor>
<interactor>
  <button name="camera1_onoff"><action>
    <func service="Surveillance.Controls">switch</func>
      <param name="camera2"/>
      <param name="camera1_onoff"/>
  </action></button>
</interactor>
</group>
```

Listing 1.4. UI description of a Mosaic component

```
<ui>
  <title>Camera mosaic</title>
    <group name="mosaic">
      <group name="camera1">&CAMERA1</group>
      <group name="camera2">&CAMERA2</group>
      <group name="camera3">&CAMERA3</group>
      <group name="camera4">&CAMERA4</group>
    </group>
</ui>
```

Notice this approach allows components to migrate and offer their services in other places. The UI integrates smoothly in the new system the component is used on. The component-based approach supports a distributed view on assembling applications out of components and generating their UI: parts of the UI are allowed to migrate together with the functionality the components offer. Finally, the UI description can be submitted to a "renderer" component in the form of an XML document.

3.2   The Rendering Component

As we take a component-based approach for designing UIs for embedded systems, there is one "basic" component: the UI renderer component. This can be compared to a web-browser: a description for an interface can be submitted to the component and it will take care of rendering this description. Nevertheless, there are some differences: the component can receive a description of a UI and render it to different kinds of output devices and widget sets. The state of the UI can be "serialised" back into XML and relocated, which makes the component approach suitable for distributed systems or remote UIs. The SEESCOA

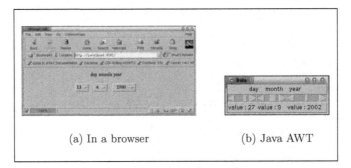

(a) In a browser   (b) Java AWT

Fig. 1. Two different views on listing 1.2, both automatically generated

component system takes care of the communication and makes it network transparent. Notice the rendering engine is also embedded in a component, so this component can also have a UI description of its own functionality. To show its UI the rendering component can send its UI description to itself.

There are several possible output formats and for each kind of output a different rendering component can be supplied. For example: there could be rendering components for a PDA (e.g. Palm, see figure 5), for Java Swing (suitable for use on a desktop PC) and a rendering component for speech synthesis. The date group presented in listing 1.2 is rendered using two different rendering components in figure 1: a HTML rendering component and a Java AWT rendering component. The rendering components are "self-contained": they do not rely on other components and are suitable to migrate individually to a particular system or software platform. Their internal working relies on the same code nevertheless.

3.3   A Case Study: A Camera Surveillance System

To illustrate how components can deliver their own UI description, we developed an example case study in the context of the SEESCOA project: a surveillance system. The example surveillance system consists of 4 cameras, each camera is represented by a component. The system also contains a Mosaic component, combining the controls for each camera in a combined control. The Mosaic component communicates with a rendering component which renders a UI to an output device. The setup is presented in figure 2. Notice each camera component has its own UI description (shown in listing 1.1) presented as an XML notation. This is shown by the trees attached to the camera components in figure 2. Each camera may offer different possibilities so they can all have different UI descriptions (The camera component is a component which abstracts the hardware and presents a real surveillance camera).

Because of the possibility to specify hierarchical groups, the Mosaic component can take the four individual controls and add them as subtrees in a new

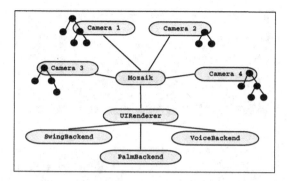

Fig. 2. Component composition example: a simple camera surveillance system

tree. The Mosaic component only needs to add a new root with 4 groups as the children of the root node. Each control can be attached to a group node (figure 3, the group nodes are coloured gray). The UI description tree produced by the Mosaic component is passed to the rendering component and rendered according to the chosen back-end. This illustrates how combining components to access their provided functionality in one application automatically results in a combined UI of these components. Notice several hierarchies can be mixed if desired: a subtree can be attached to an "open" node on another level in a new tree. This should be done with care: the chances of illogical and unusable generated UIs can increase by doing this. Our current system does not link the several subtrees across hierarchies, so no further support for mixing hierarchies is provided.

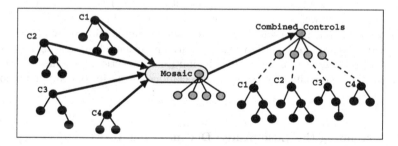

Fig. 3. The Mosaic component combining several UI descriptions

Depending on the target device the UI for the Mosaic component will be different. Suppose for example we want to access the Mosaic component using a traditional desktop computer: the rendering component for a desktop PC will load the available Concrete Interaction Objects (CIOs)[14] and try to map the

Fig. 4. The Mosaic component on a desktop

Abstract Interaction Objects (AIOs) described in the Mosaic UI description on a widget set suitable for a desktop machine: figure 4 shows this. If we want to access the functionality of the Mosaic component using our PDA, the rendering component for a PDA will do the same thing: load the available CIOs and trying to map the AIOs on this set of CIOs. This time the rendering component knows the PDA has limited possibilities, so it adapts the concrete UI to the screen space constraints. Figure 5 shows the results using a PDA (Palm IIIc). The focus of this work was not data communication but runtime UI migration, so we did not spend time investigating effective data communication between devices. The "videostream" for the PDA was actually implemented by sending separate down-scaled images to the device over its infrared connection. Of course, this can be done much more effective using other techniques or means of communication.

3.4   Extending the Case Study: Decomposing Tasks

The case study introduced in section 3.3 is a very simple "interaction session" with a single dialog. We consider an interaction session as the interaction which happens to complete a subtask, like "select camera" in figure 6 for example. Most UIs have more than one interaction session: in a dialog-based UI several dialogs are presented after each other. A design method to take this into account is required at this stage. The design method should enable the designer to decompose tasks hierarchically, and link several interaction sessions to each other

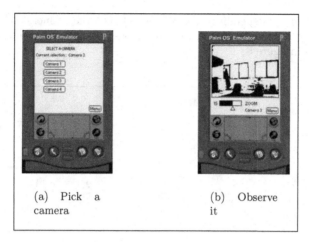

(a) Pick a
camera

(b) Observe
it

Fig. 5. The Mosaic component on a PDA

in order to achieve the postulated goal. This method should support a device independent specification of the UI.

To solve this problem, we combine ConcurTaskTree (CTT) [11] with our component-based description method. One of the advantages of the CTT notation is that we can extend it to model context-sensitive user tasks as described in [12]. Characteristics that determine the context of use include the computing platform, the available interaction devices, available screen space,... When one or more of these characteristics change, a reconfiguration of the UI may be required to adapt to the new context of use. [12] proposes a notation to model context-sensitive user tasks. Their solution consists of a CTT task model with roughly the following parts: a non-context-sensitive CTT part and context-sensitive parts depending on some conditions.

The second advantage is the asynchronous nature of the SEESCOA component system: CTT allows to describe temporal relations, and includes concurrent tasks in its notations. A third advantage is the hierarchical structure it offers: our approach also uses an hierarchical notation to describe the UI in a device independent manner.

Now suppose a human guard has access to a security system using a regular workstation or a PDA. Some tasks he can perform on the workstation are not possible on the PDA. Suppose for example that it's not possible to observe more than 1 camera at the same time on the PDA due to the minor screenspace provided by it. So it depends on the context of use (the device that's being used in this case) whether the operator can pick just one or multiple cameras to observe at a time. Obviously we can say that this is a context-sensitive task. There are also a couple of non-context-sensitive tasks in this case. The operator must logon to the system before he can pick cameras. Also he can choose to stop observing or pick other cameras to observe. While the guard is observing a camera (or cameras depending on the context) the other cameras will continue to record their video streams until the guard logs out again. The enhanced CTT tree is shown in figure 6.

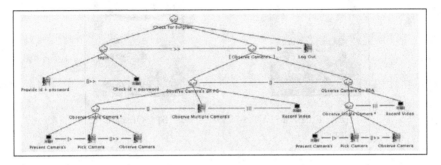

Fig. 6. ConcurTaskTree diagram: checking for burglars with the camera surveillance system in a context-sensitive way

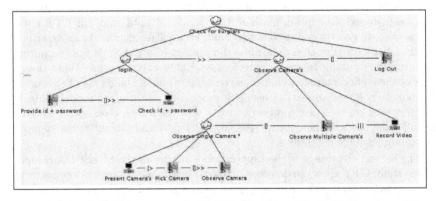

Fig. 7. ConcurTaskTree diagram: checking for burglars with the camera surveillance system

While being a good solution for modeling context-sensitive tasks there are two minor drawbacks to it. The first one is that some subtrees may appear more than once in the model. For example in figure 6 the subtree *Observe Single Camera* appears in the two different contexts of use. [12] solves this by factoring out these subtrees by placing them in the context-insensitive part of the model. The second drawback is that we still have to model every possible context of use: for each device different properties have to be taken into account. In our approach we try to avoid this by using abstract UI descriptions for an interaction task. A CTT description can be saved as an XML document, which allows us to attach our own XML description at the leafs representing an interaction task. These XML descriptions are actually the composed descriptions of the components which are used at that moment. A CTT description becomes a way to describe how we want to interact with a set of given components in a particular stage of the usage of an application. We gain a model-based approach for designing the UI, extending the component-based approach for modelling the software itself. So, instead of using a context-sensitive description as shown in figure 6 we can accomplish the same thing with a non context-sensitive description as shown in figure 7. We recognise that these are just the first steps, and the method has not been tested for a wider range of devices yet. When using totally different ways of interaction (e.g. not dialog-based), we expect we need context-sensitive parts as a consequence of particular other ways to complete the subtasks.

4   Flexible and Adaptable User Interfaces for Embedded Systems

4.1   Realising a Concrete UI

To transform the abstract UI description into a concrete one it has to pass several stages of processing in our approach:

1. a mapping stage
2. a specialised layout management stage
3. the rendering stage

The UI description, presented as a tree in memory, is passed to a rendering component, which will initiate the mapping stage: it tries to convert the AIOs into CIOs [3]. For each available widget set, the mapping choices are implemented ad hoc: the current implementation does not support user guidance. This is one of the shortcomings in our approach: we tend to solve this problem in a following iteration. The mapping stage will convert the abstract UI description to a "platform specific" description for one or several specific modalities (using XSLT[2] or an agent component).

Once the system has built a concrete representation structure, the actual screenspace needed for this presentation can be calculated. The mapping stage already involves some calculations of the weighted values of the AIOs, and the corresponding space they may require.

The final step is to show the actual UI: this is done by rendering the CIOs on screen. The widget set used to do the mapping is provided by the target platform and therefore it defines how to represent the CIOs visually.

---

[2] eXtensible Stylesheet Language Transformations

4.2   System Independent User Interfaces

Every time a new device is used as output device, the specific UI renderer component will use the device profile, containing the device constraints and its ad hoc knowledge of the target system. The renderer changes the UI presentation according to the defined limitations.

One of the consequences of adapting the UI to new device constraints is the need for an automatic layout algorithm when GUI rendering is used. When the UI moves to a new output device, the UI should be laid out in a logical way. One approach achieving this is by using layout algorithms found in diagram rendering (like graphs and state-charts). Due to the hierarchical view on the UI, we try to adopt weighting algorithms especially designed for presenting as hierarchical data like presented in [4]. Every leaf is given a *weight* indicating its complexity (primarily space needs). Recursively every group (i.e. every node that is no leaf) will get the complexity of its children and is added up with a certain constant value in complexity weight. This is a simple attempt to automate the layout algorithm, without taking into account real usability issues which arise when automating this process.

Our architecture allows each subtree of a UI description tree to use a different layout algorithm. For example; we use a layout algorithm that allocates space from left to right in a rectangular space for the first level of subtrees under the root node. The space is allocated according to the weighted complexity of each subtree. On next level, a more complex layout algorithm is used (like a GridBagLayout in the Java programming language) for each subtree. One of the .advantages of this approach is a better support for fragmented UI (several parts of the UI are accessible from several devices), multi-modal UIs and dynamically changing UIs. Currently we are integrating *spatial constraints* for 2D UI in our system, so the UI designer can indicate how AIOs should be placed in relation to each other [7].

5   Summary of Our Current Results

Current results include a rendering component, to which an XML document describing an abstracted UI can be submitted. The renderer maps this description to an actual widget set and tries to adapt the layout so the UI fits on screen. When the screen size becomes too small, the renderer will try to split different parts of the UI and put them behind each other. While doing this, logically grouped elements will not be split up. These grouping operators are specified in the abstract UI description: they group user interactions which logically depend on each other. Examples of tested target widget sets are Java *AWT*, *Swing*, *kAWT* and HTML (web pages).

The SEESCOA Components can be combined in order to make a fully functional application and their UI description can be combined automatically. An example of this was described using the Camera Mosaic application. This enables User Interfaces to become migratable: first of all their description can be rendered to other output devices and second the UI can accompany the component it represents when it is sent to another system. We have only tested the system with simple UIs, so no conclusions can be made concerning scalability.

6   Conclusions and Future Work

The new component-oriented approach suggested in this paper has several advantages for developers of embedded systems and mobile computing devices in particular. It is

Flexible : changing the UI can be done by another renderer component or letting components provide another UI description;

Reusable : providing a high level *description* of the UI related to the functionality a component offers, allows easier reusability of previously designed UIs in contrast with hard-coded UIs;

Adaptable : by abstracting the UI, device constraints can be taken into account when rendering the concrete UI.

Besides these advantages we showed how attaching abstract UI descriptions to components helps to compose User Interfaces at runtime without intervention from a programmer. This is especially important when a mobile computing device has to present a new service that it was not aware of. E.g. a PDA comes near to a printer and should be able to present the accessible functionality of this printer. All these advantages make the UIs migratable: they can be easily transported from one device to another, adapting to new environments.

Future work includes adding alternative output rendering components other then a 2D screen renderer like speech output and the implementation of context-sensitive layout algorithms. We acknowledge there is a lack of support for artistic and aesthetic influences in the creation of the UIs employing the approach we presented in this paper. It is our intention to look at alternative interaction methods besides traditional interaction methods. Due to the asynchronous nature of the SEESCOA component system, it is interesting to take time-related HCI patterns into account.

Although the focus is not on the usability of the UIs, introducing these patterns can help us to ensure a minimal usability. For introducing design-time type checks an appropriate editor for this is required. Some checks can be done if a certain amount of information of the application logic is available (the editor should know which arguments can be handled by what kind of functionality). An editor for designing the UI descriptions is not available at this moment.

Acknowledgements. Our research is partly funded by the Flemish government and EFRO[3]. The SEESCOA project IWT 980374 is directly funded by the IWT[4]. The *Vrije Universiteit Brussel (Programming Lab)* and *Katholieke Universiteit Leuven (Distrinet)* have created the SEESCOA component system.

---

[3] European Fund for Regional Development
[4] Flemish subsidy organization

References

1. Marc Abrams, Constantinos Phanouriou, Alan L. Batongbacal, Stephen M. Williams, and Jonathan E. Shuster. UIML: An appliance-independent XML user interface language. *WWW8 / Computer Networks*, 31(11-16):1695–1708, 1999.
2. Marc Abrams, Constantinos Phanouriou, Alan L. Batongbacal, Stephen M. Williams, and Jonathan E. Shuster. *UIML: An Appliance-Independent XML User Interface Language*. World Wide Web, http://www8.org/w8-papers/5b-hypertext-media/uiml/uiml.html, 1998.
3. Jacob Eisenstein, Jean Vanderdonckt, and Angel Puerta. Applying Model-Based Techniques to the Development of UIs for Mobile Computers. In *IUI 2001 International Conference on Intelligent User Interfaces*, pages 69–76, 2001.
4. David Harel and Gregory Yashchin. An Algorithm for Blob Hierarchy Layout. In *Proceedings of the Working Conference on Advanced Visual Interfaces*, pages 29–40, May 2000.
5. Elliotte Rusty Harold. *XML; Extensible Markup Language, Structuring Complex Content for the Web*. IDG Books Worldwide, 1998.
6. IBM Corporation. *MoDAL (Mobile Document Application Language)*. World Wide Web, http://www.almaden.ibm.com/cs/TSpaces/MoDAL/.
7. Simon Lok and Steven Feiner. A Survey of Automated Layout Techniques for Information Presentations. In *Proceedings of SmartGraphics 2001*, March 2001.
8. Kris Luyten and Karin Coninx. An XML-based runtime user interface description language for mobile computing devices. In *Proceedings of the Eight Workshop of Design, Specification and Verification of Interactive Systems*, pages 17–29, June 2001.
9. Andreas Müller, Peter Forbrig, and Clemens Cap. Model-Based User Interface Design Using Markup Concepts. In *Proceedings of the Eight Workshop of Design, Specification and Verification of Interactive Systems*, pages 30–39, June 2001.
10. Dan R. Olsen, Sean Jefferies, Travis Nielsen, William Moyes, and Paul Fredrickson. Cross-modal interaction using XWeb. In *Proceedings of the 13th Annual Symposium on User Interface Software and Technology (UIST-00)*, pages 191–200, N.Y., November 5–8 2000. ACM Press.
11. Fabio Paternò. *Model-Based Design and Evaluation of Interactive Applications*. Springer, 2000.
12. Costin Pribeanu, Quentin Limbourg, and Jean Vanderdonckt. Task Modelling for Context-Sensitive User Interfaces. In *Proceedings of the Eight Workshop of Design, Specification and Verification of Interactive Systems*, pages 60–76, June 2001.
13. David Urting, Stefan Van Baelen, Tom Holvoet, and Yolande Berbers. Embedded Software Development: Components and Contracts. In *Proceedings of the IASTED International Conference Parallel and Distributed Computing and Systems*, pages 685–690, 2001.
14. J. Vanderdonckt and F. Bodart. Encapsulating knowledge for intelligent automatic interaction objects selection. In *ACM Conference on Human Aspects in Computing Systems InterCHI'93*, pages 424–429. Addison Wesley, 1993.

Task Modelling in Multiple Contexts of Use

Nathalie Souchon, Quentin Limbourg, and Jean Vanderdonckt

Université catholique de Louvain, Institut d'Administration et de Gestion
Place des Doyens, 1 – B-1348 Louvain-la-Neuve, Belgium
{souchon, limbourg, vanderdonckt}@isys.ucl.ac.be

Abstract. The context of use in which users are carrying out their interactive tasks is continuously submitted to an evolution in the user population, the computing platforms used for the tasks, and the physical environment in which users are living. This evolution process raises a need for extending traditional task modelling to support multiple contexts of use simultaneously. To address this problem, this paper first provides a formal notation of a task model that is further refined to support the variation of conditions depending on multiple contexts of use. Key concepts are then introduced to support the task modelling process so as to create a clear frontier between the Context-dependent Task Model and the Context-Independent Task Model. The Context-Partially-Independent Task Model attempts to capture subtasks shared in many contexts of use, but not all. The use of these key concepts enable designers to build a Multi-Context Task Model, notably, by factoring out common parts from Context-dependant Task Models. All these key concepts are equally denoted with the introduced formal notation. In addition, they support designers in adopting the task modelling approach of their choice in multiple contexts of use, which is so far not allowed.

1 Introduction

For many years, user interfaces (UIs) have been developed assuming that the context of use in which they work remains constant over time: the user considered to have little or no variation, interacting with the same computing platform to carry out the same task in a non-changing physical environment. Today, this assumption is no longer satisfied as we observe:

1. **A multiplicity of users**: not only types of users become more numerous (e.g., more people are willing to interact with computers), but also types of user are subject to many redefinitions (e.g., users do evolve over time dynamically).
2. **A proliferation of computing platforms**: existing computing platforms, like the desktop PC, are progressively enhanced with new interaction capabilities while new platforms are emerging, such as cellular phone, Personal Digital Assistant (PDA), Pocket PC, Web Appliance, or dedicated interaction devices.

P. Forbrig et al.(Eds.): DSV-IS 2002, LNCS 2545, pp. 59–73, 2002.
© Springer-Verlag Berlin Heidelberg 2002

3. **A continuous evolution of the physical environment**: the organizational structure may change (thus leading to moving a role from type of user to another), the office location may change (thus resulting in task reallocation), the working circumstances may change (e.g., the user moves with her computing platform from one place to another).

Existing conditions in which users carry out their interactive tasks are progressively evolving, while new conditions are appearing. Therefore, the capability of task-based UI design (i.e., with a single, all-encompassing task model) to initiate the development process and to ensure user-centered design is questioned. In other words, a task model valid for a single predefined context of use may become no longer valid for multiple, possibly largely different, contexts of use or for variations of the context of use.

The aim of this paper is to address the problem of task modelling in multiple contexts of use by augmenting the capabilities of traditional single-context task modelling to support multiple contexts of use simultaneously. The remainder of this paper is structured as follows: Section 2 situates the scope of this paper and motivates it by highlighting some shortcomings of existing approaches. Section 3 selects a well-established task model that will be subject to a formal definition of its form and properties. Section 4 introduces our detailed definition of the context of use in terms of the previously defined formal notation and provides four key concepts to support an original multi-context task model. Section 5 exemplifies the above concepts on a case study in tele-medicine. Section 6 concludes the paper by reporting on the benefits of the four key concepts supporting the multi-context task modelling and suggests some future work.

2 The Development Process of Multi-context User Interfaces

To define the scope of this paper, we rely on the reference framework for plastic UIs introduced by Calvary, Coutaz & Thevenin [1]. It identifies four major levels for producing context-sensitive UIs (Fig. 1).

1. A **Concepts and Tasks Model** connects a task model and a concepts model, which describes the concepts of interest of the domain of discourse, along with their internal relationships as manipulated by the task.
2. An **Abstract UI** defines a computing platform-independent rendering of the above concepts and relationships as they are required by the task in terms of working spaces (or presentation units).
3. A **Concrete UI** transforms the above platform-independent rendering into a platform-dependent rendering.
4. A **Final UI** determines the complete piece of code required to run/execute the UI from the above concrete UI.

In any given context of use (e.g., $C1$ in Fig. 1), each level is subject to an *iteration* that is, any redefinition or recomposition performed at the same level of abstraction to accommodate with new design options. Each non-final level is subject to a *reification* that is, any transformation of an abstract level into a more concrete one with the ultimate goal of producing a final UI. A second context of use can be reached at any level of abstraction thanks to a *translation* that is, any transformation of a UI description initially intended for a given context of use into another description of the same level of abstraction, but that is tailored to another context of use.

Our approach for considering multiple contexts of use focuses on the examination of the translation at the 'Concepts and Tasks Model' level, as represented by the lens in Fig. 1. To express the impact of context variations on the task model, Thevenin [16] introduced two notions: the *decoration* which consists of expressing particular configurations of the task model depending on logical conditions representing variations of the context of use and the *factorization* which consists of expressing common configurations in part or whole of the task model depending on the same logical conditions.

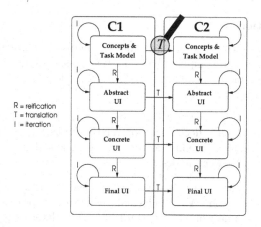

Fig. 1. The reference development process for supporting context-sensitive UIs ([1]).

The two notions of decoration and factorization can serve as fundamental atomic operations to compose various approaches to modelling tasks for multiple contexts of use. Among these approaches are the following examples:

1. A *'Specific-target-at-a-time' approach* [16]: build one task model for each context of use one after another, combine the resulting separate task models into a comprehensive one by performing factorization and decoration, respectively.
2. A *'Factoring out' approach*: build one task model for each context of use and apply factorization to separate common parts from uncommon ones.
3. A *Minimalistic approach*: build one task model containing all parts common to all contexts of use and apply decoration for all uncommon parts resulting from specific contexts of use.

4. A *Prototypicalistic approach*: build one task model for a context of use considered as representative of most cases (e.g., a more important one, a more frequent one, or a more comprehensive one) and apply decoration when appropriate.
5. A *Maximalistic approach*: build the most comprehensive task model with all subtasks for all contexts of use, derive from this maximal model a specific task model for each specific context of use by applying decoration.

The above examples show how important a simultaneous consideration of multiple contexts of use can be. Equally important are the need for a formal notation and an appropriate way to factoring out parts that are common to different contexts and for differentiating parts that are dissimilar in these contexts. They argue for the need of a sound basis for task modelling in multiple contexts of use.

3   Task Model

3.1   Introduction

A task model describes tasks that users need to perform in order to reach a goal when interacting with a computer-based system. Tasks are typically recursively decomposed into a hierarchy of subtasks. A task model can be represented by a graph structure where:

- **Nodes** are the different tasks and subtasks a user has to carry out.
- **Edges** denote either a decomposition relation (a task t_i is decomposed into several subtasks) or a temporal relation (e.g., a task must be performed before another) between nodes.

Task modelling has been extensively researched for years without any consensus on a formal notation. Various formalisms have been proposed (e.g., formal grammars, transition networks, Petri nets) that cover different types of information for different types of task model. Some are more oriented towards identifying the activities and their logical decomposition whereas others are including indications of temporal relationships and adding information related to various concepts such as task objects, rules or agents [10].

The selection of ConcurTaskTree (CTT) as a starting task model results from a careful analysis of several task models [9] based on the following rationale:

- CTT is more oriented towards software engineering than towards psychocognitive analysis (like TKS [8] for instance).
- CTT has a rich set of formally defined temporal operators (i.e. LOTOS operators) [11], probably the most extensive one.
- CTT is supported by a usable graphical tool (CCTE) which facilitates its dissemination and communication among practitioners.

This section sets the basis of a formal notation of a CTT task model in order to support task modelling for multiple contexts of use.

3.2   Definition and Properties

Let us assume that the task model is a directed graph. Let $\mathcal{RO}$ be the set of relationship operators. $\mathcal{RO}$ is partitioned into temporal and decomposition relationships. The Task Model $\mathcal{TM}$ is defined by a tuple $< TASK\,,\,t_0\,,\,T >$ where:

- $TASK$ is a finite set, called the set of tasks. $TASK = \{t_0, t_1, ..., t_n\}$ where the t_i are the different tasks and subtasks that have to be carried out.
- $t_0 \in TASK$ is the root of the graph, that is to say the initial task.
- $T \subseteq TASK \times \mathcal{RO} \times TASK$ is a set of *transitions*, which can be noted by the triplet $< t_i, ro_i, t_j >$. As it is a directed graph, t_i is the *source node* whereas t_j is the *target node*.

For example, the task tree represented in Fig. 2 would be denoted as:

$$\mathcal{TM} =< \{t_0, t_1, t_2, t_3, t_4\}, t_0, \{(t_0, ro_1, t_1), (t_0, ro_1, t_2), (t_1, ro_2, t_2),$$

$$(t_1, ro_1, t_3), (t_1, ro_1, t_4), (t_3, ro_3, t_4)\} >$$

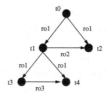

Fig. 2. Example of Task Graph.

Moreover, some properties can be asserted:

- $\forall t_i \in TASK,\ \Gamma^+(t_i) = \{t_j \in TASK \mid \exists ro_i \in \mathcal{RO} : < t_i, ro_i, t_j >\}$ denotes the set of all the successors of t_i.
- $\forall t_i \in TASK,\ \Gamma^-(t_i) = \{t_j \in TASK \mid \exists ro_i \in \mathcal{RO} : < t_j, ro_i, t_i >\}$ denotes the set of all the predecessors of t_i.
- $\forall t_i \in TASK$, father(t_i) = set of all the predecessors of t_i where ro_i is a relationship of decomposition in the triplet $< t_j, ro_i, t_i >$.
- $\forall t_i \in TASK$, child(t_i) = set of all the successors of t_i where ro_i is a decomposition relationship in the triplet $< t_i, ro_i, t_j >$.
- $\forall t_i \in TASK$, brother(t_i) = set of all the successors or predecessors of t_i where ro_i is a temporal relationship in the triplet $< t_i, ro_i, t_j >$ or in the triplet $< t_j, ro_i, t_i >$.
- the nodes of $\mathcal{TM}$ will be organized in layers from the root. We define L_i (the layer of range i) as the set of the nodes resulting from applying Deo's level decomposition algorithm [3]. Moreover, $\forall i\ \forall j,\ L_i \subseteq \mathcal{TM}_j$ can be verified. In the above example, $L_0 = \{t_0\}$, $L_1 = \{t_1, t_2\}$ and $L_2 = \{t_3, t_4\}$.

- if $\Gamma^-(t_i) = \emptyset$, then $t_i = t_0$: the root denotes the main task.
- if $\text{child}(t_i) = \emptyset$, then t_i is a leaf: a leaf denotes a basic task.
- $\mathcal{TM}_i \subset \mathcal{TM}_j$ iff $\forall < t_i, ro_i, t_j > \in \mathcal{TM}_i \Rightarrow < t_i, ro_i, t_j > \in \mathcal{TM}_j$: $\mathcal{TM}_i$ is included $\mathcal{TM}_j$ iff all the transitions of $\mathcal{TM}_i$ are included in $\mathcal{TM}_j$.

For the purpose of this paper, the following hypotheses are stated:

- $\forall t_i, t_j \in TASK$, $\exists! \, ro_i \in \mathcal{RO} \Rightarrow < t_i, ro_i, t_j >$: $\mathcal{TM}$ is a 1-graph, that is to say that there exists only one directed edge between two nodes.
- $\mathcal{TM}$ is not a tree because $\forall t_i$, $\# \, \Gamma^-(t_i) \leq 3$: a node can have up to three predecessors: its father, its brother or itself (via iteration relationship).
- $\forall t_i \in TASK$, $\text{child}(t_i) \neq 1$: there must be more than one child for each task, otherwise this task should not have been decomposed.
- $\forall t_i \in \Gamma^+(t_j)$: $\exists$ one brother(t_i), a corollary of the previous property.
- $\exists! \, t_i \mid \Gamma^-(t_i) = \emptyset$: there can be one and only one root for each $\mathcal{TM}$.

4   Task Model for Multiple Contexts of Use

4.1   Introduction to the Context of Use

Task models attempt to systematically represent the way users achieve a goal when interacting with a system. Some factors largely influence how a user performs tasks to achieve a goal. We group these factors under the term *context of use*.

The concept of context is extensively investigated in various areas of computer science, leading to no unique definition. Schilit *et al* [13] define context by three important aspects : *where you are, who you are* and *what resources are nearby*. It means that they include the computing environment, the user environment and, finally, the physical environment. Chen and Kotz [2] added to this definition the time context, because the moment the user has to perform a task is also an important and a natural factor.

Some authors consider context to be the user's context while others consider it to be the application's environment [15]. Petrelli *et al* [12] define the context as *any information that can be used to characterize and interpret the situations in which a user interacts with an application at a certain time.*

Dey and Abowd [4] define context to be *any information that can be used to characterize the situation of an entity, where an entity can be a person, a place or objects that is considered relevant to the interaction between a user and an application, including the user and the application themselves.* From this definition, almost any information available at the time of interaction can be interpreted as contextual information (e.g., social situation, physiological measurement, and schedules).

Schmidt *et al* [14] define context as *knowledge about the user's and IT device's state, including surroundings, situation and location.*

We define the *context of use* as the complete environment in which a task is carried out. The concept of context of use is partitioned into three models [4,5, 7,6,17]:

1. The *User Model* ($\mathcal{UM}$) is a finite set $\{u_1, u_2, ..., u_n\}$ where each u_i represents a specific stereotype of user.
2. The *Platform Model* ($\mathcal{PM}$) is a finite set $\{p_1, p_2, ..., p_m\}$ where each p_i represents any property of the computing platform, such as screen resolution, operating system, or network bandwidth.
3. The *Environment Model* ($\mathcal{EM}$) is a finite set $\{e_1, e_2, ..., e_p\}$ where each e_i represents a specific configuration of physical conditions (e.g., light or pressure), location-, social and organizational environment (e.g., stress level or social interactions) in which a task is carried out.

A context C_i is denoted by a tuple $< u_i, p_i, e_i >$. A context variation appears when, at least, one element of a context tuple is modified.

A Contextual Task Model ($\mathcal{CTM}$) is defined as a task model associated with a specific context of use. A $\mathcal{CTM}$ is denoted by a tuple $< TASK , t_0, T , [C_{ctm}] >$, where $[C_{ctm}]$ is a matrix of context of use which holds one element: C_i. Several $\mathcal{CTM}$s can be defined for a same application, they are referred as $\mathcal{CTM}_i$.

From the example of Fig. 2, a $\mathcal{CTM}$ can be denoted as follows:

$$\mathcal{CTM} =< \{t_0, t_1, t_2, t_3, t_4\}, t_0, \{(t_0, ro_1, t_1), (t_0, ro_1, t_2), (t_1, ro_2, t_2),$$

$$(t_1, ro_1, t_3), (t_1, ro_1, t_4), (t_3, ro_3, t_4)\}, [C_1] >$$

where C_1 would be for instance: $< u_1, p_1, e_1 >$.

If an application is used in different contexts of use, a matrix $[C]$ would have more than one element of context. Some properties of an application can be asserted from its matrix of context. An application is said to be *mono-user*, respectively *multi-user* when $(\mathcal{UM}) = 1$, respectively $(\mathcal{UM}) > 1$. By analogy an application is said to be *mono/multi-environment* and *mono/multi-platform*.

4.2   Context-Independent and Context-Partially-Independent Task Model

In task modelling for multiple context of use, we notice that some tasks or subtasks are carried out the same way in all (or several) different contexts of use. Thus, isolating context-dependent tasks from context-independent ones may be considered useful.

In this section, two new concepts are defined to support this isolation: the Context-Independent Task Model ($\mathcal{CITM}$) which is a task model valid for all considered contexts of use and the Context-Partially-Independent Task Model ($\mathcal{CPITM}$) which is a task model valid for a subset of considered contexts of use. Links between different task models will be also considered.

The Context-Independent Task Model. A *Context-Independent Task Model* ($\mathcal{CITM}$) integrates tasks and transitions that are common to all different contexts of use. The $\mathcal{CITM}$ is defined by a tuple $< TASK , t_0, T , [C_{citm}] >$, where:

- $TASK$ is a finite set of tasks $\{t_0, t_1, ..., t_n\}$ where the t_i are tasks and subtasks that belong to each CTM .
- $t_0 \in TASK$ is the root of the graph and of each CTM_i.
- $T \subseteq TASK \times RO \times TASK$ is a set of transitions common to all CTMs.
- $[C_{citm}]$ is a matrix containing all the different contexts of use.

$$[C_{citm}] = \begin{pmatrix} C_1 \\ C_2 \\ \vdots \\ C_n \end{pmatrix} = \begin{pmatrix} u_1 \ p_1 \ e_1 \\ u_2 \ p_2 \ e_2 \\ \vdots \ \vdots \ \vdots \\ u_n \ p_n \ e_n \end{pmatrix}$$

The following conditions must hold:

- $t_0 \in CITM \Leftrightarrow t_0 \in CTM_j \ \forall j$: in order to find a $CITM$, all the different CTMs need to have at least the same root. Indeed, two CTMs having parts in common but not their root can not be considered to form a $CITM$ as their main purpose is different.
- $CITM \subseteq CTM_i \ \forall i$ and $\forall t_i \in \{CITM \setminus t_0\} \Rightarrow \exists \ \text{father}(t_i)$: a $CITM$ is included in all CTMs. Moreover, each task in the $CITM$ (except the root) must have a father.
- $\# \ L_i$ of the $CITM \geq threshold$: the Context-Independent Task Model must have at least $threshold$ layers. Indeed, the number of desired layers in our $CITM$ should be adjustable by the designer. The relevancy of the $CITM$ depends indeed on the granularity of task analysis.
- if child$(t_i) = \emptyset$, then t_i is a leaf task or a fork task. A *fork task* t_i is a task which is the source node of at least one conditional relationship with a task belonging to another task model.

The Context Partially Independent Task Model. A *Context-Independent Task Model* is made up of tasks that must be carried out in **all** different contexts of use. But how do we represent a task model valid for only some of those contexts of use? For instance, if we want to develop a multi-platform application for a laptop, a desktop PC and a handheld PC, it is likely that factoring out common tasks between a laptop and a desktop PC would be useful.

A *Context-Partially-Independent Task Model* ($CPITM$) integrates tasks that are valid in a subset of considered contexts of use. A $CPITM$ is defined by a tuple $< TASK , t_0, T , [C_{cpitm}] >$, where $[C_{cpitm}]$ is a matrix containing the different contexts of use C_i with i : 1 .. m and m ≥ 2 and $[C_{cpitm}] \subset [C_{citm}]$.

Moreover, the following conditions must hold:

- $t_0 \in CPITM_i \Leftrightarrow \exists \ t_j \in \{CITM \ \text{or} \ CPITM_j\} \mid t_j$ is a fork task and $\exists$ $< t_j, ro_i, t_0 >$ where ro_i is a conditional relationship.
- $\forall j, CPITM_i \subseteq CTM_j$ where $[C_{ctm}] \subset [C_{cpitm}]$ and $\forall t_i \in \{CPITM \setminus t_0\} \Rightarrow$ $\exists \ \text{father}(t_i)$.
- if child$(t_i) = \emptyset$, then t_i is a leaf task or a fork task.

We can now define more precisely a fork task. t_i is a fork task *iff* $\exists\, t_j \in$ $\{CITM \text{ or } CTM_j \text{ or } CPITM_i\} \mid \Gamma^-(t_j) = \emptyset$ and $\exists < t_i, ro_i, t_j >$ where ro_i is a conditional relationship between two graphs ($CITM$ and CTM_j) or ($CITM$ and $CPITM_j$) or ($CPITM_i$ and $CPITM_j$) or ($CPITM_i$ and CTM_j).

Remark on $CITM$ and $CPITM$. Two properties of the general TM have been relaxed in order to obtain a transient representation that shows intersection between CTMs:

- **Unique children are allowed.** A TM is said to be *well-formed* iff the minimal number of children for a task is set to two. In other words, it does not make sense to decompose one task into a single task. In a $CITM$ or a $CPITM$, a task having only one subtask is just the sign that only one subtask is common between the different CTMs from which the $CITM$ (or $CPITM$) is constructed.
- **Isolated brothers are allowed.** Each task of a well-formed TM has to be related at least with one of his brother. In a $CITM$ (or a $CPITM$), only common transitions between CTMs are shown. As temporal relations between two brother tasks can vary from one context to another, it is admitted that two brother tasks may share no temporal relationship with each other in a $CITM$ (or a $CPITM$).

4.3   The Multi-context Task Model

The Multi-Context Task Model ($MCTM$) represents all possible variations of a task model for a given application. The $MCTM$ components are presented in Fig. 3. A $MCTM$ is the union of identified $CITM$, $CPITM$s and residual parts of CTM. All components are linked with conditional relations. The residual part of CTMs represents parts that could not be factored out in a $CITM$ or $CPITM$s.

A *residual CTM* for a context C_i is defined as the set of $t_i \in TASK$ and $< t_j, ro_k, t_l > \in T$, such that

$$\forall i,\ \forall j,\ \forall k,\ \forall l,\ t_i \text{ and } < t_j, ro_k, t_l > \in CTM \setminus (CITM \cup \bigcup_i (CPITM))$$

where $C_i \in [C_{cpitm}]$. A residual CTM can be a well-formed subgraph, a single task or a single transition.

To relate the different components of the $MCTM$, a conditional expression is introduced. This condition relates a $CITM$ to a $CPITM$ or a residual CTM; a $CPITM$ to another $CPITM$ or a residual CTM. A condition has the form X/p, where X specifies the contexts of use for which a subgraph is valid and p specifies a relationship type (decomposition or temporal) between two tasks situated on different task models (Fig. 4).

To take into account the condition, relationship type of RO must be subtyped into two types: simple and conditional. Four types are thus obtained: simple decomposition relationship, conditional decomposition relationship, simple temporal relationship and conditional temporal relationship.

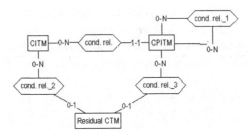

Fig. 3. Multi-Context Task Model concepts.

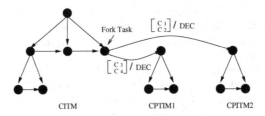

Fig. 4. Conditional relations.

5   A Case Study

To illustrate how this can be applied, a case study is introduced that refines a set of scenarios taking place in a medical institution. In all scenarios, a patient is treated in an hospital and a medical staff needs to obtain all the information relative to the patient's case. Two types of person can access this information: doctors and nurses. The computing platforms on which they have to carry out their task are various: a desktop PC, a handheld PC and a Cellular Phone. Three different contexts and associated scenarios are defined:

1. **A doctor with a desktop PC (context 1):** A doctor, in her office at the hospital, wants to prepare the visit she has to do to a patient during the afternoon. In order to do this, she logs in into the system and queries a database to access the patient's medical information (Fig. 5). This information consists in medical files which are composed of text and/or images (e.g., x-ray pictures). She may want to update this information, by adding additional observations on the patient state for instance. Moreover, for severely ill patients, the doctor also wants to monitor real-time information on the patient state (for instance, vital parameters like heart rate, body temperature).

2. **A nurse with a handheld PC (context 2):** A nurse is working in her service with a handheld PC. She wants to access the medical file of a patient. After logging in, the nurse queries the system to check the medical file of the patient. Considering the size of the screen of the handheld PC, the nurse

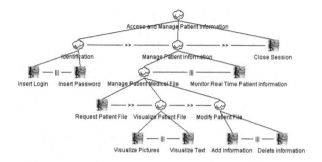

Fig. 5. The $\mathcal{CTM}$ for the doctor using a desktop PC.

can only visualize text or images one at a time. The nurse is not allowed to modify the file. Like the doctor the nurse has access to real-time parameters of a patient (Fig. 6).

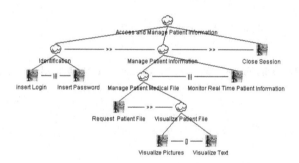

Fig. 6. The $\mathcal{CTM}$ for the nurse using a handheld PC.

3. **A doctor with a Cellular Phone (context 3):** At lunch time, the doctor wants to check a patient's medical file. After logging in into the system, she views the available textual information. As she is particularly worried about this patient, she monitors real-time information (Fig. 7).

The $\mathcal{CITM}$ is given in Fig. 8 and is valid for all the different contexts of use, it is to say that:

$$[C_{citm}] = \begin{pmatrix} Doctor & desktopPC & e_1 \\ Nurse & handheldPC & e_1 \\ Doctor & CellularPhone & e_1 \end{pmatrix}$$

The $\mathcal{CPITM}$ for context 1 and 2 (Fig. 9) is defined as: < { Visualize Patient File, Visualize Pictures, Visualize Text }, Visualize Patient File, { (Visualize

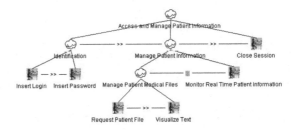

Fig. 7. The $\mathcal{CTM}$ for the doctor using a Cellular Phone.

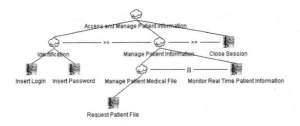

Fig. 8. The $\mathcal{CITM}$ for the three different contexts of use.

Patient File, dec, Visualize Pictures), (Visualize Patient File, dec, Visualize Text) }, $[C_{cpitm}] >$ where

$$[C_{cpitm}] = \begin{pmatrix} Doctor & desktopPC & e_1 \\ Nurse & handheldPC & e_1 \end{pmatrix}$$

Fig. 9. The $\mathcal{CPITM}$ for two contexts of use.

A $\mathcal{MCTM}$ can be defined from the different $\mathcal{CITM}$, $\mathcal{CPITM}$ and residual $\mathcal{CTM}$s (Fig. 10).

6   Conclusion and Future Work

Thanks to the approach developed in this paper, a UI intended to cover multiple contexts of use can be related to several $\mathcal{CTM}$s depending on the different contexts of use, having small or large differences depending on:

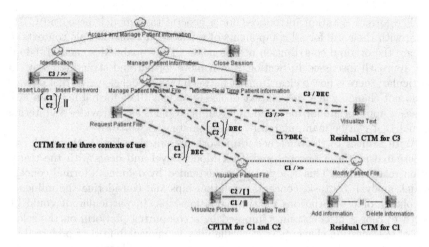

Fig. 10. Multi-Context Task Model for the Case Study.

- **tasks**: (**i**) the task remains the same while the context of use changes; (**ii**) some tasks (or subtasks) are removed when the context of use changes, because either there is no possibility to perform the removed task in the new context or some tasks appear to be unnecessary or irrelevant for a certain context of use; (**iii**) task ordering is modified without modification of the tasks themselves. In this case, only the transition differ; (**iv**) some tasks (or subtasks) are added because a new context requires more tasks to achieve the same goal;
- **relationships**: the temporal relationship between two tasks may differ from one context to another. In the case study presented in Section 5, the two subtasks of the "log in" task are concurrent in one case and sequential in another case.

In order to formally represent those possible variations, several key concepts have been defined, each of them associated with a formal notation:

- The **Context-Dependent Task Model** ($\mathcal{CTM}$) associates a task model with a context for which it applies.
- The **Context-Independent Task Model** ($\mathcal{CITM}$) represents common parts between all $\mathcal{CTM}$s of a same application.
- The **Context-Partially-Independent Task Model** ($\mathcal{CPITM}$) represents common parts between some $\mathcal{CTM}$s of a same application.
- The **Residual Context-Dependent Task Model** represents parts of the $\mathcal{CTM}$ that can not be factored out into a $\mathcal{CITM}$ or into $\mathcal{CPITM}$s.
- The **Multi-Context Task Model** ($\mathcal{MCTM}$) is a view that represents conditional relations (depending on the context variation) in the set $\{\mathcal{CITM} \cup \bigcup(\mathcal{CPITM}) \cup \text{Residual } \mathcal{CTM} \}$.

The formal notation introduced for a general task model, based on CTT, along with their use for all components of a task model for multiple contexts of use are the original contribution of this paper. They enable designers to adopt any approach discussed in Section 2 in a more formal and structured way. In particular, there is now a clear frontier between task model elements that change or do not change when the context of use is varying. The formal notation also makes it appropriate for inclusion in a tool like CTTE as it provides an internal format that can be manipulated by an automata.

With respect to the reference framework presented in Fig. 1, this work can be situated at the 'Concepts and Task Model' level and deals with the translation relationship. This study could be extended by defining a formal concept model, analyzing <task, concepts> relationships and considering the influence of context of use variations on these relationships. In particular, it could be worth to represent constraints imposed by a computing platform on the selection of presentation elements (e.g., availability vs unavailability) or preferred by a user type. Furthermore, there is a need for a formal abstract UI model and concrete UI model that could in their turn be subject to a study on context of use variation. In addition, some patterns should be identified to represent the translation relationship in prototypical context variation. Finally, the notation developed here should be extended to represent run-time adaption mechanisms, as run-time subtask switching, branching, or migrating.

References

1. G. Calvary, J. Coutaz, and D. Thevenin. Supporting Context Changes for Plastic User Interfaces : A Process and a Mechanism. In A. Blandford, J. Vanderdonckt, and P. Gray, editors, *Joint Proceedings of HCI'2001 and IHM'2001 (Lille,10-14 September 2001)*, pages 349–363, London, 2001. Springer-Verlag.
2. G. Chen and D. Kotz. A Survey of Context-Aware Mobile Computing Research. Technical Report TR2000-381, Dept. of Computer Science, Dartmouth College, November 2000.
3. N. Deo. *Graph Theory with Applications to Engineering and Computer Sciences.* Prentice-Hall, Englewood-Cliffs, 1974.
4. A.K. Dey and G.D Abowd. Toward a better understanding of context and context-awareness. Technical Report GIT-GVU-99-22, College of Computing, Georgia Institute of Technology, 1999.
5. J. Eisenstein, J. Vanderdonckt, and A. Puerta. Applying model-based techniques to the development of UIs for mobile computers. In *Proceedings of ACM Conference on Intelligent User Interfaces IUI'2001 (Albuquerque, January 11-13, 2001)*, pages 69–76, New York, 2001. ACM Press.
6. J. Gwizdka. What's in the context. In *Proc. Of CHI'2000 Workshop on Context Awareness (The Hague, April 1-6, 2000)*, Atlanta, 2000. GVU Center, Georgia University of Technology, Research report 2000-18e.
7. P. Johnson. *Human-Computer Interaction: Psychology, Task Analysis and Software Engineering.* McGraw-Hill, London, 1992.

8. P. Johnson, P. Markopoulos, and H. Johnson. Task knowledge structures: A specification of user task models and interaction dialogues. In *Proceedings of Task Analysis in Human-Computer Interaction, 11th Int. Workshop on Informatics and Psychology (Schraeding, June 9-11)*, 1992.

9. Q. Limbourg, C. Pribeanu, and J. Vanderdonckt. Towards uniformed of task models in a model-based approach. In C. Johnson, editor, *Proceedings of the 8th International Workshop on Design, Specification and Verification of Interactive Systems Workshop DSV-IS'2001 (Glasgow, June 13-15, 2001)*, volume 2220 of *Lecture Notes in Computer Science*, pages 164–182, Berlin, 2001. Springer-Verlag.

10. F. Paternò. *Model Based Design and Evaluation of Interactive Applications.* Springer-Verlag, Berlin, 1999.

11. F. Paternò, C. Mancini, and S. Meniconi. ConcurTaskTree: A diagrammatic notation for specifying task models. In S. Howard, J. Hammond, and G. Lindgaard, editors, *Proceedings of IFIP TC 13 International Conference on Human-Computer Interaction Interact'97 (Sydney, July 14-18, 1997)*, pages 362–369, Boston, 1997. Kluwer Academic Publishers.

12. D. Petrelli, E. Not, C. Strapparava, O. Stock, and M. Zancanaro. Modeling context is like taking pictures. In *Proc. Of CHI'2000 Workshop on Context Awareness (The Hague, April 1-6, 2000)*, Atlanta, 2000. GVU Center, Georgia University of Technology, Research report 2000-18e.

13. B. Schilit, N. Adams, and R. Want. Context-Aware Computing Applications. In *Proceedings of the Workshop on Mobile Computing Systems and Applications WMCSA'94 (Santa Cruz, December 1994)*, pages 85–90, Los Alamitos, December 1994. IEEE Computer Society Press.

14. A. Schmidt, K. Asante Aidoo, A. Takaluoma, U. Tuomela, K. Van Laerhoven, and W. Van de Velde. Advanced interaction in context. In *Proceedings of First International Symposium on Handheld and Ubiquitous Computing HUC'99 (Karlsruhe, 27-29 September 1999)*, pages 89–101. Springer-Verlag, 1999.

15. A. Schmidt, M. Beigl, and H.W. Gellersen. There is more to context than location. In *Workshop on Interactive Applications of Mobile Computing IMC'98*, 1998.

16. D. Thevenin. *Adaptation En Interaction Homme-Machine: Le Cas de la Plascticité.* PhD thesis, Université Joseph Fourier, 21 December 2001.

17. G. Tsibidis, T.N. Arvantitis, and C. Baber. CHI 2000 proposal for the what, who, where, when, why and how of context-awareness. In *Proc. Of CHI2000 Workshop on Context Awareness (The Hague, April 1-6, 2000)*, Atlanta, 2000. GVU Center, Georgia University of Technology, Research report 2000-18e.

Notational Support for the Design of Augmented Reality Systems

Emmanuel Dubois[1], Paulo Pinheiro da Silva[2], and Philip Gray[1]

[1] Department of Computer Science, University of Glasgow,
17 Lillybank Gardens, Glasgow, G20 6HW, United Kingdom
{emmanuel, pdg}@dcs.gla.Ac.uk
[2] Department of Computer Science, University of Manchester,
Oxford Road, Manchester M13 9PL, United Kingdom
pinheirp@cs.man.ac.uk

Abstract. There is growing interest in augmented reality (AR) as technologies are developed that enable ever smoother integration of computer capabilities into the physical objects that populate the everyday lives of users. However, despite this growing importance of AR technologies, there is little tool support for the design of AR systems. In this paper, we present two notations, ASUR and UMLi, that can be used to capture design-significant features of AR systems. ASUR is a notation for designing user interactions in AR environments. UMLi is a notation for designing the user interfaces to interactive systems. We use each notation to specify the design of an augmented museum gallery. We then compare the two notations in terms of the types of support they provide and consider how they might be used together.

1 Introduction

The integration of digital (virtual) information and actions with the physical (real) world of users through the use of augmented reality (AR) techniques is becoming a crucial challenge for designers of interactive systems. AR is becoming widely used in a number of domains, including leisure [23], maintenance [8], construction and architecture [24] and surgery [4]. Despite the increasing development of AR systems, neither tools nor methods have been proposed specifically for the design of AR systems. Furthermore, AR systems remains largely ad hoc and exploratory. In [5], we proposed a classification space for "Mixed Systems", interactive systems combining physical and digital entities, that identify two kinds of such systems:

- systems that enhance interaction between a user and his/her physical environment by providing additional computer capabilities or data to the physical objects of the environment: these are Augmented Reality systems, AR;
- systems that make use of physical objects to enhance the user's interaction with a computer: these are Augmented Virtuality systems, AV.

P. Forbrig et al. (Eds.): DSV-IS 2002, LNCS 2545, pp. 74–88, 2002.
© Springer-Verlag Berlin Heidelberg 2002

The notion of Mixed Reality, introduced by Milgram and Kishino [13], refers to systems that mix digital and physical entities into a single digital representation; for example, the representation of an interior design by merging pictures of a real chair within a 3D graphic model of the room [25]. However, this combination of digital and physical properties or entities is achieved on a monitor, so the perception of the physical world is not direct. As opposed to Mixed Reality, augmented reality approaches developed in the HCI community focus on the integration of computational capabilities with physical objects involved in the user's interaction. Users benefit from complementary computer capabilities when interacting with their usual physical tools and objects. These HCI approaches are user- and interaction-centred, although they differ in the aspects used to characterise an interaction. Four distinct aspects that may have an influence on the user's interaction with AR systems are identified in the literature: 1) Type of data provided to the user [2,8,14]: it may be textual, 2D or 3D graphics, gesture, sound, speech or haptic data; 2) Potential physical targets of enhancement to combine physical and digital data [11]: users, physical objects and the environment are the three main targets identified; 3) Adequacy of the provided data to the task, as well as the location where they are perceivable [1]; 4) Ability of the system to bridge the gap between physical and digital entities [21]. As this research suggests, developing an AR system is different from developing other sorts of interactive system. It is often neither obvious nor easy to design and implement appropriate combinations of physical and digital entities, especially in settings where (i) the user may be mobile, (ii) other artefacts may be manipulated and (iii) the interaction must be sensitive to complex aspects of the context of use. In this paper we focus on the description of such systems: without a means of specifying the features that make an AR system distinctively AR, we cannot communicate or explore design solutions that benefit from these features. We thus present two complementary notations for capturing design-significant aspects of AR systems:

- ASUR, a graphical notation that can be used to describe, characterise and support the analysis of mixed environments; and
- UMLi, a conservative extension of the Unified Modeling Language (UML) for interactive systems.

Each notation enables a designer to construct a model of an AR system. ASUR models identify the key objects and agents in an AR environment along with their physical and informational relationships. UMLi models describe behavioural and structural aspects of the software systems that make up AR systems. In particular, UMLi models include abstract descriptions of user interface presentations implemented by the software systems. These models, and the notations in which they are expressed, offer assistance in several respects:

- Making salient the AR systems-specific characteristics of a design;
- Providing a medium in which to reason about such designs and to communicate them;
- Bridging gulfs between different elements of an AR environment design.

We present the roles that each notation might play in the design of AR environments and their underlying software systems. Furthermore, we discuss the potential benefits of combining both notations to design complete AR systems. The remainder of this paper is organised as follows. First we describe the Mackintosh Project used as a case study in this paper. The next two sections describe ASUR and UMLi, and apply both notation to the case study. We then compare the modelling capabilities of ASUR and UMLi for AR systems. Finally we conclude the paper with a brief discussion of future developments.

2   The City Project Scenario

As a vehicle for introducing and comparing ASUR++ and UMLi, we use an example taken from the City Project, a project developed within the Equator consortium [7]. Based on the work of Charles Rennie Mackintosh, a Glaswegian architect of the early 1900's, the City Project has been exploring the augmentation of the permanent Charles Rennie Mackintosh Interpretation Centre, a gallery situated in the Lighthouse, an architecture and design centre in Glasgow, containing exhibits related to Mackintosh's life and work. The aim of this part of the project is to study the impact of combining multiple media to support visitors' activities, especially collaborative activities involving users in the real museum interacting with users exploring a digital version of the same museum ("co-visiting"). For the visitor to the real museum, the system being created is aimed at providing visitors with digital information tailored to visitor's current context. This information tailoring mainly relies on tracking visitor's motions in the museum and location of the exhibits. Visitor activities are thus embedded with computational capabilities. To do so, the Lighthouse has been equipped with a radio-frequency localisation system that gives the location of the visitors. There are several services that will be provided by the system in the Lighthouse. In this paper, we consider only the *FollowSelectedPath* service offered to visitors of the Mackintosh Interpretation Centre. This service provides AR support to guide visitors through a pre-defined path of exhibits. A *Path* is composed of an ordered set of Exhibits. Each *Exhibit* is at a *Location* inside the museum. In addition, the service assumes that the *Visitor* following a predefined path is already connected to the system. Under these conditions, the *Visitor* get information related to:

- The *Path* to follow: it consists of textual directions and distances separating the current position of the *Visitor* from the next *Exhibit* of the followed *Path*.
- The *Exhibits*: once the *Visitor* reaches the next *Exhibit* of the path s/he is following, the system provides her/him with information about the *Exhibit* using specific *Media*, e.g., *Image*, *Video*, that may not be perceivable in the museum (e.g. building material, previous exhibition locations, etc.)

Technically, the *Visitor* uses a PDA to perceive both kinds of information and to confirm the visit to an *Exhibit* before getting directions to the next *Exhibit* on the *Path*. Although inspired by the City Project, it is important to note that this example does not represent the design of an existing system nor is it a history of an actual design development. Rather, we have chosen this scenario because it represents a realistic design problem (viz., the design brief is a real one). However, the goals of our example scenarios don't correspond to the goals of the City Project and the design alternatives presented below are our own and don't correspond to any that have been developed during the City Project. To differentiate our example from the actual City Project, we will hereafter refer to it as the Mackintosh Project.

3   ASUR Description of the Mackintosh Scenario

ASUR (Adaptor, System, User, Real object) is a notation designed to address the need for a lightweight notation for describing AR systems. Apart from ASUR, we are not aware of any language or notation well-suited to describe AR systems. When designing AR systems, the physicality of the setting becomes crucial. The designer must consider:

- where objects are located in the physical world,
- how they might move,
- their intrinsic physical constraints, such as size, weight, position, etc.
- what can be modified or digitally enhanced,
- how users perceive, manipulate and perhaps carry objects, etc.

Existing notations, such as UML or CTT, are designed to capture properties of computational entities; there is no way to express the potential physical properties of such entities. Therefore, these notations are ill-equipped to capture exactly those aspects that make AR systems special. UMLi is an example of one way of dealing with this problem, viz., extending an existing notation. ASUR illustrates another way, starting from scratch and bringing together exactly those characteristics identified in previous interaction-oriented studies of AR systems and needed to capture AR system-related design issues.

3.1   ASUR Concepts

Firstly, an ASUR description models an interactive system as a set of four kinds of entities, called components: computer **System** (**Component S**), **U**ser of the system (**Component U**), **R**eal object involved in the task as tool or constituting the object of the task (**Component R_{tool} and R_{object}**), and **A**dapter for Input and Adapter for Output (**Component A_{in} and A_{out}**) that bridge the gap between the computer-provided entities (S) and the physical world entities, composed of the user (U) and of the real objects relevant to the task (R_{object} and R_{tool}). A relation between two ASUR components may describe a physical collocation (represented by a double line) or an exchange of information (represented by an arrow) between two components. Secondly, an interaction facet consists of an ASUR component and an ASUR relation between this component and the user. Arrows connected to the component U in Figure 1 are examples of such interaction facets. The second aspect of ASUR is the description of the interaction facets with a set of characteristics of the user's interaction. These characteristics may constitute a basis for the evaluation of usability properties. A more detailed description of ASUR is presented in [6].

3.2   Illustration of ASUR Using the Mackintosh Scenario

The diagrammatic representation of the ASUR description is presented in Figure 1. In terms of ASUR, the visitor is the component U, an exhibit is a component R_{object} observed by the visitor ($R_{objet} \rightarrow U$) and the database, represented by V-R_{object}, containing the path and the information related to the exhibits, is included in the component S. An adaptor for output (A_{out}) is required so

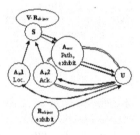

Fig. 1. ASUR Diagrammatic representation of the Mackintosh feature *"Following a path"*.

that the visitors perceives the guidance information to follow the chosen path. From this component one relation is connected to the visitor (component U), denoting the transfer of information, related to the path to follow: A_{out}(path$\rightarrow$U. Furthermore, an ASUR relation from the component S to the component A_{out} is required because information provided by the A_{out} component is issued by the database (component S): S$\rightarrow$A$_{out}$. Exactly the same reasoning applies to the transfer of information related to the exhibits, leading to the identification of a second adapter for output. However, the scenario stipulates that the PDA has to be used to carry both kinds of information. Consequently, there is only one component A_{out} but two relations from the component S to A_{out} and from A_{out} to the component U, each of them representing respectively the transfer of information related to the path to reproduce and to the exhibits. In addition, an adaptor for input ($A_{in}1$) is required to get the position of the visitor in the museum (U$\rightarrow$A$_{in}$1) and transfer it to the computer system (A$_{in}$1$\rightarrow$S). Finally, once the visitor has observed an exhibit of the path and potentially read the additional information provided by the system, s/he has to "validate" this step of the path, so that the system can provide direction information to go to the next exhibit of the path. An adaptor for input ($A_{in}2$) is thus required and establishes a bridge between the user's acknowledgment (U$\rightarrow$A$_{in}$2) and the state of the system ($A_{in}2{\rightarrow}S$). The fact that the acknowledgment and information visualisation occur on the same PDA is encoded by a double-relation between the components $A_{in}2$ (acknowledgment device) and A_{out} (screen of the PDA): $A_{in}2{=}A_{out}$. The same relation exists between the user (component U) and the components $A_{in}2$ and A_{out}, because these two last components are handheld (U=$A_{in}1$, U=A_{out}). The second main aspect of ASUR lead us now to characterise the different interaction facets, i.e. the ASUR components and ASUR relations denoting the user's interaction. Four components are involved in this case: the screen of the PDA (A_{out}), its tactile area ($A_{in}2$), the exhibit (R_{object}) and the localiser ($A_{in}1$). The location where the user will perceive and act on the two first components is his/her own hand, since the device is handheld. The visual sense is required to perceive the path and exhibit information provided by the PDA (A_{out}), while physical action, a finger click for example, will be used to acknowledge using the PDA. No information should be shared among users, since different users may have a different path to reproduce. Physical information about an exhibit is perceived on the exhibit itself. This requires a visual sense and this perception must be available for several users at the same time. Finally, the localiser gets information from a tracking area (defined by the technology used for the tracking). When moving in this tracking area, the user will implicitly communicate his/her position to the adaptor. Finally, several users may use this adaptor at the same time. These characteristics are summed up in the Table 1. Concerning the interaction facets, four relations are highlighted in the ASUR diagrammatic description of the situation: perception of the path and exhibit digital information ($A_{out}{\rightarrow}U$), perception of the physical entity ($R_{object}{\rightarrow}U$), user's localisation (U${\rightarrow}A_{in}1$) and user's acknowledgment (U${\rightarrow}A_{in}2$). The first relation carries information expressed in a textual mono-dimensional language, in a frame of reference linked to the visitor so that s/he can read it. The second relation denotes the natural observation of an exhibit: it is based on real 3D language and observed in a user-centred frame of reference. The two last relations correspond to output interaction facets. The user will act with natural 3D actions to either implicitly communicate his/her position to the localiser or click on the PDA to acknowledge. The frame of reference is again user-centred. A summary of the relation characteristics is shown in Table 2.

Table 1. Characteristics of the components that take part in the user's interaction with the system when achieving the Mackintosh project feature "*Following a path*".

Interaction components	Perceptual/Action location	Perceptual/Action sense	Information shared
A_{out} (screen)	User's hand	Visual	Should not
$A_{in}2$ (tactile screen)	User's hand	Physical action	Should not
R_{object} (one exhibit)	Exhibit	Visual	Must
$A_{in}1$ (RF-localiser)	Tracking area	Implicit	May

4   UMLi Description of the Mackintosh Scenario

Model-Based User Interface Development Environments (MB-UIDEs) are a state-of-the-art approach for modelling and implementing running user interfaces from user interface models [18,22]. MB-UIDEs provide models that are effective at capturing user interface functionality [9,16,20], but offer only limited application modelling facilities. Thus an important weakness of MB-UIDEs is in an area of specialism for UML, namely application modelling, while the main strengths of MB-UIDEs align with an area of weakness for UML, namely user interface modelling [19]. Several researchers have investigated the integration of interface modelling techniques with UML. For example, [10] discusses how interface modelling constructs, influenced by those in the TACTICS system, in particular relating to the description of tasks, might be incorporated into UML. A more recent paper [12] assesses several UML models for use in interface modelling, comparing them with a collection of specialist interface modelling notations. In [17] it is suggested how several UML models, in particular class diagrams and use case diagrams, can be used in conjunction with the CTT task model for user interface modelling. In UML for Interactive Systems (UMLi) [19], tasks are modelled using extended activity diagrams rather than through the incorporation of a completely new task modelling notation into UML. Wisdom [15] is probably more mature than the proposals in [12] and [17], in that the relationship between use cases, tasks and views are considered in the paper. UMLi also addresses these relationships but introduces fewer new models into UML and addresses more thoroughly than Wisdom the relationship between tasks and the data on which they act. Overall, the emphasis in Wisdom is probably on earlier parts of the design process than UMLi. Wisdom models tend to be more abstract than those produced using UMLi, but too abstract to generate running user interfaces. Therefore, UMLi is one approach used in this paper as a framework to incorporate AR systems facilities, leading in this way to the development of the first model-based development environment for AR systems. Finally, many aspects of an interactive system can be described by models. Therefore, many models may be combined together when describing an interactive system. However, if the intention is to build UI models that can be used, for instance to generate running user interfaces, two kinds of models

Table 2. Characteristics of the relations forming the different facets of the user's interaction with the system when achieving the Mackintosh project feature "*Following a path*".

Interaction facets	Concept	Concept Relevance	Representation Language	Representation Frame of Reference
$A_{out} \rightarrow U$	Path and Exhibit	High	1D, textual	Visitor
$R_{object} \rightarrow U$	Exhibit	High	3D, real	Visitor
$U \rightarrow A_{in}1$	User's location	High	3D, real	Visitor
$U \rightarrow A_{in}2$	Acknowledgment	Medium	3D, real	Visitor

should be included: **structural models**, that is mainly *Domain models* and *Presentation models* and **behaviour models**. We now present more precisely the domain, presentation and behaviour models of the system and illustrate them within the Mackintosh scenario, in order to explain how UMLi can be used to model the supporting system of an AR environment.

Structural Models. The UMLi class diagram represents a schema for the domain of the functional core of the Mackintosh system used to support the computational capabilities required to provide information to visitors. The classes identify the elements of the Mackintosh project previously described in the paper. To address the presentation models, user interface (UI) diagrams are introduced in UMLi to model abstract presentations of user interfaces. As explained in [16], UI diagrams are an alternative notation for class diagrams, providing additional support for interaction classes, which are the classes representing widgets. Namely, the diagram provides visual representation for containment between interaction classes and visual identification for the main role that an interaction class is playing in a particular user interface. Six UMLi constructors for UI diagrams represent different roles of interaction classes:

- **FreeContainers** (dashed cubes) are top-level interaction classes that cannot be contained by any other interaction class (e.g., a top-level window);
- **Containers** (dashed cylinders) provide a grouping mechanism that brings together interaction classes other than FreeContainers (e.g., a frame within a window);
- **Inputters** (downward triangles) receive information from users;
- **Displayers** (upward triangles) send information to users;
- **Editors** (upward rhombi), exchange information in two-ways ;
- **ActionInvokers** (right pointing arrows) receive instructions from users.

In the Mackintosh Project, the UI diagram in Figure 2 represents the *ExecutePathUI FreeContainer*, which is the abstract presentation model of the *FollowSelectPath* service UI. There, *ConfirmExhibit* is the *ActionInvoker* where visitors confirm they have reached the exhibit and *Quit* is the *ActionInvoker* used to finish the service, returning to other functionalities of the system. *Direction* and *Info* are *Displayers* describing the route to the next exhibit of the path and presenting further information about the last reached exhibit. Finally, *GetLocation* is an *Inputter* receiving information about the location of the visitors. As can be observed, *ExecutePathUI* represents relevant design decisions concerning the user interface of the service, avoiding early commitment to concrete properties of the interface. For instance, there is no specification of which kind of widget is going to implement each interaction class. Thus, the *Info Displayer* used to visualise objects of several media (using a PDA during the visit or visiting the digital version of the museum) may be implemented by more than one widget. Regarding AR systems, the *GetLocation Inputter* exemplifies an interesting kind of support that UMLi can provide to this category of interactive systems. Indeed, the *GetLocation Inputter* explicitly represents the localisation system mentioned. Thus, due to its simple mechanisms of abstraction, the UI diagram provide an appropriate description of how the localisation system, which is a component system of the AR system, interfaces with the rest of the AR system of the Macintosh Project. The UI diagram in Figure 2, along with the domain model, describe the structural properties of the AR system. A behavioural description of the *FollowSelectPath* service is required to complete its specification in UMLi.

Behaviour Models. Task models are typically used for modelling interactive system behaviours in MB-UIDEs [16,22]. However, the notion of task, as conceptualised in the MB-UIDE community, is represented by use cases and activities in UMLi [16]. Using use cases and their scenarios, designers and expert users can elicit user interface functionalities required to allow users to achieve their goals. Using activities, designers can identify the possible ways to perform actions that support the functionalities elicited using use cases. Therefore, the mapping of use cases into top-level activities describes a set of interface functionalities similar to that described by task models in other MB-UIDEs. In the Mackintosh Project, the *FollowSelectedPath* service is represented by a use case and visitors are represented by an actor who communicates with the use case. This use case is directly mapped into the *ExecutePath* activity in Figure 3. Furthermore, object flows in activity diagrams, e.g., the vs object of type Visitor and the qt object of type *ActionInvoker*, denote the use of instances of classes to perform actions in action states. For instance, the *pt.startPath()* action state is an invocation to the method *startPath()* of the class Path in the object path. Thus, using object flows, designers can incorporate the notion of state into activity diagrams primarily used for modelling behaviour. In the case of UMLi, the use of instances of interaction objects can also be described by object flows, as in the case of the qt object. However, object flow states, which are rendered as dashed arrows connecting objects to action states, have a specific semantics when used to associate interaction objects to activities and action states. UMLi specifies five categories of object flow states specific for interaction objects described as follows:

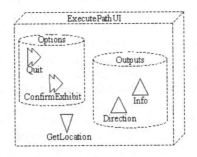

Fig. 2. The UI diagram of the *ExecutePathUI* FreeContainer.

- << *interacts* >> relates primitive interaction objects to action states, which are primitive activities. It indicates that associated action states are responsible for interactions where users are invoking object operations or visualising the result of object operations.
- << *presents* >> relates FreeContainers to activities. It denotes that the associated FreeContainer should be visible while the activity is active.
- << *confirms* >> relates ActionInvokers to selection states. It specifies that the selection state has finished normally.
- << *cancels* >> relates ActionInvokers to composite activity or selection state. It specify that the activity or selection state has not finished normally and that the flow of control should be re-routed to a previous state.
- << *activates* >> relates ActionInvoker to activity, thereby making the associated activity a triggered one, which is effectively started on the occurrence of an event.

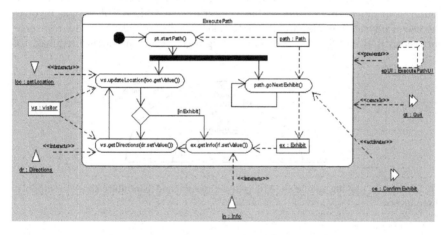

Fig. 3. The ExecutePath activity representing the behaviour of the *FollowSelectPath* service. The *FollowSelectPath* service has been modelled along with other functionalities.

The activity diagram in Figure 3 illustrates the use of most of these interaction object specific object flows. For instance, the *ExecutePathUI* FreeContainer is made visible and the *Quit* ActionInvoker is enabled when the *ExecutePath* activity is active. Then, the *loc* Inputter starts to constantly collect information about the location of visitors producing directions on the *dr* Displayer and exhibit's information on the *in* Displayer. In parallel with this process of producing directions and exhibit information, the service is able to receive a message either from the *ce* ActionInvoker saying that the visitor has reached the next exhibit in the path or from the *qt* ActionInvoker invoking the *ExecutePath* activity. The service finishes when the system control-flow leaves the *ExecutePath* activity. The following section analyses the differences and similarities of the ASUR and UMLi descriptions of the Mackintosh project and shows how both notations may be combined to support the design process of AR systems.

5   ASUR and UMLi Comparison

5.1   Model-Based Design of AR Systems

UMLi provides on top of UML the ability to express the interface presentation of software systems in an abstract way, identifying the abstract interaction objects required for the user's interaction with the underlying software system. Moreover, the UI diagram allows the composition of abstract interaction objects. Together, this constitutes a step towards an integration of user interface design with underlying system design. In the case of AR systems, however, the user's interaction with the system requires a comprehension of AR environments beyond the specification of windows-based interactions. Indeed, the designs involve the use of physical entities and it has to take into account the behaviour of such entities. ASUR can fill this gap, since it highlights the components required to

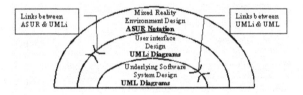

Fig. 4. Layers playing a role in AR systems design and candidate-tools to support these layers.

support the whole human-AR environment interaction, as well as the exchange of information among them, which represents the different facets of the user's interaction with the system. Moreover, ASUR characterises the entities by comparing and taking into account their physical properties. ASUR doesn't support the expression of component refinement and description of software systems of AR environments (i.e. detailed specification of computer-based components); UMLi diagrams, however, provide a solution. Furthermore, ASUR contributes to the specification of UI presentations by specifying those aspects of interaction that relate to the use of physical entities. As a result, we identify 3 layers to consider when designing an AR system (cf. Figure 4):

- **Underlying software system layer**: UML diagrams constitute an approach to design this layer, composed of a set of core components, methods and behaviours.

- **Human-computer interaction layer**: this layer corresponds to the interface presentation specification. UI diagrams proposed by UMLi along with some ASUR concepts help designers to model the presentation of software systems, augmented by other designs tools such as usability studies and guidelines.
- **Human-AR environment interaction**: this is specific to AR systems, in which a part of the interaction relies on physical entities rather than on the software system's interface. ASUR describes this part of the environment and the human-computer interaction in terms of entity-relation models and characteristics. ASUR provides a framework to support the reasoning about different design issues for AR not covered by conventional design solutions for interactive systems.

A model-based AR system design may rely on the specification of properties presented in both ASUR and UMLi notations as illustrated in this paper. The combination of these three layers and bridges among them would link both notations, resulting in a first step towards a Model-Based Design Environment for AR Systems. Thus, between the computer system and the external specification, the bridge is quite straightforward, since UMLi (external specification) is based on the UML diagrams (functional core). Bridging AR-system external specification design and conventional external specification design is required too. We detail these links in the next section.

5.2 Links between ASUR and UMLi

The use of ASUR and UMLi to model the *Following a path* service shows that these notations can be used to describe AR environments. However, the ASUR model in Figure 1 is obviously different from the UMLi models of the same service in the domain models and Figures 3 and 4. In the case of this service, the differences between the models indicate that ASUR and UMLi can support the construction of complementary models of AR environments. In fact, the ASUR model presents an AR-user-centred perspective of the same AR environment that in presented under an AR-system-centred perspective in the UMLi models. A notation for supporting the modelling of AR environments would ideally require a mix of concepts used in both ASUR and UMLi notations. Table 3 is an attempt to identify similarities between constructs used in ASUR and UMLi by comparing their constructs to concepts informally described in the **Concepts** column of the table. Thus, concepts supported in both notations indicate the similarities between ASUR and UMLi constructs. The identification of the similarities of constructs is an indication of how the notations could be used to complement each other to comprehensively support the design of AR environments. ASUR and UMLi also exhibit some mismatches, highlighted in Table 3. Thus, for example, concerning the digital space, a difference between the notations is the absence of refinement of the digital entities in the ASUR notation. Concerning the physical space, another difference resides at the level of the characteristics of the interactions and I/O devices. UMLi does not support the specification of

Table 3. A comparison of ASUR and UMLi implementation of AR-environments concepts.

Context		Concepts	Concepts Representation	
			ASUR Construct	UMLi Construct
A.R.	Physical Space	User	U	Actor
		Input device (ID)	A_{in}	Inputter
		ID interaction charact.	A_{in} charact.	
		Output device (OD)	A_{out}	Displayer
		OD interaction charact.	A_{out} charact.	
		Real tool entity	R_{tool}	
		Real object entity	R_{object}	
		Real entities characterisation	R_{object} charact.	
		Interaction(User-Real tool or object)	$R{\rightarrow}U$, $U{\rightarrow}R$	
		Interaction (Users-ID)	$U{\rightarrow}A_{in}$	<<presents>>
		Interaction (Users-OD)	$A_{out}{\rightarrow}U$	<<presents>>
		Interaction charac.	ASUR relations charac.	
Environ- ment	Digital Space	Interaction (ID-Computer system)	$A_{in}{\rightarrow}S$	Interaction object flow
		Interaction (OD-Computer system)	$S{\rightarrow}A_{out}$	Interaction object flow
		Digital entities	S	Class and Object
		Digital entity properties		Attrib. and Op.
		Relationships between digital entities		Associations + their specialisation
		Goals		Use cases
		Tasks		Use cases + Activities
		User interface presentation		UI diagram

this aspect, while ASUR does, and this aspect constitutes the basis of potential usability analysis, discussed and illustrated in [6].

6   Conclusions and Perspectives

The design of AR systems demands new notational tools to deal with the central role in AR systems, and AR systems design, of the physical properties of the interaction entities and the relationship of physical with informational entities. ASUR is a potentially useful candidate for this role but it doesn't have the capability for describing the user interface(s) that are part of such AR systems. UMLi, on the other hand, is tailored for just this job but, unlike ASUR, it cannot capture the physical properties of components and their relationships with other entities and with information flows. In our comparison of ASUR and UMLi we identified three levels of design involved in AR systems: human-AR environment interaction, human-computer interaction, functional core. ASUR and other HCI design tools deal with the first two levels. Different design alternatives can be described and subjected to analysis in terms of the physical environment (what moves, what touches), the interaction (perception, action, cognition) and the implementation (sensor deployment, wireless vs. wired). UML and UMLi, on the other hand, offer a method of specifying precisely the behavioural aspects of the interactive system. Of course, ASUR and UMLi offer a way of capturing some of the main features of AR systems, but they will probably not be sufficient on their own. We can expect that additional notations may be needed to capture other aspects of the design (e.g., motion patterns of artefacts and user). We envisage several parallel developments from this point in our work, including (1) empirical studies of the use of ASUR and UMLi with realistic AR system design problems (validating this analysis, identifying gaps in our understanding of the requirements for AR notations), (2) enhancements to the notations (adding to the expressiveness of each notation, looking at the effects of handling multiple collaborating users and augmented artifacts, dealing with scalability issues), (3) exploring further links between notations (generating transformations on descriptions), (4) providing tool support for editing but also for linking related aspects of designs, comparing alternative designs, carrying out analyses, and generating descriptions in the other notations (semi)automatically. Also, as we stated at the beginning of this paper, our ultimate goal is to develop a systematic approach to AR system design: a design method. Our exploration of ASUR and UMLi and their links constitutes a starting point towards this aim.

Acknowledgements. We would like to thank our colleagues in the Equator Consortium for the inspiration for our scenario. It was the Mackintosh Project that initially stimulated our interest in capturing alternative AR designs. We also thank L. Nigay for her constructive comments on the paper.

References

1. Ahlers, K., Klinker, G., H. Breen, D., Chevalier, P.-Y., Crampton, C., Greer, D., S., Koller, D., Kramer, A., Rose, E., Tuceryan, M., Whitaker, R., *Confluence of Computer Vision and Interactive Graphics for Augmented Reality*, in Presence: Teleoperators and Virtual Environments (Special issue on AR),6, 4: 433–451, 1997.
2. Azuma, R., T., A survey of Augmented Reality, in *Presence: Teleoperators and Virtual Environments*, 6, 4, (1997), p. 355-385.
3. Bernsen, O., Foundations of multimodal representations. A taxonomy of representational modalities, in *Interacting with Computers*, Vol. 6, 4, (1994), p. 347–371.
4. Cinquin, P., Bainville, E., Barbe, C., Bittar, E., Bouchard, V., Bricault, I., Champleboux, G., Chenin, M., Chevalier, L., Delnondedieu, Y., Desbat, L., Dessene, V., Hamadeh, A., Henry, D., Laieb, N., Lavallée, S., Lefebvre, J.M., Leitner, F., Menguy, Y., Padieu, F., Péria, O., Poyet, A., Promayon, M., Rouault, S., Sautot, P., Troccaz, J., Vassal, P., Computer Assisted Medical Interventions, in *IEEE Engineering in Medicine and Biology*, 4, (1995), p. 254–263.
5. Dubois, E., Nigay, L., Troccaz, J., Chavanon, O., Carrat, L., Classification Space for Augmented Surgery, an Augmented Reality Case Study, in *Conference Proceedings of Interact'99*, (1999), p. 353–359.

6. Dubois, E., Nigay, L., Troccaz, J., Assessing Continuity and Compatibility in Augmented Reality Systems, to appear in *International Journal on Universal Access in the Information Society, special issue on Continuous Interaction in Future Computing Systems*, (2002).
7. Equator Project Web Site: http://www.equator.ac.uk/
8. Feiner, S., MacIntyre, B., Seligmann, D., Knowledge-Based Augmented Reality, in *Communication of the ACM*, n°7, (1993), p. 53-61.
9. Griffiths, T., Barclay, P. J., Paton, N. W., McKirdy, J., Kennedy, J. B., Gray, P. D., Cooper, R., Goble, C. A., Pinheiro da Silva, P., Teallach: A Model-Based User Interface Development Environment for Object Databases. *Interacting with Computers*, 14(1), p. 31-68, (2001).
10. Kovacevic, S., UML and User Interface Modeling. In *Proceedings of UML'98*, pages 235-244, Mulhouse, France, June 1998. ESSAIM.
11. Mackay, W.E., Fayard, A.-L., Frobert, L., Médini, L., Reinventing the Familiar: an Augmented Reality Design Space for Air Traffic Control, In *Conf. Proc. of CHI'98*, p. 558-565.
12. Markopoulos, P., Marijnissen, P., UML as a representation for Interaction Designs. In *Proceedings of OZCHI 2000*, pages 240-249, 2000.
13. Milgram, P., Kishino, F., A Taxonomy of Mixed Reality Visual Displays, *Transactions on Information Systems*, E77-D(12): 1321-1329, 1994.
14. Noma, H., Miyasato, T., Kishino, F., *A palmtop display for dextrous manipulation with haptic sensation*, Conf. Proc. of Human factors in computing systems, p. 126-133, 1996.
15. Nunes, N., Cunha, J., Wisdom, A UML Based Architecture for Interactive Systems. In *Proc. 7th Int. Wshp. DSV-IS*, p. 191-205. Springer-Verlag, 2000.
16. Paternò, F., *Model-Based Design and Evaluation of Interactive Applications*. Springer, Berlin, 1999.
17. Paternò, F., Towards a UML for Interactive Systems. In *Proceedings of EHCI2001*, LNCS, pages 7-18, Toronto, Canada, May 2001. Springer.
18. Pinheiro da Silva, P., User Interface Declarative Models and Development Environments. In *Proc. 7th Int. Wshp. DSV-IS*, p. 207-226. Springer-Verlag, 2000.
19. Pinheiro da Silva, P., Paton, N. W., UMLi: The Unified Modeling Language for Interactive Applications, in *Conf. Proc. of UML00*, UK, p. 117-132, 2000.
20. Puerta, A. R., A model-based interface development environment. *IEEE Software*,8, p. 40-47, 1997.
21. Rekimoto, J., Nagao, K., The World through the Computer: Computer Augmented Interaction with Real World Environments, In Proceedings of UIST'95, 1995.
22. Szekely, P., Retrospective and Challenges for Model-Based Interface Development. In *Conf. Proc. of CADUI96*, pages xxi-xliv, Belgium, 1996. Namur University Press.
23. Szalavari, Z., Eckstein, E., Gervautz, M. Collaborative Gaming in Augmented Reality. In *Symp. Proc. on Virtual Reality Software and Technology*, (1998), p. 195-204.
24. Webster, A., Feiner, S., MacIntyre B., Massie, W. Krueger, T., Augmented Reality in Architectural Construction, Inspection, and Renovation, in *Proceedings of Computing in Civil Engineering*, ASCE, (1996), p. 913-919.
25. Whitaker, R., T., Crampton, C., Breen, D., E., Tuceryan, M., Rose, E., Object Calibration for Augmented Reality, In *Conf. Proc. of Eurographics'95*, Vol. 14, 3: 15-28, 1995.

Tool-Supported Interpreter-Based User Interface Architecture for Ubiquitous Computing

Lars Braubach, Alexander Pokahr, Daniel Moldt, Andreas Bartelt, and
Winfried Lamersdorf

Distributed Systems Group, Computer Science Department, University of Hamburg
Vogt-Kölln-Str. 30, 22527 Hamburg, Germany
{braubach, pokahr, moldt, bartelt, lamersd}@informatik.uni-hamburg.de
http://vsis-www.informatik.uni-hamburg.de/

Abstract. With the upcoming era of Ubiquitous Computing (Ubi-
Comp) new demands on software engineering will arise. Fundamental
needs for constructing user interfaces (UIs) in the context of UbiComp
were identified and the subsumed results of a survey with special focus
on model based user interface development environments (MB-UIDEs)
are presented in this paper. It can be stated, that none of the examined
systems is suitable for all the needs. Therefore a new architecture based
on the Arch model is proposed, that supports the special UbiComp requirements. This layered architecture provides the desired flexibility with
respect to different implementation techniques and UI modalities. It was
implemented in a user interface development environment called Vesuf.
Its usability was approved within the Global Info project [20], where
heterogeneous services had to be integrated in a web portal.

1   Introduction

As covered below, UbiComp applications differ inherently from conventional applications. In [8] were identified several special UI needs for this kind of systems,
which will be presented in the following. First of all it can be stated that Ubi-
Comp applications are somewhat more complex than comparable conventional
programs, because they have to cope with dynamical changes during runtime.
Therefore it should be an important objective for a UI construction system to
hide some of this complexity (simplification).

In [2] Banavar et al. explain that the application development for UbiComp
has to be device independent, because a single application should be usable from
distinct entry points, e.g. from a laptop, handheld or even phone. This implicates
some advantages for the user such as synchronous data and familiar handling
across different devices. To achieve this vision within a UI construction system it
is necessary to provide mechanisms for cross-platform user interfaces. Therefore
a clean separation between user interface and functional core is needed, as well as
mechanisms for connecting the separated parts. Moreover it should be possible
to create different interface modalities for an application (flexibility), and the

P. Forbrig et al. (Eds.): DSV-IS 2002, LNCS 2545, pp. 89–103, 2002.
© Springer-Verlag Berlin Heidelberg 2002

Table 1. Surveyed systems

Frameworks	Suggested literature		MB-UIDEs	Suggested literature
MVC-Client	[30]		Janus/Jade	[1]
SanFrancisco	[34]		Mobi-D	[28]
JWAM	[6]		FUSE	[22,5]
MVP	[27]		TRIDENT	[7]
Amulet	[23]		TADEUS	[14]
			Teallach	[15,17]
			MASTERMIND	[9,31]
			BC-Prototyper	[35]

system itself should be open for the integration of new interface modalities and implementation techniques (extensibility).

Banavar et al. further point out that the UbiComp paradigm will lead to substantial changes on how users perceive applications. They will understand the application as a composition of services, which takes into account the current context of use, e.g. the location, time or weather. To be able to support interfaces for this new kind of applications it is necessary to address the dynamic adaptation and composition of UIs.

The next section takes a look into what existing tools offer for the special UbiComp needs. In Sect. 3 a new model-based architecture and a concrete system for better accomplishing these goals are presented. Thereafter system details are introduced in Sect. 4, which help to achieve to some degree the UbiComp demands mentioned above. In Sect. 5 as an example a metadictionary service is described. Finally in Sect. 6 follows a summary of the results and an outlook.

2   Survey Subsumption

In search of a suitable system for constructing UIs of UbiComp applications several different categories of tools have been researched [8]. The two most promising approaches are frameworks and model-based systems, which were further investigated by typical representatives (see Table 1). The consolidated results of [8] as shown in Table 2 are presented next.

The goal of a *simplified* UI construction process is currently achieved by frameworks only. Because of the low abstraction level framework implementations offer a flat learning curve for the developers and additionally whitebox frameworks allow easy programmatic extension. MB-UIDEs suffer from the lack of well established standards in the field of some partial models for UIs, especially for presentation and dialogue control facets.

It is stated that the clean *separation* of UI and functional core is achieved by frameworks as well as by model-based systems. While most frameworks utilize agent-based architectures like MVC [10] and PAC [11] the MB-UIDEs accomplish *separation* in a natural way through their models. The connection between these two components, relevant for an executable interface, is established by program-

Table 2. Subsumed UbiComp-characteristics of the system categories [8]

	Simplification	Separation Connection	Extensibility UI / Connection	UI Flexibility	Adaptation	Composition
Frameworks	x	x/x	o/(x)	o	o	o
Model–Based Systems	o	x/(x)	(x)/(x)	(x)	(x)	o

x : Nearly all systems   (x): Few systems   o: None of the tested systems have the property

ming within the framework context, whereas model-based systems use descriptive techniques to link the interface to the functional core. Some of the tested MB-UIDEs like TRIDENT or FUSE do not establish the *connection* between UI and functional core, leading to substantial additional effort for manually linking the parts.

Frameworks do not address the *extensibility* with regard to various UI modalities, as there are different frameworks for different purposes, e.g. for web-services or for interactive systems. Regarding the extensibility with respect to further implementation techniques, some frameworks address concepts for integrating database systems. Model-based systems are conceptually qualified for both extensibility issues. In practice only few of the tested systems exploit the potential of the model-based approach for supporting different interface modalities, or regard extension mechanisms to integrate more than one implementation technique (like Janus and Teallach).

When considering the *flexibility* of frameworks it is obvious that these types of systems are not able to support easy mechanisms for changing interface modalities, because the glue between UI and functional core has to be programmed. Also few MB-UIDEs utilize their declarativeness for flexibility (except TADEUS). The same is true for *adaptation* and *composition* aspects, which should be considered when building constructing systems for UbiComp. MASTERMIND is the only system, which addresses adaptation with respect to display properties. No tested framework even tries to cope with one of these aspects.

From this comparison it can be concluded, that the non-declarative approaches (frameworks) are not well suited for UbiComp UI construction systems, because they do not offer enough flexibility and are settled on a too low abstraction level. Model-based systems overcome these conceptual problems and possess all features which make them appear fully qualified for UbiComp needs. Within this group the interpreter-based systems (see [12]) seem to be the most promising, because they are able to handle the UbiComp needs with respect to dynamic changes of the UI during runtime. Before utilizing model-based systems for UbiComp some problems have to be solved. One important aspect is the lack of established UI standards. Further on the support of various interface modalities must be improved, and the research in the field of adaptation and composition must be carried on.

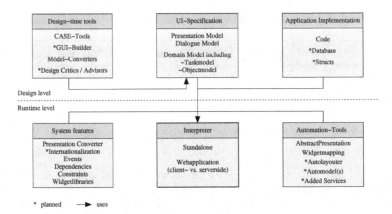

Fig. 1. Vesuf system components

3 Vesuf System

As a starting point for the design of a new system, a wide research in the field of tool-categories, techniques and architectures and their applicability with regard to UbiComp has been carried out [8], and a vision of a UbiComp development environment has been conceived [26]. This section will present the Vesuf system, a first step towards realizing the vision.

3.1 Vesuf Overview

As pointed out in the last section, interpreter-based MB-UIDEs are potentially well suited for all UbiComp requirements. Thus the Vesuf system consists of the components shown in Fig. 1. To realize an application within the Vesuf system the functional core can be implemented system independent (*application implementation*). This means that no system specific code-intrusions are necessary. In addition the different submodels for the *UI-specification* have to be created. To assist the developers in this process several tools can be used (*design-time tools*). At runtime the model-information will be evaluated by the *interpreter* which utilizes different *automation tools*. It constructs an executable UI by using further *system features* which are presented in detail in Sect. 4.

There is no fixed methodology to follow when developing applications with Vesuf and the models can be defined in an independent manner. The Vesuf system is designed to support what in this paper is called "slinky automation". This allows to start the development process with minimal specification effort, and utilize the automation tools to a high degree, in order to have executable interfaces in early design stages. During the further development the model specifications will become more elaborated, and therefore the need for automation will decrease, while the UI quality increases (see [32]). With this approach inspired by HUMANOID [33], rapid prototyping is possible.

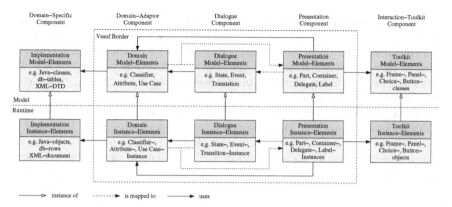

Fig. 2. Vesuf architecture

To be of use in a broad UbiComp context the system offers two different interpreter-modes. Active interpreters such as the GUIRunner and the VesufApplet are suitable for interactive applications and manage the transition between views by opening and closing application windows. Passive interpreters like the ApplicationServlet are mediator components which pass on all collected changes from the UI to the functional core and backwards.

3.2 Runtime Architecture

The layered architecture of the Vesuf system is pictured in Fig. 2. Primarily it must be stressed that a strict separation in so called model and instance elements is established in all layers. In [21] Kent et al. propose to introduce this separation as a foundation of the UML metamodel. Model elements are used to describe the various models, whereas instance elements represent concrete occurrences of the model elements at runtime.

Furthermore the horizontal partitioning in five separate components is conceived after the paragon of the Arch model [4]. The corresponding names of the Arch model components are denoted above each Vesuf layer. The Arch concept assures the independence from the implementation- and toolkit-specific side through the introduction of two adaptor components. In the domain-adaptor component all information about tasks and domain entities is encapsulated, while in the presentation component abstract and concrete display information is held. A central dialogue component is responsible for managing the global state of the UI.

In the following the models and their connections will be sketched. The domain-adaptor component is specified by a composite domain model, which consists of tasks and domain objects. This domain model is adopted from the UML metamodel and use cases are used for describing task behaviour.[1]

---

[1] It is planned to use the ConcurTaskTrees [25] as foundation for the task model in a subsequent release.

The dialogue layer contains a dialogue model, which currently is built upon the UML statechart semantics. Each application view is represented by one state. For concurrency purposes the concept of control flows is established. Each control flow is an autonomous state machine, which controls one part of the UI. To determine what will be displayed to the user, states are connected to domain entities (e.g. tasks or objects) via paths.

To map tuples of domain element and dialogue state to presentation elements a flexible mapping is used. The presentation metamodel extends the UML and is based upon functional roles. A presentation element is linked to a toolkit element which is responsible for its appearance, and to a domain element for realizing the information flow between implementation and user.

4   System Details

An overview of the proposed architecture has been presented, but it is yet to show, how it fulfills the identified requirements. Ubiquitous Computing demands the clean separation of device-specific and device-independent parts of an application. The Arch model provides five components, that can be abstractly developed and reused across a range of different environments for any application, or be specialized, e.g., to enable the use of device-specific features, according to the suitability in the application context. The border between context-, device- and user-independent and -specific parts can be flexibly shifted across the components of the Arch model. For easy integration of the components, a combination of several concepts is proposed.

These concepts heavily rely on the interpreter-style of the architecture, and therefore have not been found in recent generator-style model based systems (like Mobi-D, TADEUS, Janus, etc.). They have been inspired by other interpreter-style model-based systems such as ITS [36], HUMANOID and framework approaches like Amulet. In the following it is stated how these concepts aid in fulfilling the requirements presented in Sect. 1.

4.1   Domain-Adaptor Layer

Most model based systems try to solve the problem, how to connect the UI to the application implementation. In Vesuf the domain-adaptor layer conceals the implementation layer, and represents the application functionality from the viewpoint of the user interface.

With a flexible mechanism called "implementation accessor", any type of implementation technology (i.e. legacy system) can be integrated into the Vesuf environment. Currently the system has full support for Java implementations and prototypical support for implementations in relational databases.

The use of the UML metamodel as foundation of the domain-adaptor layer establishes a unified view on top of implementation details, and allows the specification of user interface related meta information (e.g. constraints) as first class objects together with the domain entities.

4.2   Paths

Puerta and Eisenstein [29] describe the mapping problem between what they call abstract (task, object) and concrete (dialogue, presentation) elements. They regard the solution to this problem as "essential for the construction of model-based systems". In Vesuf the connection between abstract and concrete elements is established using paths.

The Vesuf path language allows to specify navigational paths across all elements of the metamodel (e.g. classifiers, attributes, constraints). It is comparable to XPath [37] which provides navigational access to different node types of XML-documents, such as element, attribute and text. XPath introduces the concept of axes which specify DOM associations to follow (e.g. child, attribute, descendant).

The associations in the UML metamodel (e.g. attributes of classifiers) provide the axes of the Vesuf path language. For example to refer to the value of an attribute (starting from a point object), one would write `Point.<attribute>X.<value>`, or refer to the constraints of the attribute by writing `Point.<attribute>X.<constraints>`. Note that the identifiers in angle brackets are the axes that denote references of the UML metamodel, while the other identifiers (e.g. "Point") denote elements in the domain model of the application.

To be evaluated, a path is instantiated with an instance of the starting element (e.g. point). As the references in the object graph may change, the endpoint element of a path instance may also change. Paths hide the problems of dynamical changes, because they provide a static way to refer to dynamically changing elements. For example a presentation element uses a path as reference to the domain element it displays. While the displayed element may change over time (as described in Sect. 4.4), the path will always be the same.

Although paths are evaluated at runtime they are statically typed, and their correctness can be checked against the domain model at design time. Since paths can be used to navigate across all different models (object, task, dialogue and presentation model), they provide the glue, to stick together the different components of an application. Therefore most of the higher level concepts rely on paths.

4.3   Extended Constraint Semantics

In UML a constraint is a semantic condition or restriction expressed in text, represented in the metamodel by a boolean expression on an associated model element [24]. In Vesuf constraints are used to stipulate possible user interactions and valid user input. As in the Seeheim model [16] this places the validation of user input into the application interface layer and not into the presentation layer. This facilitates the reuse of input validation for all interface modalities.

The semantics of constraints are extended to allow the specification of supplementary information, that is utilized by presentation elements. For this purpose constraints include additional properties with special meanings. The additional

a) values

b) check

c) range

Fig. 3. Use of constraints for presentation elements

properties are specified as constant literals, or as paths referring to domain attributes or operations, which are evaluated dynamically at runtime. Since constraints can be realized as operations in the implementation layer, tools can be used, to generate constraint implementations, e.g., from OCL-specifications. Currently Vesuf defines five different types of constraint properties which may be used independently or together. These are described next:

valid specifies the boolean expression to validate user interaction (e.g. for operations or navigational events) or input (for attribute and parameter values). This represents the standard UML semantics of constraints.

check specifies via a path an operation, that may throw an exception, when the constraint is not valid. The exception object can include additional information, why the constraint is invalid, e.g. a text message as in Fig. 3b.

values specifies the set of possible values, e.g., for an attribute or parameter. The set of possible values can for example be used by presentation elements to create radio buttons or to fill in lists or drop-down boxes (see Fig. 3a).

range alternatively to a set of possible values a range can be specified. All Vesuf built-in data types (e.g. integer, float, date) support this. Range handling for application specific data types can be added (e.g. for IP-address). The range constraint can be used to handle interaction with scrollbars (see Fig. 3c).

active For dynamically prohibiting access to certain elements (e.g. attributes and operations) of individual objects in the domain-adaptor layer, the active constraint is used. It causes enabling and disabling of interaction elements and therefore provides a way for realizing intra-dialogue behaviour in the domain-adaptor layer, that is "inherited" (i.e. mirrored) by all specialized interface modalities.

When specified with paths, constraint properties are evaluated dynamically and internal changes are propagated by events as described in Sect. 4.4 and exemplified in Sect. 5. Besides the predefined types, custom constraint properties can be specified and then be used by the presentation layer.

The use of constraints enforces a certain level of usability, because they provide meaningful error messages. When used in conjunction with widget-mapping techniques, appropriate interaction elements are automatically selected based on the type of constraints specified for domain-adaptor layer elements.

4.4   Events and Dependencies

In Vesuf an event dispatcher component manages the collection, generation and multicasting of events. Events are initiated by instance elements in the domain layer (e.g. value of an attribute changed) or dialogue layer (e.g. a state change in a dialogue state machine). Event handlers can be registered on any type of instance element, and are used to couple loosely elements from different models. Besides propagating events to the appropriate handlers, the dispatcher manages the generation of dependent events. With dependencies the need for explicit event handlers in the presentation layer, reacting to changes in the other layers, is reduced. The system manages two types of dependencies, as described next.

Dependencies can be specified explicitly in the domain model using the UML dependency element. It is augmented by a tagged value, that specifies a path from the client to the supplier element of the dependency. The path enables the system to determine at runtime the supplier instance elements, that participate in any dependencies, and take the appropriate actions, when these supplier elements initiate events. An example for a dependency that has to be specified explicitly is the area attribute of a rectangle object, that depends on the values of the width and height attributes. When the width or the height value is changed, the dependency will cause an update of any presentation elements displaying the area attribute.

The second type of dependency arises from the use of paths for specifying properties of elements. When a section of a path changes, the endpoint of the path, and therefore the element that specifies the path (e.g. a view) also changes. When for example in a circle object a new center point is set, presentation elements displaying the x and y attributes of the old center point object are automatically adjusted to refer to the new center point. This is handled by Vesuf internally, and events for any dependent elements are automatically generated and published in the next event multicast (together with the initial event, that triggered the dependency).

4.5   Presentation Metamodel Based on Functional Roles

Since the behavioural aspects of the UI are captured in the domain-adaptor (using constraints and dependencies) and the dialogue layer, the Vesuf system features a very lightweight presentation layer, thus supporting the flexibility and extensibility requirements. The UML metamodel is extended with new elements rooted in an element called *part*. Besides this generic interface element four different types of elements are introduced (see Fig. 4). The system utilizes UIML [18] for specifying presentation models, because of its genericity and tailorability to specific environments.

The motivation behind the lightweight approach is, that the presentation elements only provide the glue between the concrete interaction elements in the

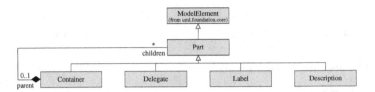

Fig. 4. Presentation metamodel

toolkit specific layer, and the application specific elements in the domain-layer. Therefore, in contrast to other proposals such as UML*i* [13], the elements of the presentation metamodel are not classified by their specific interaction capability (e.g. input, output, ...) but rather by the intention behind the element, i.e., the functional aspect of the connection between a toolkit element and a domain element. Three basic functional roles of atomic UI elements have been identified: *Delegates, labels* and *descriptions*. These elements are atomic in the sense, that they do not contain other elements.

For interaction elements, the concept of UI-delegates as self-contained representatives of domain elements, proposed by Holub in [19], is adopted. *Delegates* are the most important parts of the UI, as they enable the user to interact with elements in the other layers. In Vesuf, the actual domain-adaptor and dialogue layer elements, that are represented by a *delegate* are referenced via paths, which can be resolved at runtime to yield the corresponding instance elements. *Delegates* mediate, e.g., between attributes in the domain-adaptor layer and textfields in the toolkit layer.

The other two basic part-types (*label* and *description*) are not used for interaction, but to provide structural and usage information to the user. *Labels* are designations of elements in the other layers, usually placed near *delegates*, to designate which domain-adaptor or dialogue layer elements the *delegate* refers to. In the toolkit layer, *labels* are realized by texts, icon images or characteristic sounds. *Description* elements provide usage information related to elements in the domain-adaptor or dialogue layer, and can be used to provide context sensitive help (e.g. as tooltips). In addition to description texts these elements use information provided by constraints to inform the user about the current state of the interaction (e.g. invalid input).

To organize presentation elements in groups, *container* elements are used. They recursively aggregate the atomic presentation elements (delegates, labels and descriptions) that are to be displayed as a presentation unit. The container hierarchy is usually, but not necessarily, reflected by similar structures in the toolkit layer.

The lightweight presentation metamodel leads to simple, and easy to maintain interface descriptions. Furthermore, it allows the system to be easily extended by new interface modalities.

4.6   Interoperation of the Concepts

It has been shown, how the aforementioned concepts aid in fulfilling the requirements posed by UbiComp. The domain-adaptor component is the backbone of the architecture and features a runtime environment which manages model and instance elements with automatic handling of constraints, events and dependencies. Paths are defined on top of the modelled domain structure, to establish the connection with the other layers. The presentation elements use the potentially dynamic information of the domain-adaptor layer elements, to extract the properties of their widgets.

The dependency mechanism allows for intra dialogue control (e.g. en- and disabling of buttons) to be specified abstractly in the domain model (e.g. allowed parameter values for method invocations). The event mechanism automatically updates widgets that are dependent in this way. This mechanism of inheriting behaviour from the domain-adaptor facilitates robust and consistent behaviour in all interface modalities, and avoids redundancy in the different presentation models of an application.

5   Example

To prove the practical utilizability of the Vesuf system, it has been applied in the context of the GlobalInfo project [20]. It was used to integrate several services into the PublicationPORTAL [3]. One of these services is the metadictionary service that allows to query several online dictionary web sites (Fig. 5). The realization and integration of the services is described in detail in [8].

Using the example of the metadictionary Java application (see Fig. 5b), it is shown, how the concepts allow behaviour defined in the domain-adaptor layer to be mirrored in the presentation layer. The first example is the invocation of the *Translate* operation that uses the constraint / dependency mechanism. The operation is represented in the presentation layer using a button delegate. Choice delegates are used to represent the *To* and *From* parameters of the operation. These two delegates are self contained and not connected to each other. Nevertheless, when the user supplies parameter values, that are valid on their own but invalid in combination (i.e. a translation not supported by any dictionary), the button representing the operation will be disabled, since an appropriate constraint is specified in the domain model. This behaviour will appear in all presentations that support dynamic en- and disabling of operation delegates. In static presentations (e.g. web forms as in Fig. 5d) the user will be able to invoke operations with invalid parameter combinations, and will subsequently be presented an error page describing the constraint violation.

The second example utilizes the dynamic path concept. Consider the lower half of the metadictionary window in Fig. 5b, where a left hand side list box allows for selection of a result set, which is then presented in detail at the right hand side. This is realized in Vesuf by just using a path to the same attribute denoting the selected result set for both delegates. When the attribute value

100   L. Braubach et al.

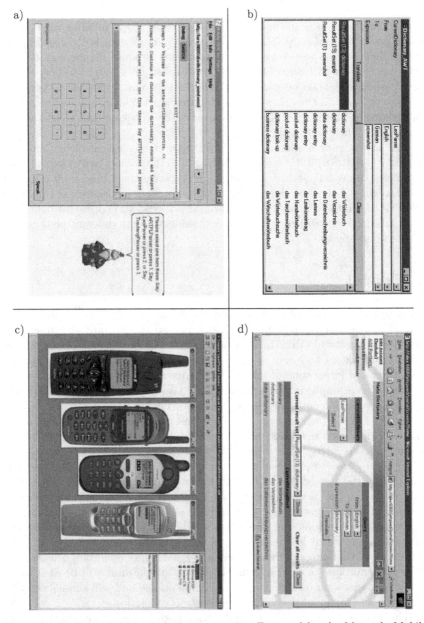

Fig. 5. Screenshots of the metadictionary service: Executed by the Motorola Mobile ADK for Voice (a), as Java application (b), displayed in the Yospace SmartPhone emulator (c), embedded in the PublicationPORTAL (d)

represented by the list box is changed, all interaction elements in the detail panel will be notified that a new result set has been selected and will therefore update their presentation appropriately. The same behaviour is exhibited in the web-portlet (Fig. 5d), where the current result set can be selected with the *Show* button and is subsequently presented at the bottom of the page.

6   Conclusion and Outlook

In this paper six major goals for UI construction tools in the context of UbiComp were presented. The proposed model-based architecture has been developed to address the arising needs. It is now shortly summarized how the architecture and the system characteristics help to fulfill these requirements.

Simplification of the development process is addressed by using standards to a high degree. The system is based on UML wherever applicable (domain-, task- and dialogue model) and uses UIML as a standard notation for the *simple* functional role based presentation model. Furthermore the development process is *simplified* by using automation tools and applying the slinky automation idea.

The architecture enforces the *separation* of the UI in five components according to the Arch model and introduces a generic mechanism (paths) to *connect* elements of these components at runtime. The *extensibility* with respect to new UI modalities is supported in a natural way by the underlying architecture and the usage of the delegate concept. To allow simple *extensions* with regard to different implementation techniques the implementation accessor concept is introduced. *Flexibility* with regard to UIs is achieved by applying constraints and dependencies. They relieve the presentation components from complex responsibilities such as input validation and intra dialogue behaviour. The resulting lightweightness of presentation components was one of the main goals with respect to UbiComp, featuring a minimum of redundancy between different UI specifications and a maximum of reusability of information rich domain models.

For *adaptation* and *composition* a sound foundation is set by the architectural separation of model and runtime layer and the interpreter-style is well suited to react to dynamical changes imposed by these demands.

Further research within the Vesuf project[2] will cover reusability aspects, especially the construction of UIs in a "LEGO" like manner. This becomes possible by the removal of all behaviour from the presentation layer and allowing UI components (LEGO bricks) to be placed on the domain-adaptor layer (LEGO ground plane). The connections between the bricks and the plane are established with paths and therefore allow to build up very complex interface elements from simpler ones in a declarative way.

References

[1] H. Balzert. From OOA to GUIs – the JANUS System. In *Proceedings of IFIP INTERACT'95: Human-Computer Interaction*, pages 319–324, 1995.

---

[2] The Vesuf project is available at: `http://vesuf.sourceforge.net`

[2] G. Banavar, J. Beck, E. Gluzberg, J. Munson, J. Sussman, and D. Zukowski. An Application Model for Pervasive Computing. In *Proceedings of the 6th Annual International Conference on Mobile Computing and Networking (MOBICOM-00)*, pages 266–274, N. Y., August 6–11 2000. ACM Press.

[3] A. Bartelt, D. Faensen, L. Faulstich, E. Schallehn, and C. Zirpins. Building Infrastructures for Digital Libraries. In *DELOS Workshop on Interoperability in Digital Libraries*, volume No. 01/W06. ERCIM Workshop Proceedings, 9 2001.

[4] L. Bass, R. Faneuf, R. Little, N. Mayer, B. Pellegrino, S. Reed, R. Seacord, S. Sheppard, and M. R. Szczur. A Metamodel for the Runtime Architecture of an Interactive System. *ACM SIGCHI Bulletin*, 24(1):32–37, 1992.

[5] B. Bauer. Generating User Interfaces from Formal Specifications of the Application. In F. Bodart and J. Vanderdonckt, editors, *Proceedings of DSV-IS'96*. Eurographics, June 1996.

[6] W.-G. Bleek, G. Gryczan, C. Lilienthal, M. Lippert, S. Roock, H. Wolf, and H. Züllighoven. Frameworkbasierte Anwendungsentwicklung (Teil 2): Die Konstruktion interaktiver Anwendungen. *OBJEKTSpektrum*, February 1999.

[7] F. Bodart, A.-M. Hennebert, J.-M. Leheureux, I. Provot, and J. Vanderdonckt. A Model-based Approach to Presentation: A Continuum from Task Analysis to Prototype. In F. Paterno, editor, *Proceedings of DSV-IS'94*, pages 25–39. Eurographics, June 1994.

[8] L. Braubach and A. Pokahr. Vesuf, eine modellbasierte User Interface Entwicklungsumgebung für das Ubiquitous Computing, vorgestellt anhand der Fallstudie PublicationPORTAL. Master's thesis, Universität Hamburg, 2001.

[9] T. Browne, D. Davila, S. Rugaber, and K. Stirewalt. Using Declarative Descriptions to Model User Interfaces with MASTERMIND. In F. Paterno and P. Palanque, editors, *Formal Methods in Human Computer Interaction*. Springer, 1997.

[10] S. Burbeck. Applications Programming in Smalltalk-80(TM): How to use Model-View-Controller(MVC).
http://st-www.cs.uiuc.edu/users/smarch/st-docs/mvc.html, 1992.

[11] J. Coutaz. PAC: An Object Oriented Model for Implementing User Interfaces. *ACM SIGCHI Bulletin*, 19(2):37–41, 1987.

[12] P. P. da Silva. User Interface Declarative Models and Development Environments: A Survey. In P. Palanque and F. Paterno, editors, *Proceedings of DSV-IS'2000*, pages 207–226. Springer, 2001.

[13] P. P. da Silva and N. W. Paton. UMLi: The Unified Modeling Language for Interactive Applications. In A. Evans, S. Kent, and B. Selic, editors, *Proceedings of UML 2000*, volume 1939 of *LNCS*, pages 117–132. Springer, 2000.

[14] T. Elwert and E. Schlungbaum. Modelling and generation of graphical user interfaces in the TADEUS approach. In P. Palanque and R. Bastide, editors, *Proceedings of DSV-IS'95*, Eurographics, pages 193–208, Wien, 1995. Springer.

[15] P. Gray, R. Cooper, J. Kennedy, P. Barclay, and T. Griffiths. A Lightweight Presentation Model for Database User Interfaces. In *Proceedings of ERCIM'98*. ERCIM, 1998.

[16] M. Green. Report on Dialogue Specification Tools. In G. E. Pfaff, editor, *User Interface Management Systems: Proceedings of the Seeheim Workshop*, pages 9–20, Berlin, 1985. Springer.

[17] T. Griffiths, J. McKirdy, N. Paton, J. Kennedy, R. Cooper, B. Barclay, C. Goble, P. Gray, M. Smyth, A. West, and A. Dinn. An Open Model-Based Interface Development System: The Teallach Approach. In P. Markopoulos and P. Johnson, editors, *Proceedings of DSV-IS'98*, pages 32–49. Eurographics, June 1998.

[18] Harmonia Inc. *User Interface Markup Language Specification, version 2.0a*, 2000.

[19] A. Holub. Building user interfaces for object-oriented systems, Part 2: The visual-proxy architecture. *Java World*, September 1999.

[20] Global Info. Globale Elektronische und Multimediale Informationssysteme für Naturwissenschaft und Technik des bmb+f. Bundesministerium für Bildung und Forschung (bmb+f), http://www.global-info.org, 2001.

[21] S. Kent, A. Evans, and B. Rumpe. UML Semantics FAQ. In A. Moreira and S. Demeyer, editors, *ECOOP'99 Workshop Reader*, pages 33–56. Springer, 1999.

[22] F. Lonczewski and S. Schreiber. Generating User Interfaces with the FUSE-System. Technical Report TUM-Info-9612, TU-München, 1996.

[23] B. Myers, R. McDaniel, and R. Miller. The Amulet Prototype-Instance Framework. In M. Fayad and D. Schmidt, editors, *Object-Oriented Application Frameworks*. Wiley & Sons, 1999.

[24] Object Modeling Group. *Unified Modelling Language Specification, version 1.4*, September 2001.

[25] F. Paterno. *Model-Based Design and Evaluation of Interactive Applications*. Applied Computing. Springer, 1999.

[26] A. Pokahr, L. Braubach, A. Bartelt, D. Moldt, and W. Lamersdorf. Vesuf, eine modellbasierte User Interface Entwicklungsumgebung für das Ubiquitous Computing. In H. Oberquelle, editor, *Mensch & Computer 2002*. Teubner, September 2002. To appear.

[27] M. Potel. Model-View-Presenter. The Taligent Programming Model for C++ and Java. http://www-106.ibm.com/developerworks/library/mvp.html, 1996.

[28] A. R. Puerta. A Model-Based Interface Development Environment. *IEEE Software*, 14(4):40–47, July/August 1997.

[29] A. R. Puerta and J. Eisenstein. Towards a General Computational Framework for Model-Based Interface Development Systems. In *Proceedings of the 1999 International Conference on Intelligent User Interfaces*, pages 171–178, 1999.

[30] R. Sanderson. MVC-Client: Putting Model-View-Controller to work. http://www.fourbit.com/resources/papers.shtml, 1999.

[31] P. Szekely. Declarative interface models for user interface construction tools : The MASTERMIND approach. In L. Bass and C. Unger, editors, *Engineering for Human-Computer Interaction*. Chapman & Hall, 1996.

[32] P. Szekely. Retrospective and Challenges for Model-Based Interface Development. In F. Bodart and J. Vanderdonckt, editors, *Proceedings of DSV-IS'96*, Eurographics, pages 1–27, Wien, 1996. Springer.

[33] P. Szekely, P. Luo, and R. Neches. Facilitating the Exploration of Interface Design Alternatives: The Humanoid Model of Interface Design. In *CHI*, pages 507–515, May 1992.

[34] P. Tamminga, D. Faidherbe, L. Misciagna, and F. Yuliani. SanFrancisco GUI Framework: A Primer. http://www.ibm.com/Java/SanFrancisco/, 1999.

[35] H. van Emde Boas-Lubsen. Business Component Prototyper for SanFrancisco: An experiment in architecture for application development tools. *IBM Systems Journal*, 39(2):248–266, February 2000.

[36] C. Wiecha, W. Bennett, S. Boies, J. Gould, and S. Greene. ITS: A Tool for Rapidly Developing Interactive Applications. *ACM Transactions on Information Systems*, 8(3):204–236, July 1990.

[37] World Wide Web Consortium (W3C). *XML Path Language (XPath), version 1.0*, November 1999.

Combining Compound Conceptual User Interface Components with Modelling Patterns – A Promising Direction for Model-Based Cross-Platform User Interface Development

Erik G. Nilsson

SINTEF Telecom and Informatics, Norway
egn@sintef.no

Abstract. In this paper we examine why model-based user interface development languages and tools only have had a limited dissemination outside the research communities, and argue that there will be an increasing need for cross-platform user interface development in the future. To meet these needs, user interface development languages and tools must use new approaches. We examine some alternatives, and conclude that an approach based on pattern-based abstract compound user interface components as building blocks is the most promising. We describe this approach in some detail, and give an example showing how three quite different instantiations of one modelling pattern may be mapped to different running user interfaces using a number of mapping rules to two different implementation platforms with significant differences. Then we discuss what is needed for modelling languages and tools following the described approach to be successful and give some concluding remarks.

1 Introduction

Model-based user interface development [15, 19, 23, 27, 28, 29, 30] has an unexploited potential – the principles hold possibilities to obtain large gains, but these gains have not been fulfilled by any language or tool yet. Some years ago, the user interface modelling field was trying to solve very small or non-existing problems. Now, important real-world problems have emerged for which user interface modelling is indeed an appropriate solution – but the community is still trying to solve the problems using the same approaches as the ones used to solve the non-existing problems. Expressed in a less polemic way, one may say that the increased focus on mobility and ubiquitous computing has on the one hand made user interface modelling much more important than before. But on the other hand it has made the problems that need to be solved much more complicated. This causes a need for new approaches to user interface modelling.

In the late eighties and early nineties, the market focus on cross-platform user interfaces was quite high, as many organizations was in a transition phase from terminal based to graphical user interfaces. During the nineties, the market focus on and needs for cross-platform user interface development decreased as MS

P. Forbrig et al. (Eds.): DSV-IS 2002, LNCS 2545, pp. 104–117, 2002.
© Springer-Verlag Berlin Heidelberg 2002

Windows emerged as *the* standard user interface platform on desktop computers. The last years, one may say that cross-platform user interface development face a potential renaissance – and the focus will be even stronger in the future.

One of the most important trends that are likely to enhance the needs for cross-platform user interface development is *user mobility*. Access to and dissemination of powerful ultra portable equipment used in high capacity wireless networks, enables users to operate far more nomadic than what is feasible with mainstream equipment today. This trend will cause increased variety in what type of equipment users will exploit. This applies both to equipment exploited by a given user in different situations, but even more to an increased degree of variety in types of equipment used by different users. It will no longer be possible to presume that most users have equipment based on the same technological platform (which has been the case for desktop computing the last five to ten years). Thus, there will be an increasing need for developing user interfaces that must be available across a set of machine platforms, user interface styles and / or a varying set of modalities, etc. [16].

Another trend that supports this is a move to increased flexibility in how work is performed. Firstly, the physical location on which the work is performed gets more diverse. Secondly, the division between work and leisure time becomes less distinct – i.e. work can be done on more diverse moments in time. Both these aspects of increased work flexibility cause a need for accessing applications and services (both used in work and private contexts) in various situations, exploiting different versions of the user interface for the application/service exploited. A way of seeing this is that *where the user is* and *what the user does* to an increasing degree is uncoupled.

The challenge addressed in this paper is to have specification languages and tools that render it possible to have common specifications when developing user interfaces (UIs) that are to run on UI platforms with significant differences regarding screen size, available modalities, and/or available UI components. This means that the specifications should at least cover common specifications of UIs on traditional GUI platforms, on Web platforms, on Personal Digital Assistants (PDAs) and on mobile phones. It is also a presumption that the languages and tools shall facilitate specification of UIs that are "richer" and more dynamic than what is possible using HTML/XML technology today [16, 14].

Further on in this paper, we examine why model-based user interface languages and tools fail to meet these new challenges for cross-platform user interface development and outline an approach which has the potential to solve them. By this we also propose a direction for the user interface modelling field to move in the future.

2   Problems with Model-Based User Interface Development Languages and Tools

Recently, work within user interface modelling has put an increasing focus on modelling mobile user interfaces [5, 6, 11, 12, 18, 21]. Despite this, model-based user interface development has an unexploited potential as a means for supporting cross-platform user interface development. The main reason for this is that the conceptual level offered in the languages and tools is too low and that the building blocks are too simple.

Offering abstractions based on simple building blocks (like buttons, text fields, menus, etc.) are done on different abstraction levels. At a low level, a language may offer a *radio group* concept that is an abstraction of a set of radio buttons in a frame component on different implementation platforms. At a higher level, a language may offer a *choice element* concept that is an abstraction of radio group, drop-down list box, list box, etc. On different implementation platforms only a number of the concrete components may be available, but as long as at least one of them are available, the abstract specification may be mapped to the platform.

Using this scheme, a user interface specification is an instance hierarchy of such modelling constructs on the given abstraction level. This works well as long as the same instance hierarchy is applicable on all the platforms. Problems arise when this is no longer the case. If the specification is to work across platforms with a certain level of differences – e.g. with large differences in screen size – there may be a need to have different instance hierarchies on each platform.

One way of handling this is to divide the specification of a given user interface in two parts, one describing the commonalities across the platforms and one describing the specialities on each platform. Of course, there will one common model and a certain number of platform-specific ones. In many languages and tools, e.g. in UIML [26] – one of the languages with broadest platform support – this division between the common and the platform-specific models must be done at a quite early stage in a user interface specification [15]. Furthermore, the amount of specification code constituting the platform-specific parts tends to be much more voluminous than the common part. In such a situation, it is relevant to question whether a model-based approach gives any benefit over the most relevant alternative, which is to develop the user interface on each platform from scratch [16].

A second problem with most model-based user interface modelling languages and tools is a lack of usability in user interfaces generated from the models [23, 17, 34]. Part of the problem is that the user interfaces do not exploit all specialities available on the target platforms. Abstractions across a number of platforms tend to use concepts that are closer to the intersection than to the union of the possibilities on the different platforms. A related topic is to what degree the concrete user interfaces adapt to the look and feel standard on the various platforms. It is argued that solutions developed across platforms to a lesser degree follow the look and feel standards on the individual platform than solutions developed from scratch.

A third problem with most model-based user interface modelling languages and tools is that they are fairly restricted with regards to which type of user interfaces that may be expressed. A common restriction is to forms-based data base applications [2, 3, 10, 13, 20, 22].

3   Approaching a Possible Solution

The main challenge for a modelling language that shall work across platforms
with significant differences is to have abstraction mechanisms that combine being
general enough to cover the different interaction mechanisms on the different
platforms, yet being powerful enough to act as a meaningful specification for the
concrete platforms. Thus, there is a need for a combination of generalization and
specialization.

A model-based language that is abstract enough to be able to describe UIs
with significant differences may run the risk of being *banal*. By this we mean
that the model is not able to describe sufficient number of aspects of the user
interfaces in a way that renders it possible to transform the models to concrete
user interfaces without adding so much additional information to the mapping
process for each platform, that the interfaces might as well have been developed
from scratch on each platform. Which indeed is the same problem we described
above for languages and tools on a lower abstraction level. To avoid this pitfall we
need something in between abstractions of fairly similar "atomic" components
and models that are abstract in the sense that they are stating that there exist
some dialogs, but not much about the contents of them. One approach may be
to use *compound* user interface components.

Compound UI components on a concrete level work very well as a means
for *reuse*. But as with reuse in other contexts, it is only useful when the reuse
problem is the same as or a specialization of the original problem that the component was design to solve – or it solves some subtask that is orthogonal to the
main problem (like a file open dialog). I.e. if we have implemented a compound
component for handling time sheets, this component will hopefully work well in
different applications where the users are to report time expenditure, but cannot be used in an application for reporting expenses, even though the underlying
model may have a quite similar structure.

This example points towards the need for patterns [1] support – as the similarities between the applications may possibly reveal a common model structure.
So, the solution is maybe user interface patterns [4, 9, 24, 25, 31, 32., 33]. Most
work on user interface patterns operates on a concrete realization level, and is
usually quite guidelines-oriented (i.e. if you have this type of problem, you may
use one of a number recommended designs – usually for an isolated subpart of
a user interface design). In this way the use of user interface patterns is closer
to the original architectural use than to the conceptual modelling and systems
design use [8] – which has proved to be more successful than the architectural
use(!) For our need in a user interface modelling language, general conceptual
modelling patterns turn out to be more useful than concrete user interface patterns.

4   The Proposed Modelling Approach

Our proposed solution – which has some similarities to work by Trætteberg
[25] – is to use abstract patterns-based compound (or composite) user interface

components as building blocks in user interface modelling languages and tools. The core concept in this is *modelling patterns*. As a modelling pattern usually involves a number of objects, a user interface supporting a modelling pattern must be a *composition* of different user interface components (each being simple or composite). As the user interface supporting the modelling language shall work on a number of user interface platforms, the compound (or composite) user interface components must be at a certain *abstraction level*.

This approach as it is just described is banal in the sense banal was described in the previous section. To solve this, transformation rules from the abstract, compound components to a concrete implementation on the different deployment platforms must be part of the modelling framework. It is essential to stress that these transformation rules describe how the *modelling patterns* are to be realized on various platforms. This means that the transformation rules must be instantiated with the same concrete objects or classes that the patterns are instantiated with.

To utilize the potential of this modelling approach, it must include a number of different mapping to concrete representations for each abstract compound user interface component on each platform, both based on preferences, desired user interface style, modalities, etc. Fig. 1 shows how the different main parts of the modelling approach are connected – expressed using a Unified Modelling Language (UML [7]) class model.

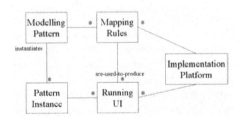

Fig. 1. Connections between the concepts in the modelling approach

To illustrate how the modelling approach may work, we look at a simple example. A typical modelling pattern that should be supported in a modelling language is the *Composite pattern* [8]. Fig. 2 shows this pattern. The pattern consists of a generalized Component that may either be a *Composite* component of a *Leaf* component. The Composite component may have a set of children, which are Components – i.e. either Composite or Leaf components. The *children* aggregation is recursive in an arbitrary number of levels.

This modelling pattern may be used e.g. for modelling a file system (see Fig. 3), a mail system (Fig. 4), and a department structure in a large organization (Fig. 5).

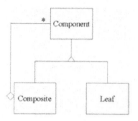

Fig. 2. The Composite Pattern

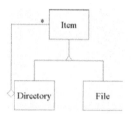

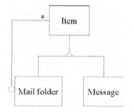

Fig. 3. File system instantiation of the Composite pattern

Fig. 4. Mail system instantiation of the Composite pattern

Fig. 5.   Department structure instantiation of the Composite pattern

The user interface model for each of the pattern instances is the instantiation of the pattern, choices of which platforms the pattern shall be implemented, and also which of the available mappings that are to be used on each platform. Before we look at how each instantiated patterns will be transformed to a running user interface, we present examples of how the mapping rules could be for the given pattern.

For traditional GUI presentation one mapping could be to present the *Composites* and the *Composite children* in tree view to the left and to present all children of a node selected in the tree in a list view to the right. Details about the *Leaf children* are presented in a separate window (e.g. using a forms based presentation) when the user double-clicks on Leaf items in the list view. Fig. 6 shows this mapping scheme.

An alternative mapping for GUI presentation could be to present the *Composites* and the *Composite children* in tree view to the left. On the top right, only *Leaf children* of a node selected in the tree are presented in a list view. On the bottom right, details for the node selected in the top right list view are presented (e.g. using a forms based presentation). Fig. 7 shows this mapping scheme.

On a PDA platform one mapping could be to present the *Composites* and the *Composite children* in a tree view (occupying the whole screen), while the *Leaf children* are presented in a list view (also occupying the whole screen). Selecting an item in the list view opens this item in a new view (also occupying the whole screen). Fig. 8 shows this mapping scheme.

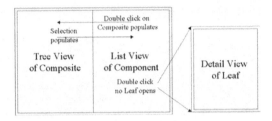

Fig. 6. First mapping scheme for GUI presentation

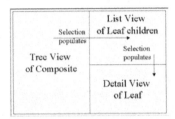

Fig. 7. Second mapping scheme for GUI presentation

An alternative mapping for the PDA platform could be to present the all *Components* on one level of the tree structure in a list view (occupying the whole screen). Navigating down in the tree structure is done by selecting a *Composite* item in the list view (which causes all its children to be shown in the same list view). Navigating up in the tree structure is done with a dedicated drop-down list-box showing all ancestors of the items in the list view. Selecting a *Leaf* item in the list view opens this item in a new view (also occupying the whole screen). Fig. 9 shows this mapping scheme.

Given these (and of course a number of other) mappings on these (and possibly other) platforms, each of the instantiated model patterns may now be

Fig. 8. First mapping scheme for PDA presentation

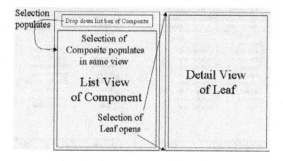

Fig. 9. Second mapping scheme for PDA presentation

mapped to a desired number of arbitrary mappings (often only one per platform) on the desired platforms (mostly more than one).

In this way the file system instantiation of the model pattern may be realized using the first mapping on the GUI platform and the second mapping on the PDA platform. Similar, the mail system instantiation may be realized using the second mapping on both platforms, while the organization model instantiation may be realized using the second mapping on the GUI platform and could be available in both mapping on the PDA platform – based on user preferences.

Fig. 10 shows how the file system implementation may look on the GUI platform, while Fig. 11 shows it on the PDA platform (details views are omitted). Fig. 12 shows how the organization model implementation may look on the GUI platform, while Fig. 13 and Fig. 14 show the two alternative implementations on the PDA platform. The detail view for the chosen Employee in Fig. 14 is omitted as it is identical to the corresponding view in Fig. 13 (the rightmost screen dump).

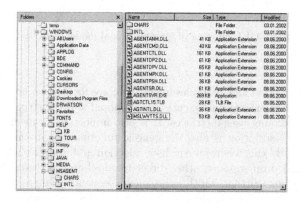

Fig. 10. GUI mapping of File System instantiation (detail view omitted)

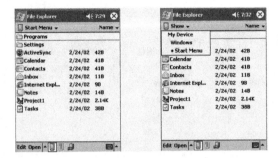

Fig. 11. PDA mapping of File System instantiation (detail view omitted) – right view shows navigation to ancestors

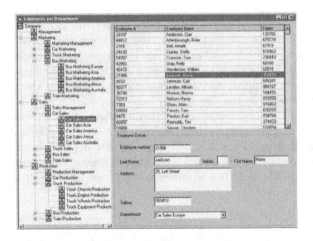

Fig. 12. GUI mapping of Organizational model instantiation

In the description and examples above, we have focused on how the abstract compound user interface components are composed and the structure of various mappings to running user interfaces. It is also important to mention that part of a mapping description is also the generic functionality in the implemented user interface. By this we mean e.g. how selection and double click on elements work, drag and drop support, other direct manipulation features, functionality on table headings (sorting, width adjustment, sequence changes, etc.).

The instantiation of a model pattern also includes determining necessary visual and functional details like icons to use (e.g. in a tree view), column headings, sorting of lists, menus, toolbars, layout style for detailed presentations, mapping

Fig. 13. First PDA mapping of Organizational model instantiation

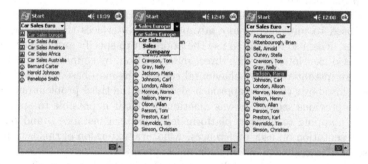

Fig. 14. Second PDA mapping of Organizational model instantiation – detail view omitted (identical to rightmost view in Fig. 13) – middle view shows navigation to ancestors

from data types of attributes to presentation styles, actions for element etc. These issues should as much as possible be part of the pattern instantiation, not of the mapping process (and thus be specified on a conceptual level) – but in some cases it may be necessary to give some details of this kind specifically for a given mapping on a given platform.

Modelling languages and tools following the approach described in this section also need to include mechanisms for how the abstract composite components (i.e. the pattern instances) may be coupled to build user interfaces consisting of more than one pattern instance. Preferably, the coupling mechanism should also be based on modelling patterns, and ideally it should be recursive, where the top level is the dialog structure of the application.

5   Discussion

The goal of the approach presented in the previous section is that by using pattern-based abstract composite user interface components with connected mapping mechanisms it is possible to have a common specification of a UI that work across platforms with significant differences – without having to have major amounts of extra specification for the variant on each platform. This solves the main problem with model-based user interface languages and tools today as outlined earlier in this paper. And an extra benefit is that the approach also solves the two other problems outlined.

As both the number of abstract, compound components (i.e. supported modelling patterns), the number of mappings for each pattern, and the number of implementation platforms are limited, it is possible to optimise the mappings with regard to usability and exploiting special features on each platform. In this way, the approach solves the usability problem encountered in user interfaces generated with many model-based languages and tools today – which was the second problem outlined.

As showed in the examples in the previous section, the presented approach may be used to implement more advanced user interfaces than simple forms-based ones. It is also feasible to use the approach to specify and implement e.g. a map-based user interface with direct manipulation, by coupling elements from the pattern instantiation to behavioural rules in the map-based mapping mechanisms. This shows that the approach also solves the third problem outlined.

In the previous section, it was mentioned that it is possible to apply more than one mapping to a given platform for a pattern instance – and base the actual presentation on user preferences. A natural extension of this is to use the same scheme to realize an adaptation mechanism.

To make the proposed modelling approach successful, it is of critical importance to find the right set of abstract patterns-based compound user interface components. It is also very important to define a good set of mappings for each pattern to the chosen set of implementation platforms – but this is much easier. Choosing the appropriate set of platforms is more of a market than a technical issue.

As mentioned, the main challenge is to find the right set of abstract components. It must be a limited set to make the modelling language comprehensible and to limit the amount of work needed to define all appropriate mappings. Yet the set must be sufficient comprehensive to render it possible to use the modelling language to specify an arbitrary user interface. It is of limited help to be able to specify and implement the wrong user interface very efficiently on a vast variety of platforms.

A way of making this choice less critical is to make the modelling language expandable – both regarding new modelling patterns/abstract components and how they are mapped to implementation platforms.

6   Conclusions

If we consider a probable future development, we foresee that a combination of increased bandwidth available for wireless communication, increased requirements on security, a huge multitude of mobile devices, a fairly large variety of client platforms, and enhanced maturity of new modalities will increase the needs for developing applications and services that must be able to run on a number of quite different platforms. This will cause an increased need for languages and tools that support cross-platform user interface development.

For model-based user interface development tools to meet these needs, different approaches than the ones used today are needed. Basing user interface modelling on simple (yet abstract) concepts may work quite well across platforms that are quite similar, but when the user interface models are to work across platforms with significant differences (regarding screen size, available modalities, and/or user interface components) this scheme falls apart. The result in many modelling approaches is that the abstract models must be supplemented by additional platform specific models describing how the user interface are to be tailored to the various platforms. Even worse, these platform specific models tend to dominate the specification with regard to the specification volume.

To solve this, and a number of other problems with model-based user interface development languages and tools, we have proposed a modelling approach using abstract composite user interface components based on conceptual modelling patterns. Supplementing these pattern-based, abstract, compound user interface building blocks with a number of well defined, usability-optimised mappings to a set of implementation platform (as part of the modelling scheme) it is possible to have models that are both conceptual and powerful. These models will work as specifications towards platforms with significant differences without having to supplement the abstract models with a lot of platform-specific models.

It is our hope that this paper will serve as an inspiration for the user interface modelling community when determining directions for new languages and tools for model-based user interface development.

Acknowledgement. The paper is partly based on results from the MOGOP project, which is funded by the Norwegian Research Council and Genera A/S.

References

1. C. Alexander, S. Ishikawa, M. Silverstein, M. Jacobson, I. Fiksdahl-King, S. A. Angel: A Pattern Language. New York: Oxford University Press. 1977.
2. H. Baltzert: From OOA to GUI – the JANUS System. In "Proceedings of Interact '95"
3. H. Balzert, F. Hofmann, V. Kruschinski, C. Niemann: The JANUS Application Development Environment – Generating More than the User Interface. In "Computer-Aided Design of User Interfaces – Proceedings of CADUI '96"
4. J. Borcher: A Pattern Approach to Interaction Design. Wiley 2001.
5. J. Eisenstein, J. Vanderdonckt and A. Puerta: Adapting to Mobile Contexts with User-Interface Modeling. In "Proceedings of IEEE Workshop on Mobile Computing Systems and Applications WCSMA'2000"
6. J. Eisenstein, J. Vanderdonckt and A. Puerta: Applying Model-Based Techniques to the Development of UIs for Mobile Computers. In "Proceedings of ACM Conference on Intelligent User Interfaces IUI'2001"

7. M. Fowler (with K. Scott) UML Distilled (2ed): A Brief Guide to the Standard Object Modeling Language Addison-Wesley, 1999

8. E. Gamma, R. Helm, R. Johnson, and J. Vlissides: Design Patterns – Elements of Reusable Object-Oriented Software. Addison-Wesley, 1995

9. Å. Granlund, D. Lafrenière and D. A. Carr: A Pattern-Supported Approach to the User Interface Design Process. In Proceedings of HCI International 2001. Available at http://www.sm.luth.se/ david/papers/HCIInt2001Final.pdf

10. M. B. Harning: An Approach to Structured Display Design - Coping with Conceptual Compexity, In "Computer-Aided Design of User Interfaces – Proceedings of CADUI '96"

11. K. Luyten and K. Coninx: An XML-Based Runtime User Interface Description Language for Mobile Computing Devices. In "Proceedings of The Eighth Workshop on the Design, Specification and Verification of Interactive Systems, 2001"

12. A. Muller, P. Forbig and C. Cap: Model Based User Interface Design Using Markup Concepts. In "Proceedings of The Eighth Workshop on the Design, Specification and Verification of Interactive Systems, 2001"

13. C. Märtin: Software Life Cycle Automation for Interactive Applications: The AME Design Environment. In "Computer-Aided Design of User Interfaces – Proceedings of CADUI '96"

14. E. G. Nilsson: Using application domain specific run-time systems and lightweight user interface models – a novel approach for CADUI. In "Computer-Aided Design of User Interfaces II – Proceedings of CADUI '99"

15. E. G. Nilsson: Modelling user interfaces – challenges, requirements and solutions. Proceedings of Yggdrasil 2001 – Norwegian Computer Society's annual conference on user interface design and user documentation.

16. E. G. Nilsson: User Interface Modelling and Mobile Applications – Are We Solving Real World Problems? Proceedings of Tamodia'2002.

17. A. Puerta: Work Group Report: Issues in Automatic Generation of User Interfaces in Model-Based Systems, In "Computer-Aided Design of User Interfaces – Proceedings of CADUI '96"

18. C. Pribeanu, Q. Limbourg, J. Vanderdonckt: Task Modelling for Context-Sensitive User Interfaces. In "Proceedings of The Eighth Workshop on the Design, Specification and Verification of Interactive Systems, 2001"

19. D. Roberts, D. Berry, S. Isensee, J. Mullaly: Designing for the User with OVID: Bridging User Interface Design and Software Engineering. Macmillan Technical Publishing, 1998

20. E. Schlungbaum and T. Elwert: Automatic User Interface Generation from Declarative Models. In "Computer-Aided Design of User Interfaces – Proceedings of CADUI '96"

21. K. Schneider and J. Cordy: Abstract user interfaces: A Model and a Notation to Support Plasticity in Interactive Systems. In "Proceedings of The Eighth Workshop on the Design, Specification and Verification of Interactive Systems, 2001"

22. P. Szekely: P. Sukavikiya, P. Castells, J. Muthukumarasamy, and E. Salcher: Declarative Interface Models for User Interface Construction Tools: the MASTERMIND Approach, in Proceedings of EHCI95, 1995

23. P. Szekely: Retrospective and Challenges for Model-Based Interface Development. In "Computer-Aided Design of User Interfaces – Proceedings of CADUI '96"

24. J. Tidwell: COMMON GROUND: A Pattern Language for Human-Computer Interface Design. Available at http://www.mit.edu/

25. H. Trætteberg: Model based design patterns, Position paper for CHI'2000 workshop on user interface design patterns. Available at
http://www.idi.ntnu.no/ hal/publications/design-patterns/CHI00-position.pdf
26. Universal Interface Technology: White paper: The UIML Vision. Available at
http://www.universalit.com/uiml/UIMLVisionWhitePaperV4b.pdf
27. J. Vanderdonckt: Computer-Aided Design of User Interfaces - Proceedings of the Second International Conference on Computer-Aided Design of User Interfaces, 1996
28. J. Vanderdonckt: Current Trends in Computer-Aided Design of User Interfaces. In "Computer-Aided Design of User Interfaces - Proceedings of CADUI '96"
29. J. Vanderdonckt and A. Puerta: Computer-Aided Design of User Interfaces II – Proceedings of the Third International Conference on Computer-Aided Design of User Interfaces, 1999
30. J. Vanderdonckt and A. Puerta: Introduction to Computer-Aided Design of User Interfaces. In "Computer-Aided Design of User Interfaces II - Proceedings of CADUI '99"
31. J. Wesson: A Pattern Language for Forms-based UI Design. Available at
http://www.cs.ukc.ac.uk/people/staff/saf/patterns/gallery/wesson.doc
32. M. van Welie and H. Trætteberg: Interaction patterns in user interfaces. PLOP'2000. Available at
http://www.cs.vu.nl/ martijn/patterns/PLoP2k-Welie.pdf
33. M. van Welie, G. C. van der Veer, A. Eliëns: Patterns as Tools for UI Design. Available at http://www.cs.vu.nl/ martijn/gta/docs/TWG2000.pdf
34. S. Wilson: Work Group Report: Reflections on Model-Based Design: Definitions and Challenges, In "Computer-Aided Design of User Interfaces – Proceedings of CADUI '96"

Multiple User Interfaces: Towards a Task-Driven and Patterns-Oriented Design Model

Ahmed Seffah[1] and Peter Forbrig[2]

[1] Human-Centered Software Engineering Group, Department of Computer Science,
Concordia University
1455 de Maisonneuve Blvd. West, Montreal, Quebec, Canada H3G 1M8
seffah@cs.concordia.ca
[2] Software Engineering Group, Department of Computer Science,
University of Rostock
Albert-Einstein-Str. 21, 18051 Rostock, Germany
pforbrig@informatik.uni-rostock.de

Abstract. The convergence of the Internet, mobile telephony, and hand-held technologies has led to the emergence of new kinds of internet-based interactive systems. Such systems can allow a single or a group of users to interact with the server-side services using different kinds of devices. In this technological context, a Multiple User Interface (MUI) refers to an interactive system that provides both multiple views of the information and coordinates the services provided to a user. The desired views are made available on different platforms, operating systems, user interface toolkits and on a large array of devices. Each view should take into account the specific capabilities and constraints of the platform. This paper begins by describing a set of constraints and characteristics intrinsic to multiple user interfaces, and then by examining the impacts of these constraints on the specification, design and validation processes. Then, it describes the research opportunities in important topics relevant to MUI development and usability including cross-platform usability, adaptation, task model-based and pattern-oriented design.

1 Introduction

Multiple user interfaces are proliferating in a variety of fields, such as cooperative engineering, e-commerce transaction, on-site equipment maintenance, remote software deployment and support, contingency management and assistance, as well as distance education and telemedicine. For example, a civil engineer can use a PDA for gathering information when inspecting a new building. Then, a mobile telephone can be used for adding comments and faxing or uploading all information gathered to the headquarter office. Finally, the same engineer or any other employee can use an office laptop to analyze the data and prepare a report. During this workflow, the engineer interacts with the same information and service using different variations of a single interface. These variations can support different "look and feel" and to a certain extent, different interaction

P. Forbrig et al. (Eds.): DSV-IS 2002, LNCS 2545, pp. 118–132, 2002.
© Springer-Verlag Berlin Heidelberg 2002

styles. This different "look and feel" should take into account the constraints of each device, while maintaining cross-platform consistency.

McGreere [9] summarized the usage of a MUI as follows:

"One can imagine having multiple interfaces for a new version of an application; for example, MSWord 2000 could include the MSWord 97 interface. By allowing users to continue to work in the old interface while also accessing the new interface, they would be able to transition at a self-directed pace. Similarly, multiple interfaces might be used to provide a competitor's interface in the hopes of attracting new customers; for example, MSWord could offer the full interface of a word processor such as Word Perfect (with single button access to switch between the two), in order to support users gradually transitioning to the Microsoft product."

However, even if the runtime infrastructure and the related development environment for developing the MUI on each platform is already available or will be in the near future, the following are the major design, specification and validation questions that should be addressed both by academia and industry researchers:

- Should we strive for uniformity in the services offered, dialogue styles and presentation formats, or should we adapt the interfaces and services to the constraints and capabilities of each device and/or each context of use?
- When designing multiple user interfaces, what is the best way to take the constraints related to each type of device into account while assuring the maintainability and cross-platform consistency of this interface mosaic?
- How can we make it possible for users to customize a multiple user interface device they are using in terms of accessibility to resources, tools, services, etc? When it is done from one device, how can such customization be reflected on all other devices that the user can use?
- How can we implement and validate N interfaces for M devices without writing N*M programs, training an army of developers in L languages and UI toolkits, and maintaining N*M architectural model for describing the same UI?

This paper is an attempt to clarify these questions. It is in three parts: a characterization of the essence of MUI; a brief summary of early results obtained during a workshop we organized [15], and a guided tour of fertile research topics awaiting investigation.

2   Multiple User Interface – Definition and Characterization

We introduced the concept of MUI during the HCI-IHM workshop [15]. The term multiple user interface is being used by others [9] and [18]. Intuitively, a MUI:

- Allows users to interact with the server-side services and information using different interaction/UI styles. For example, our requirement engineer uses pen and gestures for a PDA, function keys or single characters for a mobile phone and direct manipulation for desktop.
- Allows an individual to achieve a sequence of interrelated tasks using different devices. For example, a requirement engineer can use a mobile telephone on the road to confirm an appointment, use his desktop to email information about the interview, use his PDA to gather information about the user needs when he is interviewing stakeholders and finally use his laptop/desktop computer at to synthesize the information and write the requirement report.
- Presents features that behave the same across platforms, even though each platform/device has its specific look and feel.
- Feels like a variation of a single and cross platform interface for different devices with the same capabilities.

More formally, a Multiple User Interfaces (MUI) refers to an interactive system that provides both multiple views of a model and co-ordinates the user actions gathered from different devices/computers. The model may reside in a single information repository, or may be distributed among independent systems. Each view can be seen as a complete user interface for a specific platform (hardware, operating system, user interface toolkit) because all devices are able to present features of the system. However, all these mosaic interfaces form a unique and single multiple user interface. The interaction style and the displayed information/feedback can vary from one to another platform.

2.1   Multiple User Interface Styles

There are, at least, three user interface styles that a MUI may implement:

GUI Style or WIMP interfaces. This style, the most popular and dominant, employs four fundamental elements: windows, icons, menus, and pointers.

A Web browser-based user interface (WUI). The Web was originally conceived as a hypertextual information space; but the development of increasingly sophisticated client and server sides' technologies has fostered its use as a remote software interface. A WUI is generally a mixture of markup (in say HTML, XML syntax), style sheets, scripts (in say ECMAScript, VBScript) as well as embedded objects such as Java applets, plug-ins. An application using WUI style information is typically displayed in a single GUI window called a browser, though multiple browser windows can be used by an application to display information. The browser provides basic navigation. Different browsers for small devices and mobile phone are being developed. Such browsers are able to display a customized version of a WUI. The Yahoo Stock Manager is an example of a WUI that has a customized version for mobile phones. The Web clipping architecture and WAP frameworks provides basic services for dynamically generating customized HTML documents that can be displayed on mobile phones.

Handheld user interface (HUI). There are two major classes of PDAs in use today - those using a true GUI style of appearance and behavior and those that use a GUI or WUI subset. Both classes of UI employ a gesture-based interaction using a stylus and/or a touch screen. Even if it is not yet clear what style of UI will dominate handheld, the use GUI and WUI models should be reevaluated because of the lack of screen space and the low bandwidth.

Fig. 1. GuruNet: an example of a MUI implementing different UI styles (GUI for PDA, WUI for desktop, WUI for Mobile phone)

We expect that in the near future designers will be asked to combine these three different styles. Fig. 1 shows an example of a MUI that uses GUI and WUI styles. GuruNet is a pop-up application to retrieve reference information (dictionary, thesaurus and encyclopedia) and real-time information (e.g. news, sports, weather or stock quotes) across the Internet from inside any application. GuruNet offers a Web browser-based user interface and an optimized GUI version for PDA and mobile phone. Dealing with different UI styles complicates both the development and the validation of the MUI.

2.2   Characteristics and Constraints

The following are the fundamental intrinsic characteristics of a multiple user interface:

Abstraction. All information/services should be the same across devices of the same or larger category, even if not all information/services is shown or needed for all platforms. For example, a product listing may include only the best-selling items on a small narrowly device with the rest relegated to a secondary "more products" page. For an office desktop, the product includes all the selling items. We can use a different text color to highlight the selling items.

Cross-Platforms Consistency. A MUI can have different look and feel while maintaining the same behavior over different platforms. For example, all user preferences must be preserved across the interfaces. For example, if the end-user uses one access mechanism today and another one tomorrow, then the changes made in one user interface are reflected in the other.

Uniformity. A MUI should offer the support of the same functionality and feedback even if certain special features or variations are eliminated in some platforms [12]. For example, an airline reservation system may make choosing a flight and buying the ticket in two separate steps. This separation should be preserved in all versions instead of having the simplified version unify choosing and buying into a single step.

User Awareness of Trade-Off. It would be OK to have an advanced version including additional features (such as specifying a seating preference) that were not in the simplified version. Missing these features is a trade-off that the user would make in return for the benefits of being able to use the system under various limited circumstances.

Conformity to Defaults Standards. It is not necessary for all features to be available in all access mechanisms. For example, a PDA interface may eliminate images or it may show them in black-and-white. Similarly, text may be abbreviated on a small display, though it should be possible to retrieve the full text through a standardized command.

These characteristics and constraints are not artifacts of current development technologies, but are intrinsic to the MUI concept. Together, they characterize a MUI and complicate its development. They also justify the need to rethink the existing approaches to usability engineering.

3   Relevant Background Works

Remarkably, though focused research on multiple views and multi-devices interaction can be traced to the early 1980s. There are relatively few examples of successful implementations [7]. Perhaps the main cause of this poor success rate, are the difficulties of integrating the overwhelming number of technological, psychological, and sociological factors that affect MUI usability into a single unified design.

In the evolution of user interface ranging from the hardware to the concept of a multi user interface [7], the fifth stage (1990s to present) is the most relevant for our discussion. A multi-user interface supports groups of devices and people cooperating through the computer medium. A MUI can be considered as a multiuser interface. Our single user in the context of a MUI is what a group is for multi-user interfaces. He or she is asynchronously collaborating with himself. Even if a user is physically the same person, he can have different characteristics while working with different devices. . For example, a mobile user is continuously in rush, impatient and he cannot wait [12]; he needs immediate, quick, short and concise feedback. The same user, when he is in his office, can wait a few seconds for more details and explanations.

Another important relevant work to MUI is the concept of context-sensitive or oriented user interface. This area is still an active research domain and many models are emerging. The concept of a plastic user interface [17] or moderator [18] are two promising models. In a recent essay, Winograd also compared different architectures for adapting a user interface to the context of use [19]. As we characterized it in the previous section, a MUI is a context-sensitive user interface. This does not mean that a MUI should adapt itself magically at runtime to the context of use and in particular to the platform capabilities and constraints. It can be adaptive or adaptable. As we will discuss it in the next section, the adaptation can be done by the end-user or developer during the specification, design, and development, or before or after the deployment.

Compound document is also a useful technology that can support the development and integration of the different views that a MUI offers. A compound document framework can act as a container in which a continuous stream of various kinds of data (components) can be placed [13]. In certain extent, a compound document is an organized collection of user interfaces that form a single integrated perceptual MUI. Each form of content has associated controls that are used to modify the content in place. During the last decade, different frameworks have been developed such as Andrew, OLE, Apple OpenDoc, Active X and Sun Java Beans. Compound document frameworks are important for the development of a MUI for different reasons. It allows the different parts of a MUI to co-exist closely. For example, it makes data from one to another be "active", unlike Cut and Paste. It also eliminates the need for an application to have a viewer for all kinds of data; we just need to invoke the right functionality and/or editor. Views for small devices don't have to implement redundant functions. For example, there is no need for Microsoft Word to implement a drawing program; views can share a charting program. Compound document frameworks can also support asynchronous collaboration between the different views and computers.

4   Fertile Topics for Exploration

We now turn to the discussion of promising research topics in MUI design, development and usability. By its very narrative nature, this section of the paper is highly speculative and will raise far more questions than it answers. Further, this is a selective list of topics; it is certainly not intended to be exhaustive. Rather, our goal is to give the reader a tantalizing glimpse of the rich problem space defined by MUI.

4.1   Vertical versus Horizontal Usability

Vertical usability refers to the usability requirement specific to each platform while horizontal usability is concerned with the cross-platform usability issues of a MUI. What kind of tool can be used to support these two dimensions of usability?

Many system manufacturers have issued design guidelines to assist designers in developing usable applications. These guidelines can be categorized according to whether they prescribe a design model, i.e. "do this" or whether they discourage a particular implementation, i.e. "don't do this". Palm Inc. has put forth design guidelines to address navigation issues, widget selection, and use of specialized input mechanisms such as handwriting recognition. Microsoft Corporation has also published usability guidelines to assist developers with programming applications targeted at the Pocket Windows platform. For example

Microsoft recommends giving "the user immediate and tangible feedback during interaction with an application. Appropriate feedback includes acknowledging a request, pointing out an error, or tracking the progress of an operation." They also suggest "although auditory feedback can be useful for attracting a user's attention, it should be used sparingly." Such feedback is either broadly specified or too simplistic. Compounding this problem is the fact that in many cases it would appear that the usage of different guidelines could create many inconsistencies. Some guidelines can come into conflict and making a tradeoff not an easy task for MUI developers. The Java "look-and-feel" developed by Sun aims to be a cross-platform guideline that can fix the limitation of platform-dependant guidelines. However, this guideline does not take into account the particularities of each specific device, and in particular the platform constraints and capabilities.

To be consistent across platforms, an application does not hard-code its UI components for a particular look and feel. For example, the PL&F (Pluggable Look and Feel) is the portion of a Swing component that deals with its appearance (or look), is distinguished from its event-handling mechanism (its feel). When you run a Swing program, it can set its own default look by simply calling a UIManager method named setLookAndFeel.

4.2   Adaptation Strategies

Adaptation refers to the ability to tailor and optimize an interface according to the context in which it is used. Adaptation requires a MUI to sense changes about the context of use, make inferences about the cause of these changes, and then reacts appropriately. There are two visions of adaptation.

Adapting to technology variety. Technology variety implies supporting a broad range of hardware, software, and network access. The first challenge in adaptation is to deal with the pace of technology change and the variety of equipment that users employ. The stabilizing forces of standard hardware, operating systems, network protocols, file formats, and user interfaces are undermined by the rapid pace of technological change. This variety results also in computing devices, in particular mobile phones that exhibit drastically different capabilities. For example personal digital assistants (PDA) use a pen based input mechanism and have average screen sizes in the range of 3 inches. On the other hand, the typical PC uses a full sized keyboard, a mouse and has an average screen size of 17 inches. Coping with such drastic variations implies much more than mere layout changes. Pen based input mechanism are magnitudes slower than traditional keyboard and thus are inappropriate for applications such as word processing that require intensive user input.

Adapting to context of use diversity. A second challenge to broadening participation is the diversity of users [8]. Accommodating users with different skills, knowledge, age, gender, disabilities, disabling conditions (mobility, sunlight, noise), literacy, culture, income, etc., is the source of a further complication. For example, walking down the street, one user may use his mobile telephone's Internet browser to lookup a stock quote. However, it is highly unlikely that this same user review the latest changes made to a document using the same device. Rather, it would seem more logical and definitely more practical to use a full size computer for this task. It would therefore seem that the context of use is determined by a combination of internal and external factors. The internal factors primarily relate to the user's attention while performing a task. In some cases, the user may be entirely focused while at other times he may be distracted by other concurrent tasks. An example of this latter point is when a user driving a car, operates a PDA to reference a telephone number. External factors are determined to a large extent by the device's physical characteristics. It is not possible to make use of a traditional PC as one walks down the street. The same is not true for a mobile telephone. The challenge to the system architect is thus to match the design of a particular device's user interface with the set of constraints imposed by the corresponding context of use.

A fundamental question is when a multiple user interface can be or should be tailored as a single and unique interface. The range of strategies for adaptation is delimited by two extremes. Interface adaptation can happen at the factory, that is, developers produce several versions of an application tailored according to different criteria. Tailoring can also be done at the user's side, for instance, by system administrators or experienced users. In the other extreme, individual users might tailor the interfaces themselves, or the interface could adapt on its own by analyzing the user's context of use. As a major conclusion of the workshop we organized [16], we consider the adaptation of a MUI should investigated at the different steps of the entire design, deployment and exploitation lifecycle.

User customization during usage. Tailoring operations are the entire responsibility of the user. While this laissez-faire approach avoids the need for system support, it lacks a central arbitrator to resolve incompatible and inconsistent preferences between devices. The arbitrator should have the ability to make global changes (cross-platform changes) based on local adaptations. This makes MUI more difficult to write, and fails to amortize the development cost of support for adaptation.

Automatic adaptation at runtime. The idea to write one UI implementation that magically adapts itself, at runtime, to any device or platform, is not a realistic approach. The drawback of this strategy is that there may be situations where adaptation performed by the system is inadequate or even counterproductive.

Just-in-time customization during development or deployment. Developers can use one high level language to implement an abstract and device independent user interface model. Then, they can use a renderer to generate the code for a specific platform. The user interface markup language (UIML) aims to support such approach.

Customization during design and specification. This needs to use an appropriate design methodology and a multi-platform terminology to properly build a task model of a MUI. Tailoring operations can happen at the abstract interface specification where the dialogue gets modified, for example to shortcut certain steps, to rearrange the order for performing steps, etc.

Model-Based Adaptation. A task model describes the essential tasks that the user performs using a user interface. A typical task model is a hierarchical tree with different subtrees of the tree indicating the different tasks that the user can perform. Task models are a very convenient specification of the way problems can be solved. They are able to specify different problem domains on different abstractions. Our early investigations show us that in the case of a multiple user interfaces, we should make a distinction between four kinds:

– General task model for the problem domain
– General task model for software support
– Device dependent task model
– Environment dependent task model

The general task model for the problem domain is the result of a very accurate analysis of the problem domain. It describes how a problem can be tackled in general. All relevant activities and their temporal relations are described. Such a model can be considered as the representation of the knowledge of an expert. The state of the art is captured within this model.

The general task model for software support contains activities that have to be executed by humans by principle or because of financial reasons. It contains all activities that have to be executed by a software system or in an interactive way. In some sense this model is the first design decision. Later on the behavior of the developed software has to be consistent to the specified behavior of this task model.

The capabilities of a device are the most restrictive once in the context of use of a software system. This is the reason why the relation between task models and devices is especially stressed. As we already mentioned there are approaches to transform whole applications from one platform to another one without looking at the tasks that will be supported. But sometimes it is wise to look at the tasks first and to decide which tasks can be supported in an optimal way by a special device. This information is captured in the device dependent task model.

The environment dependent task model is the most specific one. It is based on several design decisions in previous models and describes computer-supported tasks for a special device. This model describes the behavior of a system based on the available tools, resources and the abilities of the user. It can be interpreted statically (influences are fixed during design time) or dynamically (influences are evaluated during run time).

There are different possible scenarios for the usage of task models in a client/server environment, which is the case of Web applications with a MUI. Often such models are used implicitly only. The implementation is done in a manual way. But it is possible to generate software based on task models. The idea for the modularization of task models was described in [6]. It is based on the usage of process algebra and allows the specification of temporal specifications by equations [4].

The kernel model describes the general approach of solving a problem with all flexibility. Constraints describing actual restrictions (available tools, user disabilities, etc.) are used to adapt the model to a specific situation. This adaptation can be done statically during generation or dynamically at run time.

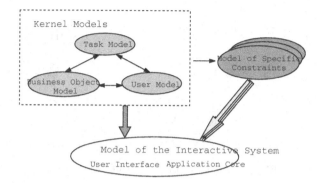

Fig. 2. Ontology of a model-based approach

If the resources on the client side are large enough then the interpretation of a task model can be done there. If there is a lack of resources the interpreter should run on the server side. In this case the client is informed about all tasks that can be performed in the next step. One of these tasks is selected and executed. The server is informed about this selection and computes a set of tasks that can be executed after this actual task.

In a client server environment there is the question whether the adaptation has to be performed on the client or on the server side. We will have a look at this problem for the task models at these various levels.

Models and Mappings. The most abstract model is the general task model for the problem domain. It is more or less for analysis reasons only. A usable model for a computer is the general task model for software support only. Allocating tasks to humans or machines is the first design decision. It results in the general task model for software support. This mapping can be done by attaching information to the nodes. This development step is omitted in this discussion. It is very similar to the transformation from the general task model for software support to the device dependent task model.

Tasks are attached to devices (more or less stereotypes or roles of devices only). This mapping specifies which type of device supports, which task. The restrictions are due to the input/output features of devices. They are not because of computational abilities. If the computational power is not strong enough then the computation can be performed on the server side. But because of small displays and keyboards it makes no sense to perform tasks with a lot of data transfer.

It is assumed that the stereotypes of the devices can be put into a "relation. This relation expresses the input-output capabilities of a device (e.g. Personal computer PC > Palmtop PT > Mobile phone MP). If the stereotype of a device is attached to a node this task and all nodes of the sub-trees can be performed on a corresponding machine. If a stereotype S is attached to a node then all devices belonging to a stereotype T with T > S can be used to perform the corresponding

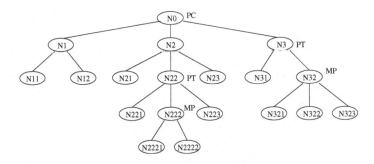

Fig. 3. General device dependent task model

task as well. We assume that real execution of a task is performed in the leafs only. Let us have a look at an example.

The whole task model can be performed on a personal computer (see Fig. 3).

If only a palmtop is available it makes no sense perform tasks related N11, N12, N21, N23 and N31. You need the full screen of your computer. With a mobile phone at hand it makes only sense to perform N2221, N2222, N321, N322 and N323. These tasks can be performed of course using a personal computer or a palmtop as well. The model does not specify that you need a mobile phone it specifies that you at least need such a device.

This general device dependent task model allows an extraction of the specific task model for a palmtop and a mobile phone (see Fig. 4). The question arises whether all mappings of tasks to devices are possible.

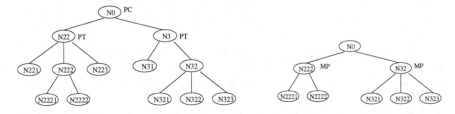

Fig. 4. Device dependent task model a) for a palmtop, b) for a mobile phone

This is not the case because temporal relations of the model have to be considered. If the successful performance of a task not attached to a device is a precondition of a task attached to this device the specification has an error of course. If task N1 is in the temporal relation of a sequence to task N2 the model for the palm top (Fig. 4) can't be correct. Such kinds of mistakes can be detected by looking at the constraints of the model.

Task Models and Client Server Architecture. The task model can be interpreted on the client or on the server side. It makes sense to consider it as specification of a workflow. In this case the execution of a task model starts with the instantiation of the model. This instance plays the role of a repository or mediator. It controls the workflow in a CSCW application. One person cooperates via different devices.

The question arises whether one can continue in executing a task on a different device. Is it e.g. possible to continue writing an email on a mobile phone? It could make sense if the body of the mail is already written and only the address is missing. In this case the address could be added at that moment the mail has to be delivered. This can be initiated via a mobile phone.

Two scenarios are possible representing the extreme situations.

1. The task models are interpreted on the PC and on the mobile phone. The server is only informed about the state of the execution. It plays the role of a mirror or proxy.
2. The task model is interpreted on the server and the clients are used as a kind of display only.

For case 1 the server works as a mirror of the work of the clients. If a new device is switched on a view of the relevant tasks is downloaded to the device. This means that the state of the execution of the tasks is stored on the new device. If states are changed on the client the server is informed and vice versa. It depends on the temporal relations whether tasks can be performed or not. States of subtrees that are not supported by the device cannot be changed by this client.

In case 2 the server controls the execution of tasks. It has to consider which tasks are supported by which device and has to send the corresponding information to the device.

Two mixtures of both scenarios are also possible.

All approaches can be combined with the idea of specifying specific features of a device by separate models. This idea is discussed in [10].

subsectionPattern-Oriented Design

Another perspective that can facilitate the development and validation of MUI is the concept of pattern-oriented designs. In the user interfaces design community, there have been vigorous discussions on usability patterns and pattern languages worldwide since 1997, and there are many groups devoting time to the development of patterns and patterns languages for different kinds of user interfaces. Amongst the heterogeneous collections of usability patterns, "Common Ground", "Experience", "Brighton" and "Amsterdam" play a major role in this field and have significant influence [17], [14].

For example, the Web Convenient Toolbar pattern provides direct access to frequently used pages or services. A typical Web convenient toolbar includes navigation controls for What's New, Search, Contact Us, Home Page, Site Map, and so on. Fig. 5 shows two design solutions and implementations of this pattern for a Web browser and PDA platforms. For PDA, it is implemented as a combo box using Wireless Markup Language (WML). For a Web browser, it is implemented as a toolbar using HTML and JavaScript or a Java applet. The implementations should take into account the context of use including platform constraints and capabilities. This is why the combo box implementation is suitable for the PDA.

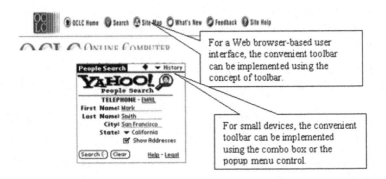

Fig. 5. The Convenient Toolbar Pattern on a Web Browser and a PDA

Patterns should not be considered just as an alternative design tool to guidelines. In the context of MUI development, we perceive them as a high-level tool for compiling experience gained through end-user feedback as well as for transferring, by means of software tools, the knowledge from usability experts to software engineers unfamiliar with usability principles. For instance, CASE tools have long been available to assist software developers to integrate the many aspects of Web application prototyping. However, the majority of them do not provide any mechanism for explicitly ensuring the usability of the developed application. In addition, it is not clear how usability knowledge should be integrated with existing development tools in order to maximize the benefits of usability patterns. Tidwell pointed out that the latest technology and design tools can help the designer to build much more creative Web applications than in the past. However, there is stillroom for improvement in the design process and in usability issues [17].

Given the wide variety of applications, usability pattern implementations should exist in various formats. An editor, should provide advice to pattern users in terms of selecting the suitable implementations for their context. Selection rules should be embedded in the tool.

Furthermore, rather than using different programming languages for coding the different implementations, we are investigating XML as a unified and device-independent language for implementing patterns. By using XML-compliant implementations, patterns can be translated into scripts for script-based environments like HTML authoring tools, beans for Java GUI builders like VisualAge, and pluggable objects like Java applets and ActiveX components. Generating a specific implementation from an XML-based description is now possible because of the availability of XML-based scripting languages. Among them, the User Interface Markup Language, UIML (http://www.uiml.org) is a potential candidate [1],[20]. UIML descriptions of a user interface can be rendered in HTML, Java and WML. Tools like the IBM-Automatic code generator [2] from design patterns encourage us to investigate the generation of code from XML-based pattern implementations as well as for automating the development of patterns-oriented designs. The UPADE editor we are developing aims to support such design approach [20].

5   Conclusion

In the current technological context, the concept of Multiple User Interfaces (MUI) is essential. As outlined in this paper, an effective MUI design must consider both cognitive and social factors in addition to the usual technological constraints. Architectures that neglect these matters cannot effectively cater to the requirements of the different users. Unfortunately, adoption of a MUI application is contingent on the acceptance of all the stakeholders.

Research has put forth several approaches to assist developers in creating effective MUI designs. Generally, these methods work well for regular software development and have thus been adapted for the case of multiple user interfaces. However, this approach usually results in tools that do not capture the full complexity of the task. Pattern hierarchies seem to be an exception to this finding. Whereas an individual pattern provides a solution to a specific problem, organized as a hierarchy, patterns guide the developer through the entire architectural design. In this way, they enforce consistency among the various views and breakdown complex decisions into smaller more comprehensible steps.

Acknowledgements. This paper is the result of two years of discussion and brainstorming with many people including the participants of the workshop on multiple user interfaces we organized. We are grateful to Fabio Paterno, Gerome Canals, Paul Ashutosh, Franck Tarpin, Jean Vanderdonckt, François Oger, Valsilos Zarikas, Antonio da Silva Filho and Homa Javahery.

References

1. Abrams, M., Phanouriou, C.: UIML: An XML Language for Building Device-Independent User Interfaces. Proc. XML 99, Philadelphia (1999)
2. Budinsky F. Finnie, F.J., Vlissides J.M., Yu P.S.: Automatic Code Generation from Design Patterns. Object Technology Vol.35, No.2 (1996)
3. Dey, A.K., Abowd, G.D.: Towards a Better Understanding of Context and Context-Awareness. In: Proc. of CHI'2000 Workshop on Context Awareness (The Hague, April 1-6), Research report 2000-18e, GVU Center, Georgia University of Technology, Atlanta (2000)
4. Dittmar, A.: More precise descriptions of temporal relations within task models. DSVIS 2000, Limerick (2000)
5. Eisenstein, J., Vanderdonckt, J., Puerta, A.: Applying Model-Based Techniques to the Development of UIs for Mobile Computers. In: Proc. of ACM Conf. on Intelligent User Interfaces IUI'2001 (Albuquerque, Jan. 11–13, 2001). ACM Press, New York 69–76 (2001)

6. Forbrig, P., Dittmar, A.: Software Development and Open User Communities. HCI 2001, New Orleans, August (2001)
7. Grudin, J.: Groupware and Social Dynamics: Eight Challenges for Developers. Communications of the ACM vol. 37, no. 1: 92–105 (1994)
8. Stephanidis, C.: User Interfaces for all: Concepts, Methods, and Tools. Lawrence Erlbaum Associates (2002)
9. McGrenere, J., Baecker, R., Booth, K.: An evaluation of a multiple interface design solution for bloated software. ACM CHI 2002, Minneapolis, 20–24 April (2002)
10. Müller, A., Forbrig, P., Cap, C.: Model-Based User Interface Design Using Markup Concepts. DSVIS 2001, Glasgow, June (2001)
11. Myers, B., Hudson, S., Pausch, R.: Past, Present, Future of User Interface Tools. Transactions on Computer-Human Interaction, ACM, 7(1), March 2000, pp. 3–28 (2000)
12. Nielsen, J., Ramsay, M.: WAP Usability Déjà Vu: 1994 All Over Again Report from a Field Study in London. Fall 2000 Nielsen Norman Group (2000)
13. Orfali, R., Harkey, D., Edwards, J.: The Essential Distributed Objects Survival Guide. Wiley (1996)
14. Pemberton L., Griffiths, R.: The Brighton Usability Pattern Collection. 1999, http://www.it.bton.ac.uk/cil/usability/patterns, 1998.
15. Seffah, A., Radhakrishan, T., Canals, G.: Workshop on "Multiples User Interfaces over the Internet: Engineering and Applications Trends. HM-HCI: French/British Conference on Human Computer Interaction, September 10–14, Lille, France (2001)
16. Thevenin, D., Coutaz, J.: Plasticity of User Interfaces: Framework and Research Agenda. In: Sasse, A., Johnson, Ch. (eds.): Proc. of IFIP TC 13 Int. Conf. on Human-Computer Interaction Interact'99, Edinburgh, August 1999. IOS Press, London 110–117 (1999)
17. Tidwell, J.: Common Ground: A Pattern Language for Human-Computer Interface Design. http://www.mit.edu/~jtidwell/common_ground.html (1997)
18. Vanderdonckt, J., Oger, F.: Synchronized Model-Based Design of Multiple User Interfaces. Workshop on "Multiples User Interfaces over the Internet: Engineering and Applications Trends, HM-HCI: French/British Conf. on Human Computer Interaction.
19. Winograd, T.: Architectures for Context. http://hci.stanford.edu/~winograd/papers/context/context.pdf, HCI Journal (2001),
20. Seffah, A., Javahery, A.: A Model Usability-Patterns Oriented Designs. Tamodia Conference (2002)

Foundations of Cognitive Support: Toward Abstract Patterns of Usefulness

Andrew Walenstein

Department of Computer Science,
University of Victoria, Victoria, B.C., Canada
walenste@csr.uvic.ca

Abstract. Computer tools for cognitively challenging activities are considered useful, to a great extent, because of the support that they provide for human thinking and problem solving. To analyze, specify, and design cognitive support, a suitable analytic framework is required. Theories of "distributed cognition" have been offered as potentially suitable frameworks, but they have generally failed to plainly articulate comprehensive theories of cognitive support. This paper seeks to clarify the intellectual foundations for studying and designing cognitive support, and aims to put them in a form suitable for design. A framework called RODS is described as a type of minimal, lightweight intellectual toolkit. Its main aim is to allow analysts to think in high-level cognition-support terms rather than be overwhelmed by task- and technology-specific implementation details. Framing usefulness in terms of cognitive support makes it possible to define abstract patterns of what makes tools "good". Implications are drawn for how the framework may be used for the design of tools in cognitively challenging work domains.

1 Introduction

A universal and critical design goal for tools is to make them *useful*. In the realm of physical labour, critical aspects of usefulness are understood in terms of *mechanical advantage*. For example a lever is understood to be useful primarily due to its ability to reduce the force needed to raise a mass. For cognitive work domains such as software debugging, financial forecasting, and writing composition, a key aspect of a tool's usefulness relates to how it improves cognition. For instance, we should expect that useful software visualization systems will make program comprehension easier, faster, or better in some way. Thus in highly cognitive work domains, usefulness is closely associated with the provision of *cognitive support*—i.e., with the ways in which cognition is helped, aided, or otherwise assisted by artifacts. Tools for cognitive work domains may fail to be usable in many ways (e.g., they may be hard to learn), but they cannot fail to provide cognitive support.

In order to systematically analyze, specify, and design cognitive support in tools, the fundamental principles of cognitive support must be known and effectively wielded. This is not easily done. Many common shortcomings of HCI

P. Forbrig et al. (Eds.): DSV-IS 2002, LNCS 2545, pp. 133–147, 2002.
© Springer-Verlag Berlin Heidelberg 2002

theories and guidelines are by now well known (see e.g., Carroll [6]). Four inadequacies are of particular interest in this paper. First, existing theories may be too costly to learn and apply [4]. Second, they can be too task- or technology-specific. This greatly hinders the specification of reusable and science-grounded patterns of successful design [25]. Third, the theories can fail to adequately address usefulness in terms of cognitive support. Frequently the objective adopted for HCI theories is to identify *usability problems*, instead of identifying the forms of cognitive support which render a tool worthwhile using in the first place. Fourth, the theories may be ineffective for generating design advice. The theories must work in the absence of a prototype solution if they are to be especially useful in design; they must identify steps one might take to add cognitive support.

These four shortcomings currently hamper the application of distributed cognition (DC) theories. DC has been portrayed as a promising general theoretical framework for analyzing cognitive work domains [10]. Several researchers have recently adopted DC as an umbrella approach for HCI research and design (e.g., Wright *et al.* [30], Hollan *et al.* [10], Rogers *et al.* [20]). The key tenet in DC is that cognition is not localized to a single individual, but is instead a process distributed amongst various artifacts and humans. But knowing how any cognitive system works is only a prelude to changing it by introducing new tools. It is reasonable to expect that theories of *cognition* (even *distributed* cognition) will primarily explain or predict how existing cognitive systems work. In contrast, a theory of *cognitive support* is a theory of intervention: it tells one how cognitive systems are improved via the introduction of artifacts. It is important to be able to clearly articulate the principles underlying these interventions in a way that is technology- and task-independent, and such that learning and application costs are minimized.

This paper outlines an attempt to satisfy these goals by proposing a high-level cognitive support theory. At its heart is a general cognitive support analysis framework called RODS. RODS integrates and adapts existing theories from DC and elsewhere. It is essentially a high-level and general theory of cognitive support together with an overarching framework for analysis. The central resource within RODS is a list of four support principles identifying distinct classes of cognitive support. These four classes of support give RODS its name.

RODS is proposed as a resource for designers to use throughout the design and development process, but it is expected to be especially helpful during design envisionment. Our long range goal is to facilitate various phases of design, but our current focus is on relatively informal design reasoning such as might occur during design brainstorming sessions. Our aims are thus similar to those of the cognitive dimensions (CDs) work which "raise the level of discourse" [9, pg. 132] of designers. In particular, we wish to specify theory-derived patterns of cognitive support which are task- and technology-independent. These would allow designers to avoid "death by detail" [9, pg. 131] and yet still proceed towards essential design insights. If we are successful, we expect such "broad-brush" theories of cognitive support to have broad implications for HCI development.

The rest of the paper is structured as follows. First, requirements for generating a suitable theoretical framework for cognitive support are outlined in Sec. 2. Six desirable traits are extracted from this analysis. Section 3 describes RODS and shows how it embodies these six desirable traits. Section 4 briefly overviews how RODS has been used to view various tool implementations as instances of patterns of cognitive support. Related work is overviewed in Sec. 5, and implications and conclusions are drawn in Sec. 6.

2   Leveraging Mechanical Support Theory

Identifying fundamental principles is a critical undertaking for any field of research. Fundamental principles frequently provide deep and general insights that are as important as the fine details. This fact was noted by Newell and Simon [16] in their 1975 ACM Turing Award lecture. They noted that the essential characteristics of a discipline can often be stated in short, general sentences. They highlighted, in particular, the importance of the cell doctrine in biology, the theory of plate techtonics in geology, and the germ theory of disease. These are all gross qualitative theories which are critical for understanding a domain. They tie together, relate, and organize multitudes of facts. The fact that they are not specific theories capable of generating precise predictions does not diminish their importance. High-level, generalized truths can be enormously valuable in understanding a broad range of phenomena at a high level.

The arguments raised by Newell and Simon likely apply to cognitive support theories. For designers in HCI, there is, in fact, a particular reason for needing a high-level, qualitative theory of cognitive support: cost of application. There exists a "cost gulf" [4] which can prevent otherwise helpful theories from being applied. High-level, qualitative theories are usually "lightweight" and widely applicable. Consequently, they can be expected to provide the analyst with the most benefit for the least investment in theory learning and application. Colloquially speaking, high-level, qualitative theories may yield the best "bang for the buck" for the analyst. Thus, articulating such an overarching qualitative theory for cognitive support should be given a high priority—ahead of, say, specific theories pertaining to one form or implementation of cognitive support.

Where will such a general, qualitative theory come from? Distributed cognition (DC) is one possible source. DC theory contains many insights into the ways in which tools affect and support thinking. It identifies key principles underlying DC such as the fact that artifacts are key resources used to represent and propagate knowledge. Our concern here is particularly on generalizable principles for how artifacts support cognition. Although DC is a prime candidate to be able to describe such principles, they have yet to be clearly and comprehensively elucidated. What are principles of cognitive support? How are these foundations best highlighted in a designer-oriented framework?

One way to approach these questions is to look to previous successful frameworks for inspiration. Here we shall turn to mechanical support theory for insights. Compared to cognitive work, the realm of physical work is very well understood. We now understand a great deal about how to assist physical work.

Consider our understanding of *levers*. A lever is a *simple machine*—an "atomic" machine of sorts. It can be defined in structural terms as a movable *pivot* rotating about a fixed *fulcrum*. The total amount of work done is not reduced when using a lever. Instead, the lever is merely a *force-amplification* device, meaning that it reduces the force needed to move a load. However the assistance is not completely free: overheads are introduced by the fact that the lever must be depressed a greater distance than the mass needs to be raised. These overheads are perfectly acceptable when the leverage is needed.

There is much to admire about our relatively mature understanding of mechanical advantage. We know that the key principle for a lever's usefulness is *mechanical advantage*. The concept of mechanical advantage can be stated simply as a way of trading off distance traveled for a reduction in required force. It is a general concept which is defined in abstract terms, and is thus removed from the particulars of its *implementation* (materials, sizes, etc.) or its use (lifting people, water, planets, etc.). Furthermore, the fundamental concept has a succinct and memorable name: "leverage". Catalogues of various simple machines have been described (inclined plane, pulley, etc.). These, in combination, form a type of "language" for building more complicated physical labour saving devices [18]. With such a language we can decompose complex machines into their component machines, and compose new complicated machines out of simpler ones.

Our scientific understanding of the principles of mechanical support is now well-established. Designers of new machines can rely on these theories as justification for their design decisions without having to reestablish their veridicality. Even without complicated materials models and physics equations, the gross, qualitative theories are valuable. The basic concepts of simple machines are easy to learn and readily applied without deep analysis or scientific knowledge. It does not take a PhD in physics to apply the concepts during real design.

It would be highly desirable to be able to tell a similar tale for understanding cognitive support at the broadest levels. We can use our understanding of *mechanical* support as an intuition pump for deriving desiderata for understanding *cognitive* support. In particular, we can expect it to be helpful to have the following:

1. **Core theory**: this would explain the basic idea behind cognitive support. It would be the analogue to concept of mechanical support.
2. **Small vocabulary of advantages**: this would describe "atomic" principles of cognitive advantage. Ideally, this would identify *orthogonal* principles that can discussed independently. These principles, in turn, would generate equivalence classes identifying tools implementing a common type of cognitive support. These cognitive support classes would be analogues of the classes of simple machine (lever, pulley, etc.).
3. **Composition language**: this would explain how the various primitive types of support can be composed. It would be an analogue of mechanical composition (e.g., attaching a pulley to a lever).

4. **Mnemonic, evocative names**: the names of the cognitive support principles would ideally have helpful names that are easy to understand and remember. Ideally the names would index into deep expert knowledge concerning related issues.
5. **Abstract, generalizable description level**: cognitive support would be ideally defined at an abstract, functional level which is removed from particulars of the tool or its uses.
6. **Analysis framework**: this framework would serve as a foundation for applying the cognitive support principles during analysis. It would allow the analyst to decompose complicated tools into their component types of cognitive support. It would also allow the designer to do the reverse, i.e., to compose simple supports into more complicated ones.

In the future, as DC and HCI mature, we may expect to someday build detailed models of cognitive support and perhaps even be able to quantitatively predict cognitive benefits. But for now, it would be very helpful merely if the above six desiderata could be addressed in some adequate way such that the basic forms of cognitive support can be loosely analyzed. Ideally, such cognitive support analyses could be done without requiring an advanced degree in cognitive science. The following section describes RODS, an attempt to provide such a framework.

3   The RODS Analogue to Mechanical Support

RODS is a high-level, qualitative theory of cognitive support. The name "RODS" comes from the four main classes of cognitive support it identifies: task **R**eduction, algorithmic **O**ptimization, **D**istribution, and **S**ubstitution. The framework is described in more detail below. It is introduced by arguing how it addresses the six desiderata from the previous section.

3.1   Core Theory of Cognitive Advantage

The central tenet of DC theory is that cognition is not a process localized to an individual human mind, but one that is spread out amongst possibly many humans and artifacts [11]. Various artifacts, including computers, can therefore be viewed as parts of a single cognitive system. Critically, DC argues that a cognitive system will operate better or worse depending upon whether the appropriate external artifacts are available, and depending upon how they are designed. This insight is memorably noted by Norman who said "it is *things* that make us smart" [17].

Since DC generally explains cognition in terms of computation, the explanation of cognitive assistance must surely also be computational in nature. The essential argument is that a computation that utilizes a *computational advantage* may be *substituted* for another equivalent one which does not. By "computational advantage" we mean some way of improving the computation according to some measure (speed, memory use, etc.). Cognitive support can therefore be understood entirely in computational terms: support is the provision of computational advantage. Newly introduced artifacts reengineer the overall computations involved in a DC system. Thus designing cognitive support means reengineering computational systems such that the system's cognition is improved.

From these considerations, a general, qualitative theories of cognitive support can be stated as follows: *The cognitive support provided an artifact is the computational advantage that it provides.*

3.2   Small Vocabulary of Advantages

A staggering vareity of cognitive artifacts are used by humans. Software developers, for instance, use a wide assortment of diagrams, compilers, analyzers, visualizers, editors, and so on. Yet it would be surprising if each variation in cognitive artifact would require a wholly different explanation. A more plausible situation is that is that some relatively small set of principles are *in combination* sufficient to account for the many varieties of cognitive support. Variations and combinations of those "atomic" principles might be seen to generate the enormous design space of cognitive artifacts.

Given that cognitive support is considered computational reengineering, the atomic support principles will be associated with distinct principles of computational advantage. The trick, of course, is settling on a suitable set of principles. Ideally, these would identify orthogonal computational advantages. We have found it useful to settle upon just four commonly understood computational principles. Each of these induce a class of support types; these support types are termed "task reduction", "algorithm optimization", "distribution" and "substitution". These support classes are listed in Figure 1, and described below.

Task Reduction. It is sometimes possible to eliminate work that is unnecessary. For example a pathologically designed programmer's editor might insist on having the developer re-read every line of code in a program before each and every edits she makes (e.g., by forcing a line-by-line scroll through the program). In most (all?) circumstances this would be a waste of time and effort. Computationally speaking, the problem is that there are unnecessary computations being performed; from an HCI point of view, the task can be reduced by eliminating unnecessary steps. Removing unproductive work will decrease the amount of cognitive work done and thus should influence performance.

This form of task and performance "enhancement" is quite obvious, but it is included in RODS because in some cases it is helpful to reduce real task demands. For instance, it may be possible to require only "good enough" answers from users. Moreover, it is critical to include task reduction in RODS so that one cannot confuse any of the other support types with a simple reduction in the work done. Thus the remaining principles will all insist on maintaining some form of equivalence in work.

Algorithmic optimization. Algorithmic optimization relies on the fact that differences in encoding or procedure in can create differences in performance

$\boxed{\mathcal{R}}$ **task Reduction**

Cmpt Principle: some functions are easier to compute
Substitution Type: substitute simpler tasks for more complicated ones
Example (cmpt): removing redundant or unused computations
Example (HCI): eliminating unnecessary steps
Design Principle: remove unnecessary work; relax task demands

$\boxed{\mathcal{O}}$ **algorithmic Optimization**

Cmpt Principle: functionally identical algorithms differ in efficiency
Substitution Type: substitute equivalent methods, ADTs, or encodings
Example (cmpt): changing to doubly-linked list; switching sorting algorithm
Example (HCI): switching to Roman numerals
Design Principle: optimize cognitive processes for task & infrastructure

$\boxed{\mathcal{D}}$ **Distribution**

Cmpt Principle: distribution adds memory or computing resources
Substitution Type: substitute external resources for internal ones
Example (cmpt): caching memory to a hard drive; client-server architecture
Example (HCI): writing down a shopping list; automating constraint checking
Design Principle: distribute (i.e., *redistribute* or *offload*) data or processing

$\boxed{\mathcal{S}}$ **Specialization**

Cmpt Principle: specialized routines or processors can be more efficient
Substitution Type: substitute specialized processors for more general ones
Example (cmpt): use a FPU or accellerated graphics card
Example (HCI): enable visual search to substitute for "manual" search
Design Principle: change representation to make use of specialized hardware

Fig. 1. Summary of RODS cognitive support classes.

without changing the essential outcome—i.e., without changing the "function" being computed [13]. For succinctness, we shall gloss over the many possible variations in terminology (e.g., "data structure" instead of "encoding", "algorithm" instead of "procedure", etc.). Normally, differences in encoding and procedure go hand-in-hand. For instance, for two different encodings of some data, different processes are normally needed to compute equivalent functions. Because of the intimate relationship between procedure and encoding (e.g., see Rumelhart *et al.* [21]) they are both considered to be variants of a single principle. The term "algorithmic" is adopted because it is a term used in analogous works in computing theory (e.g., see Aho *et al.* [1]). Where the meaning is clear, the term "algorithmic" will be dropped.

The principle identifies the class of cognitive support that works by *optimizing* the algorithm when given some particular task and computing infrastructure. This use is consonant with optimization in computing science, which normally fixes the function being computed and the underlying computational infrastructure [2]. Performance can be optimized according to a variety of measures (e.g., speed, memory usage, etc.). In changing data encoding, the *information content* is presumed to be unchanged [13]. In computing science, a familiar example is the change from singly-linked lists to doubly-linked lists. Such a change can make various list operations simpler and quicker to perform.

In cognitive support terms, optimization normally means the introduction of artifact designs that reduce cognitive burdens on users (memory use, processing, etc.) by changing the encodings that are used. In other words, it frequently involves *re-representation* [31]. One instance of optimization is the difference made to arithmetic tasks when switching from Roman numerals to Arabic numerals or vice versa [17]. For example, Roman numbers are easier to add because the algorithm involved in adding Arabic numbers is complicated (involving symbol substitution).

Distribution. In the ordinary sense of the term, computational systems are called "distributed" when they have multiple, loosely-connected distinguishable computing resources. Distributing computations amongst multiple computing resources can have several types of performance advantages. Having multiple processing elements do the computation means that the work can be divided, thereby reducing the work done by each processor. This can also speed up the execution because frequently the work can be done in parallel. Distribution can also mean that computations with resource requirements exceeding the capabilities of one limited processor might still be performed if the excess load can be taken up by other elements. In computing science, a familiar example of distributed computing is a client-server architecture. One important reason for moving to client-server architectures is that the burdens on the client are greatly reduced.

In its application to HCI, distribution of computation can be interpreted in cognitivist terms [30]. Thus, instead of "data", one can speak of "representations", "mental state", or "knowledge". Instead of "processing", one can speak of "reasoning", "inferencing", or "thinking". For example, using an external memory [17,23] distributes knowledge. Distributing processing analogously means either having the artifact perform or embody the processing, or having a user process symbols externally. An example of the former is a type-checking compiler. Type-checking compilers externalize the test of constraints on a program [5]. An example of the latter is the manipulation of a slide rule to compute a mathematical function [11].

Substitution. The principle underlying substitution is the fact that computing facilities can be adapted specially to restricted sets of tasks. The specialization means that they can be made more efficient. In computing terms, it means they compute fewer functions or operate over a restricted input domain. For instance it is common to have specialized processing hardware such as a floating-point unit (FPU), digital signal processor, vector processor, or graphics accelerator.

Unlike the CPU (which is a general, reprogrammable processor), such special computing hardware computes only a restricted set of functions and has limited programmability. The analogue in cognitive terms is the existence of efficient but specialized mental capabilities. These may either be "hardware" (built-in) or various forms of optimized "software" (learned or over-learned skills) [29]. A classic example is perceptual operators [7]. These are fast, effort-free, and execute at least partially in parallel [19]. They stand in contrast to deliberate reasoning which is slow, serial, and effortful.

The principle of specialization creates a category of cognitive support that operates by allowing more specialized processing to substitute for more general, deliberate reasoning. This substitution is a staple of the visualization literature. The essential quality of many accounts of visualization efficacy is that specialized perceptual mechanisms substitute for more complicated inferences (see Larkin *et al.* [13], Casner [7]). One standard example is the use of a line chart to enable *visual search* to substitute for deliberate search [7].

3.3 Compositional Language

A single cognitive artifact can be associated with multiple cognitive supports. For instance, when knowledge is distributed from the head and onto an artifact, perceptual substitutions might be enabled for operations over that knowledge. This implies that many of the varieties of more complicated types of support may be reducible to compositions of computational substitutions identified by RODS. Although this cannot be exhaustively demonstrated, we can illustrate the compositionality of RODS principles by deconstructing composite instances of support according to their constituent support types. Here we consider here Larkin's analysis [12] of *display-based problem solving* (DBPS).

Larkin [12] invented the term "display-based problem solving" to describe a form of problem solving that makes extensive use of external displays. It is clear that to Larkin [12] there are three essential qualities of *display-based* problem solving: (1) that all or almost all of the relevant problem solving state can be read from the display, (2) that because of the nature of external displays, perceptual inferences can be used in places where otherwise more taxing logical inferences would need to be made, and (3) that little planning or deliberation is required for any of the steps—the solver employs very local control. Using this conception, DBPS involves a combination of *distribution* and *substitution*. The distribution involves distributing the current state of the problem. Substitution is involved because the solver is able to use perceptual skills to make inferences concerning problem implications, goal selection, or problem constraints. Substitution is also involved because learned rules are cued by rapid recognition of current system state, eliminating the need to deliberately reason about what operations to perform next. Once DBPS is deconstructed in this manner, a variety of different variations on DBPS can be entertained.

3.4   Mnemonic, Evocative Names

RODS is couched in terms familiar to most computer scientists. This does not guarantee that the terms will be more understandable, memorable, or more evocative of important implications. However the odds are that, unlike their cognitive science analogues, the computing terms will be at least meaningful to the average computer science student. Furthermore the terms may index into deep computer science knowledge of computing optimization. This may allow non-specialists to reason by analogy about various forms of cognitive support.

3.5   Abstract, Generalizable Description Level

RODS defines four categories of cognitive support and their underlying principles in cognitivist terms (knowledge, inferencing, etc.) and computational terms (memory, processing, etc.). Both of these are description levels are abstract and independent of their implementations. In particular, cognitive support categories are defined without reference to a task or even a particular cognitive model. For instance, distribution is defined without referring to the specifics about what are being redistributed. Plans, constraints, goals, and processing history might be distributed (e.g., see Wright *et al.* [30]). This means RODS can be used on whatever issues of cognition the analyst considers important (goals, social roles, etc.). In addition, the computational principles referenced are abstracted away from their implementation. For instance, any number of artifacts may play the role of an external memory (white boards, computers, even other people [23]). Thus RODS is independent of both task and technology: how they are used depend on the analyst's application context.

3.6   Analysis Framework

The "output" of a cognitive support theory is an explanation of cognitive benefits provided by artifacts. The analysis of benefit is necessarily comparative: the benefits of an artifact may be understood only in comparison to what is implied by its absence, substitution, or modification. One way of thinking about this comparison is to suggest that there is a continuum of different levels of support that ranges from the completely unsupported (entirely mental) to the completely automated (no human thinking involved). In between are cases where cognition is spread between humans and artifacts. In practice, both extreme ends of the spectrum will be unattainable for interesting tasks. Still, it is instructive to imagine what, in principle, the unachievable extremes of the spectrum would entail. In particular, starting at the completely unsupported end of the spectrum will allow us to use RODS to define a structured space of cognitive support types.

In order for the *entirely* mental end of the continuum to hold up under close inspection, all of the user's problem, evolving solution, and mental state information would need be held internally; all of the processing of such information would also need to be done internally. Distribution begins to change that picture. As distribution of cognition is increased, the locus of cognition expands away from the individual mind and is dispersed. As various parts of the computation are distributed, substitution and optimization changes can be added. That is, once data of any sort is distributed, processing can be distributed, substitutions can be enabled, and optimizations can be performed. For instance, Sharples noted that writing things down unlocks other types of support:

> So long as ideas, plans, and drafts are locked inside a writer's head, then modifying and developing them will overload the writer's short-term memory. By putting them down on paper (or some other suitable medium) the writer is able to explore different ways of structuring the content and to apply systematic transformations... [24, p. 135]

The above observations suggest one conceivable method for generating the space of all possible cognitive supports for some task (conceptually, at least). The generation is effectively by *recursive application of RODS transformations*: start with the set of all possible distributions of data and, one-by-one, apply each type of cognitive support to generate new compositions. For instance in Sharples' writing example, one could begin by enumerating the possibilities of distributing ideas, plans, drafts, goals, and so on. Then one might consider various ways of processing these externally, substituting efficient perceptual operators for more complicated ones, and of making changes to encodings and methods.

The procedure described above also suggests a way of improving design methods. Although an exhaustive generation of the design space would impossible for real tasks, a restricted analysis might be both feasible and helpful. One would need: (1) a particular cognitive task analysis for how an unaided mind would perform a task (i.e., an analysis of the of data and processing required), (2) a list of known perceptual operators that might substitute for deliberate reasoning, and (3) a catalogue of common principles for re-representing data to optimize cognitive processing. Then #1 could be stepped through for ways of distributing data and processing, and then ways of applying #2 and #3 could be envisioned. This sort of analysis has proven feasible even for non-trivial tools such as software engineering tools [28].

In the case of the above sort of analysis, the process described generates a restricted space of design options. This might be used to make design envisionment more systematic. Alternatively, design options might conceivably be analyzed automatically (much as, for instance, how Casner automated perceptual substitution design [7]). The design space analysis might also eventually lead to improved designer resources. For instance, design heuristics and cookbooks might be produced which codify successful implementations of each known type of cognitive support.

4   Toward Mining Patterns *and* Theory

A philosophy guiding our development of RODS was that it will be fruitful to crystallize design knowledge by simultaneously considering our rich wealth of successful design within the context of our existing theories of cognitive support.

Our belief is that a good place to begin looking for patterns of good design is in the intersection between craft wisdom and scientific knowledge.

Towards this goal we have been applying RODS to extracting design insights from the world of software engineering tools. While doing this we have been building and refining RODS itself. Essentially we have tried to examine successful tools from the field while looking towards DC theory to justify the patterns we have found [27]. Our results are very preliminary, but we have found that RODS is helpful for giving the "gist" of an enormous variety of different types of support. At the same time, we have found that classifying a tool idea as an instance of cognitive support tends to pull in related literature that may be used to justify or refine the idea.

An excerpt of the results so far hints at the type and breadth of analysis. Table 1 lists several exemplars of tool features, a categorization of these as support implementations, and a list of literature that might be linked to the idea based on its association with the support type. Work has been started on using cognitive models to generate a finer classification system for cognitive support types [27].

5   Related Work

This work builds upon and synthesizes select aspects of many prior works from HCI, DC and cognitive science. These include works by Hutchins [11], Zhang and Norman [31,17], Wright *et al.* [30], and Rasmussen [19]. The main point of departure from prior works is the emphasis on clearly articulating a small, comprehensive, and orthogonal set of computational principles underlying the different support classes.

There exist several attempts at synthesizing a generalized, abstract understanding of cognitive support and related cognitive design issues. Neuwirth *et al.* [15] produced an analysis of how artifacts can assist in several cognitive tasks in hypertext authoring. Scaife *et al.* [22] try also to provide a synthetic account of the cognitive benefits of graphical representations. Both of the above

Table 1. Examples of the types of RODS analyses explored.

Support	Sample Literature	Exemplars
distribution (data)	Zhang & Norman [31], Wright *et al.* [30]	code inspection checklists, diagramming constraints, undo history, link visitation history
distribution (processing)	Zhang & Norman [31], Scaife & Rogers [22]	type checking, compiler error list generation
substitution	Casner [7] Larkin & Simon [13]	browser link colouring (visual search), algorithm animations, call graph visualizations

analyses consider several instances of the cognitive support types identified by RODS. Many other works touch on a smaller or more restricted collection of cognitive support types. These include frameworks and summaries by Tweedie [26] and Narayanan *et al.* [14].

Another collection of related works consider generalizable, high-level cognition-related design issues. The most prominent of these is probably the "cognitive dimensions" framework [8,3] (CDs). The CDs are intended to represent orthogonal dimensions of usability tradeoffs in notational systems [8]. The CDs framework itself seems essentially orthogonal to RODS. Each class of cognitive support identified by RODS generates design considerations for notational systems. Thus the CDs may be a very helpful resource for identifying design tradeoffs while reasoning about cognitive support.

A third stream of related work is the proposal by Sutcliffe *et al.* [25] for producing a reusable federation of psychological claims together with their theoretical justifications. The most obvious surface difference between their work and RODS is that their claims libraries are proposed to be built up through a taxonomy-driven claims abstraction and collection process, whereas RODS is borne directly from prior theories. Nevertheless their approach aligns well with RODS. Notably, it might be possible for each of the cognitive support classes identified by RODS to be considered as abstract, reusable claim in some future extension of the work of Sutcliffe *et al.*.

6   Conclusions and Implications

DC is a theoretical framework which appears to have significant promise for application in HCI. One need which has to date been inadequately met is for a clear articulation of a general framework for analyzing cognitive support. RODS takes steps towards providing such a framework. The framework defines primitive support classes and outlines a general method for generating a restricted design space consisting of various compositions of cognitive support types (subject to some particular analysis of a cognitive task). This capability has far reaching implications for the specification, design, and evaluation of interactive systems.

One set of implications stem from the succinct but inclusive definition of cognitive support. With such a definition it is conceivable to try to specify at design time the cognitive support desired or required and then work systematically during implementation to satisfy these requirements. For instance, a usability engineer might specify that a certain amount of memory offloading must be provided. Tests might be run periodically to ensure that usability targets (i.e., "usefulness targets") are being met. We have performed a preliminary exploration of this possibility in the context of a study of observing and measuring plan and planning distribution in commercial software development environments [27].

A second set of implications stem from the fact that cognitive support identifies ways of actually improving cognition. Thus "good" design moves are defined and reified (made concrete). Reifying "good" design moves can be expected to be helpful [30]. It may help systematize design space exploration and thus help eliminate designer oversights, thereby reducing the dependence on early usability testing. Our analysis of a reverse engineering tool [28] (using a variation of RODS) lends evidence to this supposition. Our analysis showed that applications of cognitive support theory (based on RODS) could anticipate design changes made by the tool's designers only after receiving user feedback.

In conclusion, we must emphasize that the importance of RODS may be in terms of a high-level, qualitative theory for understanding an entire field. If the analogy to mechanical support is apt, RODS may make it possible for HCI designers to forgo talking about usability blunders at the implementation level, and begin to speak directly in terms of usefulness at the cognitive level.

References

1. A. V. Aho, J. E. Hopcroft, and J. D. Ullman. *Data Structures and Algorithms.* Addison-Wesley, Reading, MA, 1983.
2. D. F. Bacon, S. L. Graham, and O. J. Sharp. Compiler transformations for high-performance computing. *ACM Computing Surveys*, 26(4):345–420, Dec. 1997.
3. A. F. Blackwell, C. Britton, A. Cox, and T. R. G. Green *et. al.* Cognitive dimensions of notations: Design tools for cognitive technology. In M. Benyon, C. L. Nehaniv, and K. Dautenhahn, editors, *Instruments of Mind: Proceedings of The Fourth International Conference on Cognitive Technology*, volume 2117 of *Lecture Notes in Artificial Intelligence*, pages 325–341, Berlin, 2001. Springer-Verlag.
4. S. Buckingham Shum and N. Hammond. Delivering HCI modelling to designers: A framework and case study of cognitive modelling. *Interacting with Computers*, 6(3):314–341, 1994.
5. L. Cardelli. Type systems. In *Handbook of Computer Science and Engineering*, chapter 103, pages 2208–2236. CRC Press, 1997.
6. J. M. Carroll, editor. *Designing Interaction: Psychology at the Human-Computer Interface.* Cambridge Series on Human-Computer Interaction. Cambridge University Press, 1991.
7. S. M. Casner. A task-analytic approach to the automated design of graphic presentations. *ACM Transactions on Graphics*, 10(2):111–151, 1991.
8. T. R. G. Green. Cognitive dimensions of notations. In A. Sutcliffe and L. Macaulay, editors, *People and Computers V: Proceedings of the Fifth Conference of the British Computer Society Human-Computer Interaction Specialist Group*, pages 443–460. British Informatics Society, Cambridge University Press, 1989.
9. T. R. G. Green and M. Petre. Usability analysis of visual programming environments: A 'cognitive dimensions' framework. *Journal of Visual Languages and Computing*, 7(2):131–174, 1996.
10. J. Hollan, E. Hutchins, and D. Kirsh. Distributed cognition: Toward a new foundation for human–computer interaction research. *ACM Transactions on Computer-Human Interaction*, 7(2):174–196, June 2000.
11. E. L. Hutchins. *Cognition in the Wild.* MIT Press, 1995.
12. J. H. Larkin. Display-based problem solving. In D. Klahr and K. Kotovsky, editors, *Complex Information Processing: The Impact of Herbert A. Simon*, chapter 12, pages 319–341. Lawrence Erlbaum Associates, Hillsdale, NJ, 1989.
13. J. H. Larkin and H. A. Simon. Why a diagram is (sometimes) worth ten thousand words. *Cognitive Science*, 11(1):65–99, 1987.

14. N. H. Narayanan and R. Hübscher. Visual language theory: Towards a human-computer interaction perspective. In K. Marriott and B. Meyer, editors, *Visual Language Theory*, chapter 3, pages 87–128. Springer-Verlag, 1998.
15. C. M. Neuwirth and D. S. Kaufer. The role of external representations in the writing process: Implications for the design of hypertext-based writing tools. In *Proceedings of the 2nd Annual ACM Conference on Hypertext*, pages 319–341, 1989.
16. A. Newell and H. A. Simon. Computer science as empirical inquiry: Symbols and search. *Communications of the ACM*, 19(3):113–126, Mar. 1976.
17. D. A. Norman. *Things That Make Us Smart: Defending Human Attributes in the Age of the Machine*. Addison-Wesley, Reading, Massachusetts, 1993.
18. H. Petroski. *The Evolution of Useful Things*. A. Knopf, New York, NY, 1992.
19. J. Rasmussen. Skills, rules, knowledge: Signals, signs, and symbols and other distinctions in human performance models. *IEEE Transactions on Systems, Man, and Cybernetics*, 13(3):257–267, 1983.
20. Y. Rogers and J. Ellis. Distributed cognition: an alternative framework for analysing and explaining collaborative working. *Journal of Information Technology*, 9(2):119–128, 1994.
21. D. E. Rumelhart and D. A. Norman. Representation in memory. In R. C. Atkinson, R. J. Herrnstein, G. Lindzey, and R. D. Luce, editors, *Stevens' Handbook of Experimental Psychology*, volume 2: Learning and Cognition, pages 511–587. John Wiley & Sons, New York, 2nd edition, 1988.
22. M. Scaife and Y. Rogers. External cognition: How do graphical representations work? *International Journal of Human-Computer Studies*, 45(2):185–213, 1996.
23. W. Schönpflug and K. B. Esser. Memory and its Graeculi: Metamemory and control in extended memory systems. In C. A. Weaver III, S. Mannes, and C. R. Fletcher, editors, *Discourse Comprehension: Essays in Honor of Walter Kintsch*, chapter 14, pages 245–255. Lawrence Erlbaum, 1995.
24. M. Sharples. Writing as creative design. In C. M. Levy and S. Ransdell, editors, *The Science of Writing: Theories, Methods, Individual Differences, and Applications*, pages 127–148. Lawrence Erlbaum Associates, 1996.
25. A. Sutcliffe. On the effective use and reuse of HCI knowledge. *ACM Transactions on Computer-Human Interaction*, 7(2):197–221, June 2000.
26. L. A. Tweedie. Interactive visualisation artifacts: How can abstractions inform design? In M. A. R. Kirby, A. J. Dix, and J. E. Finlay, editors, *People and Computers X, Proceedings of HCI'95*, pages 247–265. Cambridge University Press, 1995.
27. A. Walenstein. *Cognitive Support in Software Engineering Environments: A Distributed Cognition Framework*. PhD thesis, School of Computing Science, Simon Fraser University, May 2002.
28. A. Walenstein. Theory-based cognitive support analysis of software comprehension tools. In *Proceedings of the 10th International Workshop on Program Comprehension (to appear)*, 2002.
29. C. Ware. The foundations of experimental semiotics: a theory of sensory and conventional representation. *Journal of Visual Languages and Computing*, 4(1):91–100, 1993.
30. P. C. Wright, R. E. Fields, and M. D. Harrison. Analyzing human–computer interaction as distributed cognition: The resources model. *Human Computer Interaction*, 15(1):1–41, Mar. 2000.
31. J. Zhang and D. A. Norman. Representations in distributed cognitive tasks. *Cognitive Science*, 18:87–122, 1994.

User Interface Design Patterns for Interactive Modeling in Demography and Biostatistics

Sergiy Boyko[1,2], Peter Forbrig[2], and Anatoli Yashin[1]

[1] Max Planck Institute for Demographic Research,
Doberaner Str. 114, D-18057, Rostock, Germany
{boiko, yashin}@demogr.mpg.de
[2] University of Rostock, Department of Computer Science,
Albert-Einstein Str. 21, D-18051, Germany
peter.forbrig@informatik.uni-rostock.de

Abstract. The paper is focused on the interface design patterns for interactive modeling and it is an effort to systematically describe the usage of UID patterns in this area. Main objectives were to develop the UID patterns to increase the usability of the software for numerical computing and to make the process of numerical simulation highly interactive.

On the basis of these UID patterns authors developed reusable software components in several programming languages: Java, Python, C++ and Matlab. The patterns described in the paper were verified in the development of practical software tools for demographers and biostatisticians, but can be readily applicable to other domains of numerical computing.

1 Introduction

Computers were conceived to perform numerical calculations. More then 60 years have passed since the moment of invention of the first digital computer[1]. Nowadays scientists working in the area of numerical computing use modern software and languages that gradually replace old-fashioned Fortran, error prone C, or hard to master C++.

But how much HCI has changed in that area during the last 10 years? Has numerical modeling experienced the revolutionary changes that took place in the design of GUI driven software during that period? The answer is twofold. On the one hand, it is positive due to a wide spread of integrated modeling environments like Matlab, Matematica, and Mathcad with rich and powerful libraries of numerical procedures and extensive visualization facilities.

On the other hand, Fortran, C and C++ still predominate in the numerical computing area, they have a rich set of useful generic-precision intrinsic functions. There is a vast body of existing code written in these programming

---

[1] In 1939, Stibitz and S.B. Williams built the Complex Number Calculator, the world's first electrical digital computer. Its brain consisted of 450 telephone relays and 10 crossbar switches and it could find the quotient of two eight-place complex numbers in about 30 seconds.

P. Forbrig et al. (Eds.): DSV-IS 2002, LNCS 2545, pp. 148–158, 2002.
© Springer-Verlag Berlin Heidelberg 2002

languages. Unfortunately, even with the help of modern modeling environments scientific programmers mostly create code operating in the batch mode, neglecting the possibility to create GUI for their programs and leverage the power of interactive modeling.

Let's introduce some terminology. We will refer to the *modeling* as to the act of the formal representing of a system, biological object, effect, etc. We will focus on the mathematical *models* which is a set of assertions about properties of the object.

We will refer to the *design* to represent the act of defining an object. And finally, we will refer to the *simulations* as to results of executing of the *models*, or put it another way, as to output the model produces, which reflects the modeled experimental data.

This paper describes user interface design (UID) patters for interactive modeling, i.e. the patterns for the communication with models, rather than UID patterns used by the software for numerical simulations. Our objectives were to develop UID patterns to increase the usability of the software for numerical computing and to make the process of numerical simulation highly interactive.

These patterns were verified in the development of practical software tools for demographers and biostatisticians. However, all patterns described in the paper are readily applicable to other domains of numerical computing.

2   Two Levels of Interaction

There are two levels of user interactions in numerical computing: the first level is the interaction with the modeling software, and the second level, on which this paper is focused – is the interaction with models. Let's consider the following example that clarifies this point. Let's assume that the user (scientist) simulates the model, described by a set of ordinary differential equations. The typical scenario could be the following:

1. Open the Modeling Environment [2]
2. Load the model, stored in a file
3. Select the differential equation solver
4. Set the solver parameters
5. *Set model parameters*
6. Save the model
7. Run the simulation
8. *See the results*
9. *Make modification of the model*
10. Repeat steps 2-10

Items in italic correspond to the second level of user interaction. On steps 1–3 the user interacts with the modeling environment, he uses menus and dialogs to

---

[2] In the simplest case it is a source code editor

navigate the directory tree and to open a file in which the model is stored. Then he selects a solver suitable for the given model, and sets its parameters.

When the user changes model parameters he is starting to interact directly with the model (step 5).

Then again, the user interacts with the software saving the model and running the simulation (steps 6,7). On step 8, the user interacts with the model observing its outputs and if necessary makes additional modifications of the model, for instance, changing a relation between model inputs (step 9).

However, such an interaction with the model is not highly interactive. Modifications of the model are frequently performed simply by editing source files. Changes of model inputs may be performed only between the simulations [6].

To understand user's goals and expectations about functionality of interactive modeling tools we need to develop a more comprehensive specification, based on task-oriented analyses of user interaction with the system [3,4,7].

3   Data-Centric Modeling

Because of the central role of experimental data for the mathematical modeling in demography and biostatistics, the following HCI pattern may be used as a generalization. We refer to this pattern as the "Data-centric Modeling Circle" to stress the importance of the experimental data.

The circle may be formally divided into several phases, each of which requires specific activities of the user.

Preliminary Analysis. This phase usually includes extensive work with the raw data stored in a database. During this phase the user performs more or less standard statistical procedures. He transforms the data to a form that emphasizes those effects, which are of most interest. On this stage the data are frequently represented visually as charts, diagrams, etc.

Mathematical formalization of the model. This is the most difficult part of the process. Almost everything happens in the investigator's head. The scientists combines his knowledge about phenomena. He formulates a theory consistent with the new data and tests new hypothesis about the mechanisms of observed phenomena.

Simulation and testing. As soon as the model has been designed, time to learn the solutions is coming. On this phase the model should be transformed to a form suitable for computer representation using the modeling software of choice.

On this phase the user interacts with the model, studies its flexibility and suitability for the description of the experimental data. The user, most probably, makes numerous changes in the model structure. Thus, one of the very important criteria is how fast these changes may be incorporated into the model, which in turn depends on the tools used for modeling.

Evaluation. On this phase the user performs the evaluation of the model and compares simulation results with the experimental data described by the model.

4 UID Patterns for Analysis, Visualization, and Simulation

Thus, user interaction with the model and data may be separated into three categories: analysis, visualization, and simulation. We generalized user interaction scenarios [7] based on a real-life episodes and developed the UID patterns for interactive modeling and reusable software components [6,2] that were verified in several interactive modeling tools used to solve real-life problems in the fields of demography and biostatistics.

The main objectives of this work were:

1. Increase the usability of modeling tools
2. Prevent users from possible errors
3. Let the user make use of his expertise and creativity without having to spend time on the programming
4. Decrease time of the data-centric modeling circle
5. Develop reusable software components for interactive analysis of data, interactive visualization of data and interactive simulation of data.

The following sections provide more detailed specifications of user tasks and the UID patterns that model them. Each section consists of several subsections. Objective subsection provides a short description of the problem. Example subsection illustrates the problem using real-world problem, usually from demographic domain. Solution subsection explains the UID pattern that is used to solve the problem. Discussion subsection provides the explanation of usability principles on which the given UID patters is based. And finally, Example of usage demonstrates the application of developed UID patterns to solve real-world problems.

5 Two-Panel Selector

5.1 Objectives

The user needs to select a subset of data. This selection is made on the basis of user expertize. Formalization of the selection procedure is complex, or impossible. User wants to work with different subsets, changes should be easily accomplished.

5.2 Example

After the Chernobyl accident numerous measurements of thyroid activities have been performed [1,5]. Some of these measurements are of very low quality. The user needs to select trajectories suitable for evaluation of average thyroid doses based on these measurements.

5.3   Solution

To solve this problem, the Two-Panel selector has been developed. The Two-Panel selector Fig.1(a), 1(b) is a generalization of the pattern widely used in user interface design. Perhaps, the most well-known example is Norton Commander utility. The user has two panels and may select files or directories on one panel and copy or move them to another.

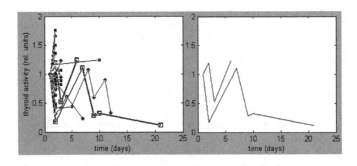

(a) Normal mode

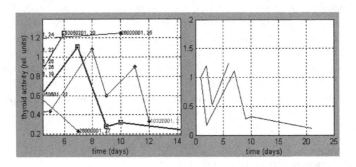

(b) Left panel is zoomed, grid and information tags are shown

Fig. 1. Graphical Two-Panel Selector Pattern

The Two-Panel selector was mainly inspired by this example. We used two graphical panels: one panel to show the whole data set and another panel to show selected data. The left panel is used to show all data. Selections are activated by the mouse click. Selected trajectories immediately appear on the right panel. To make selected trajectories visually distinctive, they are displayed using lines of double width, and their nodes are highlighted. If the user made a mistake, it is possible to reselect a trajectory clicking on it in the right panel. To make the selection of data more convenient, the user may zoom a rectangular area on the left panel. The right panel remains unzoomed to simplify a navigation and selection since in this way a user has a close-up and a general view of the data. Additionally, each trajectory has an associated information tag that may contain arbitrary information to specify the selected trajectory. The bottom panel on Fig.1(b) demonstrates a zoomed panel with information tags turned on.

5.4 Discussion

The Two-Panel selector greatly improves the usability and may be applicable to the design of systems for interactive analysis of data, when the user has to select subsets of data. Sometimes this selection is made on the basis of user knowledge and the development of selection algorithms may be an extremely complex task, because rules on which the formalization could be made are hard to articulate. Usage of this pattern significantly increases the interactivity, since the user can easily manipulate the data. Thus, time needed for data analysis may be substantially minimized. The two-panel selector also greatly increases the system feedback.

5.5 Example of Usage

The Two-Panel selector was firstly used in the software for the evaluation of thyroid activity for the population of Ukraine irradiated to the aftermath of Chernobyl accident [1,5].

6 Interactive 2D User Input

6.1 Objectives

On the stage of verification the user wants to test how the model behaves when input parameters have specific shapes. The user wants to make these changes with the mouse, and to observe these changes immediately. The system must restrict the user behavior to prevent him from possible errors.

6.2 Examples

Simulation of the stress in the human and experimental animal populations. This pattern also finds its usage for interactive determination of initial guesses for non-parametric and semi-parametric optimization problems [10].

6.3   Solution

To solve this problem we developed the 2D Interactive Input Pattern. According to the objectives this pattern may be either restrictive or non-restrictive. The restrictions may have different forms and are based on mathematical requirements. The most interesting application of this pattern is the optimization of non-parametric or semi-parametric models. One of the most complex tasks is determination of the initial guess. Instead of guessing and trying different inputs coded in functional or tabular forms, the user may simply draw an initial guess by the mouse so that it will be close to the values of the empirical data.

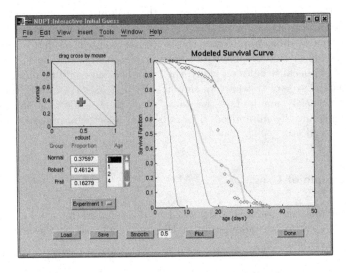

Fig. 2. Restricted and Non-Restricted 2D Input Patterns

Fig.2 demonstrates a dialog of the software for numerical optimization of non-parametric discrete heterogeneity model used in the analysis of stress experimental data for nematode worms [9]. The graphical panels are different forms of the restricted 2D Input Pattern.

The left panel allows the user to change values of two parameters, restriction is imposed in the form $p_1 + p_2 \leq 1, p_1 \leq 1, p_2 \leq 1$, Graphically it means that parameters may have only those values that are below the diagonal of the square (shown on the panel). Current values of parameters are shown as a cross on the left panel and their exact values are displayed in the text fields.

The right panel demonstrates another form of the restricted user input. Thin lines on the right panel are used to give initial guesses for the optimization procedure. The thick line is the resulting modeled curve approximating the empirical data plotted as diamonds. The user may arbitrarily change the shape of thin lines with the mouse. The only restriction is that these curves must monotonically decrease. Obviously, this interactive procedure greatly simplifies the process of the initial guess finding. Being non-interactive, the initial guess determination would take a reasonable amount of time and could be a problem of its own.

Another interesting example of the restricted 2D Interactive Input is shown on Fig.3. In the given case a restriction is the shape of the signal. The user may change signal shape only so that the signal is a combination of rectangular steps (meanders).

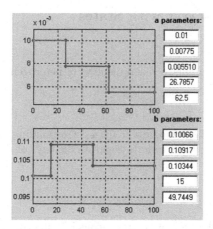

Fig. 3. The Restricted 2D Input pattern

The user may change the shape of the signal by dragging different segments of the curve by the mouse. Additionally, some frequently performed actions may be activated by double-clicks. For instance, a double-click on the left horizontal segment positions the right horizontal segment on the same level as the left one; a double-click on the central horizontal segment flattens the signal so that it becomes the straight line. Corresponding values may also be changed using edit text fields.

6.4   Discussion

Usage of the 2D Interactive Input highly increases the interactivity level of the simulation. The user changes model parameters with the mouse, and may provide complex shapes of input without coding. This significantly improves the flexibility. Additionally, the user immediately observes the input in a visual form that eliminates possible errors and increase the feedback of the system. The user is prevented from input errors when the restricted form of the Interactive Input Pattern is used.

Another interesting aspect of the 2D Interactive Input is simulations in real time. Using this pattern it is possible to change values of model parameters in the course of simulations [6].

6.5   Example of Usage

The Interactive Input Patterns were used in the software for non-parametric estimates of discrete heterogeneous model [9].

7   Multiple Observer with States

7.1   Objective

The user wants to accumulate visual displays of heterogeneous data.

7.2   Example

The user works with the demographic data corresponding to different countries and different ages. He wants to have separate displays of data for each country grouped by genders.

7.3   Solution

To simplify the visualization of heterogeneous information the UID pattern that we called Multiple Observer with States can be used. The Multiple Observer consists of several displays, each of which can be in several states: active state, when it is ready to visualize the next set of data, and inactive state. Besides, the display may react differently on user actions: displayed data may be accumulated or each next data set may replace the previous one.

States may be changed by the user. For instance, the user may click on the display to make it active, or the display may be data-aware, when it knows the data it should visualize.

7.4   Discussion

Usage of Multiple Observer with States allows the user to easily accumulate displays of heterogeneous data, this pattern improves the performance time and user's satisfaction. The main usability principle on which this pattern is based is immediate feedback. It also minimizes user actions. Usage of the data-aware Multiple Observer prevents the user from possible errors and increases safety.

7.5   Example of Usage

The Multiple Observer with States is used in the interactive modeling tool for the simulation of age-dependent dynamics of longevity in the human population [10].

8   Summary

This paper is an effort to systematically describe the usage of GUI for interactive numerical computing in terms of user interface design patterns.

One of the most important objectives that we pursued was to develop UID patterns to increase the usability of the software and make numerical modeling interactive. Usability of the software can be measured by usage indicators: learnability, memorability, speed of performance, error rate, satisfaction and task completion [8]. To become a UID pattern the pattern should improve all user indicators. All presented UID patterns seems to satisfy these criteria.

Another aspect of this work was to demonstrate that GUI may significantly simplify the process of numerical modeling. The efforts spent on the development of user interface are often rewarding, because they decrease the time of Data-Centric Modeling circle.

At the same time the development of graphical user interfaces requires additional skills, knowledge and time. Every so often the developer and the user of the modeling software is the same person. That is why the development of user interface should be based on high-level software components [6,2] that do not require substantial efforts on learning and usage.

With the software components, the developer can encapsulate pieces of models, and in order to use these components the developer does not have to know their internal details.

Frequently UID patterns may be mapped to the reusable software components or a combination of them. All described patters were implemented as reusable software modules using several programming languages, namely C++, Java, Python and Matlab. We used well proved design patterns, such as MVC, State, Chain of Responsibility, etc [4].

Developed components provide clean and straightforward external interfaces for the developer and can be easily combined together with standard widget components to create complete interactive modeling tools. This has been demonstrated on numerous examples of real-world applications from the domain of demography and biostatistics [1,5,9,10].

References

[1]   S. Boyko. Reconstruction of fetal thyroid activity for those exposed in utero to the aftermath of the Chernobyl accident. 1997 AAAS Annual meeting 1997, Seattle, Washington, A-91

[2]   W. Brinkman, R. Haakma, D. Bowhuis, Usability Evaluation of component based user interfaces, Human-Computer Interaction –Interact '01, pp. 767–768

[3]   J.M. Carroll. Making use: scenario-based design of human-computer interactions. Cambridge, MA: MIT Press, 2000

[4]   E. Gamma, R. Helm, R. Johnson, and J. Vlissides, Design Patterns: Elements of Reusable Object-Oriented Software, Addison-Wesley, Reading MA, 1995.

[5]   Likhtarev I.A., Tronko N.D., Bogdanova T.I., Kairo I.A., Boyko S.I., Chepurny N.I., Shpak V.M., et al. Methodological recommendation for thyroid dose reconstruction for the population of Ukraine, exposed in the result of Chernobyl accident. Kiev, publishing of Ukrainian Ministry of Emergency Situations and Chernobyl, 1997

[6]   Lie Liu and Edward A. Lee, "Component-based Hierarchical Modeling of Systems with Continuous and Discrete Dynamics," Proc. of the 2000 IEEE International Conference on Control Appli-cations and IEEE Symposium on Computer-Aided Control System Design (CCA/CACSD'00), Anchorage, AK, September 25-27, 2000. pp. 95–100

[7]   M.B. Rosson, J.M. Carroll. Scenarios, object and points of view in user interface design.

[8]   van Welie, M., van der Veer, G. C., and Eliës, A. (1999), Breaking down Usability, Proceedings of Interact '99, Edinburgh, Scotland.

[9]   Yashin, A. I., Cypser, J. W.,Johnson, T. E., Michalski, A. I., Boyko, S. I. and Novoseltsev, V. N. (2001). Ageing and survival after different doses of heat shock: the results of analysis of data from stress experiments with the nematode worm Caenorhabditis elegans. Mechanisms of Aging and Development 122:1477–1495

[10] A.I. Yashin, A.S.Begun, S.I.Boiko, S.V.Ukraintseva, J.Oeppen (2001). The new trends in survival improvement require a revision of traditional gerontological concept. Experimental Gerontology, 37: 157-167.

User Interface Conceptual Patterns

Pedro J. Molina[1], Santiago Meliá[1], and Oscar Pastor[2]

[1] CARE Technologies S.A.
Pda. Madrigueres, 44.
03700 Denia, Alicante, Spain
{pjmolina|smelia}@care-t.com
[2] Information System and Computation Dept.
Technical University of Valencia
Valencia, Spain
opastor@dsic.upv.es

Abstract. User Interface Patterns are not sufficiently explored at the Conceptual phase. Work in area of User Interface patterns is predominantly done at design phase but not enough work is dedicated to analysis patterns. This paper shows different examples of abstract user interface patterns and explores the impact of such patterns in the software lifecycle. Conceptual User Interface Patterns can be used for direct specification of device independent interfaces that can be refined using UI design patterns, or moreover, used to automatically obtain prototypes of the user interface specified in several devices.

1 Introduction

Patterns have proven their utility in different fields of appliance. Design patterns [6] or architectural patterns [2] are well known uses of successful patterns in computing. Patterns provide, in a given field, a common *interlingua* (or *lingua franca* [4]). At the same time, patterns document problems and its correspondent best solutions. Pattern languages are excellent tools for expressing the concepts involved in a given domain. Therefore, they constitute a valuable way to express distilled experience from real life.

In the User Interface field, most works deal with design patterns [12,14]. However, in this paper we advocate for starting employing patterns in early phases (requirements and analysis) and propagating them in later phases (design and implementation). Covering in this way, a pattern oriented development over the whole life-cycle following a similar approach as proposed in PSA[7].

In the last four years, we have been exploring first at the Technical University of Valencia and later at CARE Technologies the field of User Interface Specification based on patterns. As a result of such research, we have discovered a collection of patterns useful to deal with the specification of UI of information systems. The discovered patterns are useful to describe abstract user interfaces, guiding the design phase and providing automatic code generation strategies for fast prototyping. Such patterns are the elemental concepts described in Just-UI [9] (a model for abstract UI specification). A CASE tool implements the

P. Forbrig et al. (Eds.): DSV-IS 2002, LNCS 2545, pp. 159–172, 2002.
© Springer-Verlag Berlin Heidelberg 2002

model assistance in the specifications and we have also developed translators to automatically transform abstract specifications to implementations.

This work presents a way for applying patterns in the Conceptual phase in the area of User Interfaces. Section 2 introduces UI Conceptual Patterns and provides examples of them. Section 3 describes the role of the patterns in the specification process. Section 4 introduces a refining approach. Sections 5 and 6 cover design and implementation phases, respectively. Section 7 provides examples of code generation from conceptual patterns. Then, related work is presented. Eventually, conclusions and references are given.

2   UI Conceptual Patterns

Patterns are widely used in the User Interfaces area. Some works like Trætteberg [12], and van Welie [14] provide collections of patterns to deal with problems in the design and implementation of user interfaces. However, we are going to focus on the conceptual phase.

Following the approach of Fowler [5], we propose to apply the concept of pattern at the conceptual phase. Moreover, we follow a pattern-oriented approach in each phase of the software development as it is used in PSA[7].

At the analysis phase, while developing the Conceptual Modelling, we can detect and document valuable patterns. Such patterns appear in the domain where users and analysts talk about the requirements of the system to be built. Particularly, applied to the User Interface context, we can typify the User Interface Conceptual Patterns such as those patterns related to user interface topics that appear in the requirements gathering at the conceptual phase.

Conceptual patterns are clearly focused on *what* (the problem space) and not focused in *how* (the solution space). Accordingly, they expressly discard design and implementation issues. The rationale is to prevent taking any design or implementation decision at the analysis phase. Such topics will be covered after at the correspondent design and implementation phases.

The pattern language developed (Fig. 1) is oriented to detect common necessities or requirements from users. The patterns help analysts indicating what information must be gathered and how it must be organized. In this sense, they provide a common language between users and analysts to describe the requirements in terms of patterns. At this phase, each pattern supplies the accumulated experience of previous UI analysis. Furthermore, such patterns imprint structural, static and behavioural restrictions that must be taken into account in the following phases (design, implementation, and maintenance).

In the classical software life-cycle, it is better to detect errors in early phases than in the later ones. Patterns, like errors, provide more advantages if they are detected and applied in early phases.

Finally, the use of User Interface Conceptual Patterns provide the same advantages as patterns, but applied at the Conceptual phase: documented analysis concepts, provide a common language for analysis, and easy reuse of analysis concepts.

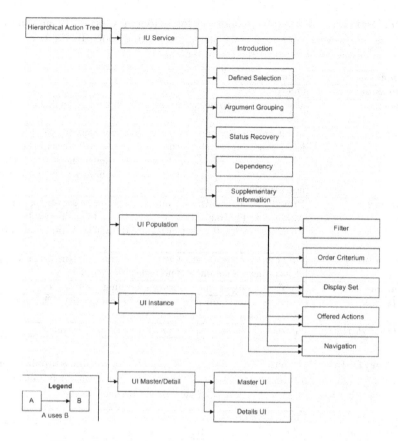

Fig. 1. Conceptual pattern language and use relationships.

2.1   Examples of UI Conceptual Patterns

To illustrate the idea of UI Conceptual Patterns we are going to describe three examples using a classical tabular form. For each pattern we will provide a *name*, an *also known as* (other names), the *problem* to be resolved, the *context* (express the conditions needed for pattern application), the *forces* (different opposing requirements), the *solution* (a core solution, not details), the *restrictions*, an *example*, the *rationale* and other *related patterns*.

Filter Pattern. A filter is a condition for searching objects. In information systems, users need very frequently specific searching tools. In the conceptual phase, analysts must capture such requirement.

Name	Filter
Also known as	Query
Problem	The user needs to browse and search objects belonging to a large set.
Context	In information systems is a very frequent task to search for objects. Powerful search mechanisms are needed to help the user.
Forces	The number of objects in the set may hinder the searching process. A complex query interface can be hard to understand for not experienced users.
Solution	Provides a mechanism to query the objects satisfying certain conditions. The analyst can express it in a OQL-like syntax with variables, letting the user introduce data in such variables in run time.
Restrictions	Objects to be searched must be comparable (in other words, objects have a common type to be comparable).
Example	Web searching engines, library searching facilities, etc.
Rationale	Provides a mechanism to reduce the complexity. The user can incrementally narrow the searching scope.
Related Patterns	Order Criterium, Display Set, Population observation.

Master/Detail Pattern. This pattern is typical for business applications. Head information and depicted data in a composite presentation increases the usability with respect to a solution with two single presentations.

Name	Master/Detail
Also known as	Master/Slave, Director/Details
Problem	The user needs to work with different sets of information units linked by a relationship. The main information unit (the master) determines the slave information units (details).
Context	Applications normally contain scenarios with several aggregated objects. The user needs to interact with all of them.
Forces	Layout may discourage a master/detail presentation. Less important information can be accessed throughout navigation. On the other hand, Master/Detail maintains the information synchronized and jointly.
Solution	Provides a unique composed scenario presenting master and detail data at the same time. Synchronizes data in the details when master data changes.
Restrictions	Details are synchronized with master information units.
Example	Invoice/Lines is a typical case of master/detail.
Rationale	The joint presentation of two or more information units allows the user to work in a unique scenario capable of performing several tasks and, at the same time, the scenario maintains the details synchronized with respect to the master component.
Related Patterns	Object observation, Population observation.

Defined Selection Pattern. If the analyst can detect a closed set of values for a given range (domain), the use of this pattern allows to reduce user errors, avoiding the introduction of invalid values.

Name	Defined Selection
Also known as	Closed selection
Problem	The user needs to select one or more items from a list of elements.
Context	The selection set is closed and known in advance.
Forces	The number of elements could be high. The selection key could be hidden to the user. Localized aliases should be shown instead of keys.
Solution	Provides a table to gather the codes and aliases for each item. Ask for the default values and the minimum and maximum number of items selectable.
Restrictions	Items must be known in advance.
Example	Marital status or sex are classical examples of defined selection in UIs. Defined selection is frequently implemented as combo-boxes or radio-buttons.
Rationale	The user requirements can be gathered using a simple tabular form with an item per row. The number of items may encourage different implementations to maintain the usability. This pattern can prevent user-errors: it only provides to the user the valid values.
Related Patterns	Introduction.

Fig. 1 shows the user relationships among the patterns in the pattern language developed. The complete collection of patterns can be consulted in [8, 9].

3   Using Patterns at the Analysis Phase

The conceptual pattern language can be a key concept in a model for abstract user interface specification. As described in [9] we have developed a Model-based User Interface Development Environment based in conceptual UI patterns. Patterns are employed as *bricks and blocks* (created, composed, and/or reused) to build the UI specification. Such specifications maintain the good properties of the conceptual patterns:

- Target platform independence: No design or implementation decisions have been taken in the specification.
- Describe the problem in terms of well-documented concepts.
- Reuse work form previous cases.

A CASE[1] tool is implemented supporting the gathering of complete object-oriented conceptual specifications comprising: system logic and abstract user interfaces. Such tool is being used in industrial developments with success.

---

[1] SOSY Modeler is the industrial CASE tool developed at CARE Technologies S.A.

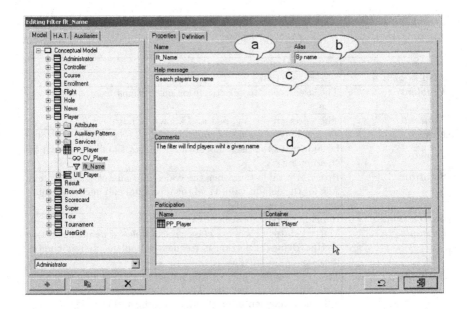

Fig. 2. Example of pattern template.

The capture of each pattern in the modeler tool is driven by a form template. The analyst can fill the template with the appropriate values to instantiate the pattern. Fig. 2 shows an example of template for gathering the *filter pattern*. In Fig. 2, fields labeled as a-d: collect a name (a), an alias (b), a help message(c), and observations(d), respectively. The pattern is instantiated by filling its template. Once instantiated (created), it can be applied to a specific context, composed with others, reused, or destroyed. Finally, the composition of patterns following the structure showed in Fig. 1 constitutes the complete UI specification of a system.

The modeler tool supports the validation of the specification. Each pattern contains a template that must be filled. When a compulsory field is empty the validation process can detect such errors in order to obtain a complete specification. Furthermore, there are rules for correct composition of patterns and type checking[2]. The validation process also checks these rules, thus providing a verification of correctness. The validation process provides a list of errors and warnings. Once the specification is finished and produces zero errors in the validation process, the specification is ready for the next phase.

---

[2] The validation process is out of the scope of this paper. The number of validation rules is very high, so it is not described here for brevity.

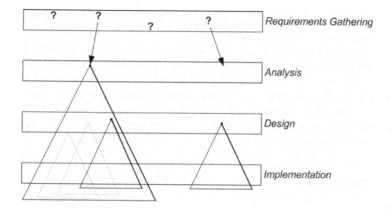

Fig. 3. The Δ effect. Implications of early pattern gathering.

4   Refining the Specification

Once the analysis specification is built and validated, the next phase is the design. At this point, designers must decide about configuration, distribution, and other topics. After that, programmers have to take additional decisions about implementation.

Following an approach similar to [7], it is a good idea to employ patterns in different phases. For example, design patterns [14,12] could be applied at design phase to maintain a pattern-oriented development.

Moreover, we propose to refine patterns in a series of successive steps from analysis to design and from design to implementation. Such refining allows adapting the solution to a specific implementation environment. The initial specification can be refined in these phases to add such decisions for a given design and then for a given implementation. Once again, this working method is an excellent way to maintain the system documented.

4.1   The Δ (Delta) Effect

Some questions arise due to the refinement-based approach: *What implications imposes a decision taken at the conceptual phase? How do UI conceptual patterns applied at the analysis phase influence the subsequent phases?*

As stated before, a pattern can supply semantic, behavioural and structural restrictions. Such restrictions have a *conical scope* or Δ (delta) effect (Fig. 3): the decision has implications from its definition to refined parts in later phases. These parts are constrained by the pattern application decision taken at upper phases. The question marks in Fig. 3 represent questions made in the Requirements phase. Such questions with its correspondent answer can instantiate conceptual patterns in the analysis phase. Fig. 3 shows the scope of such decisions as Δ-form triangles where parts of the subsequent phases are constrained or guided by such decisions.

In this sense, decisions taken in upper phases (conceptual patterns selected at analysis phase) can guide, or help to resolve decisions at the design phase where design patterns must be selected. A wizard can help to select patterns in the design phase guided from the information captured in previous phases. For example, a wizard could suggest the reification of the Conceptual Pattern *Master/Detail* [9] at the design phase with the design pattern *Container Navigation* [12,14] and *Navigation Spaces* [14].

5   Design Approaches

Decisions taken at the analysis phase have implications and constrain the possible alternatives in the following phases. Nevertheless, to perform the design phase and implementation, there are different approaches. This section describes how conceptual patterns are useful in order to make good design choices. The most important design approaches are: Manual Design, Semiautomatic Design, and Automatic Design.

5.1   Manual Design

At the moment, OO methodologies require additional tuning in the design phase. This refinement must be provided by a designer. Designers base their decisions in knowledge and acquired experience. In this case, conceptual patterns could help the designer to constrain the population of the possible design patterns to choose from. Therefore, conceptual patterns provide experience and simplify the selection of valid alternatives for design.

5.2   Semiautomatic Design

Design is not done manually in this case. On the other hand, it is assisted by design model-based tools or by means of wizards, which guide designers to obtain designs and implementations. The implementation could be obtained in an automatic way by means of code generation. Bell [1] defines a kind of generators named translative in which, analysis domain is accompanied with design templates. It allows to get a set of architectural and design patterns for a certain architecture, and it guides the designer to choose the most adapted templates for the system. The main advantage is that it allows the intersection between a set of M domain analyses with a set of A architectures, obtaining therefore the cartesian product $M \times A$ of different possible sets of implementations. In this approach, mapping decisions between the conceptual and design patterns are not made in an automatic manner. With respect to our approach, the designer could select the templates in the design phase which are compliant to the patterns specified in the analysis phase. In such a task, this phase can be guided by an assistant like in SEGUIA [13,15].

5.3   Automatic Design

Nevertheless, we discuss in Just-UI [9] the mapping that converts from the conceptual patterns to design patterns using different transformation techniques. It normally takes a number of decisions based on design experience, speeding up and simplifying the design and implementation process. This approach is currently been developed at the CARE-T firm, using the OO-Method methodology [10] to automatically obtaining not only the UI but also system logic and persistence. The fundamental advantage is that it only requires collecting information in the requirements and analysis phases, thus obtaining in a very early phase tangible results using automatic code generation. It also eases an early development costs estimation since it allows Function Points counting [11] using these conceptual patterns. Therefore, the final productivity obtained with this approach is better with respect to the previous ones.

Table 1. Design Approaches.

	Manual Design	Semiautomatic Design	Automatic Design
Design Effort	High	Medium	Low
Design Choices	Many	Many	Few
Error prone	Yes (high)	Yes (moderate)	No
Mappings form Conceptual Patterns	It depends on designer	It depends on designer, but assisted	Always
Prototyping speed	Slow	Medium	Quick
Customization	High	Medium	Low
Fiability	It depends on designer	Medium	High

Table 1 summarizes the main characteristics of the three approaches presented for design.

Automatic design is our preferred choice. However, pure automatic translation could not be applicable or not desirable for each system, especially, when the system is out of the scope of the translator (out of the context it is based in) or an optimization must be introduced. Each system could require additional tuning that may imply changes in the automatically generated artifact. In such cases, manual design will be necessarily complemented with one of the previous approaches.

6   Deriving Implementations

Implementation phase can be also performed following different implementation approaches: Manual Programming, Code Reuse, and Code Generation. Usually, mixed approaches of these three ones are also employed.

6.1   Manual Programming

This is the most traditional but, at the same time, the most error prone and slowest approach. Here, programmers manually write part or all of the application code. A big problem appears when it is necessary to develop a system as quick as possible but the implementation is built from the scratch. Furthermore, manual programming introduces errors in this phase so it is important to complete it with exhaustive debugging and testing tasks.

6.2   Code Reuse

On the other hand, we can use software reuse for speeding up the development. The reused artifacts are obtained from previous developments and must have been highly tested. There are different code reuse artifacts like components, frameworks or idioms. In the user interface field, CIOs (Concrete Interface Objects [13]) or widgets, libraries, ActiveX and JavaBeans components are the natural artifacts to be reused. Nevertheless, for any software reuse technique to be effective, it must be easier to reuse the artifacts than developing the software from scratch. Moreover, in order to reuse an artifact, you must know what it does, where it is, and if it has been tested. Therefore, it is crucial the use of repositories to increase the reuse in development teams.

6.3   Code Generation

Translators and code generation techniques can be applied to transform analysis and design patterns to an executable program in a given platform, architecture and language. Of course, in order to derive the implementation, coding decisions must be taken automatically. Therefore, a code translator must be parameterized to support variations in the implementation produced in order to change decisions about configuration, components to employ or code topics.

In our approach we have adopted a mixed solution. On one hand, we have used code generation in domain dependent software. On the other hand, we have reused frameworks in domain independent software. We have built translators for the most used platforms at CARE Technologies. There is a desktop solution implemented in Visual Basic. The Web platform is covered with ColdFusion and JSP technology. And the Java platform is implemented using JFC/Swing.

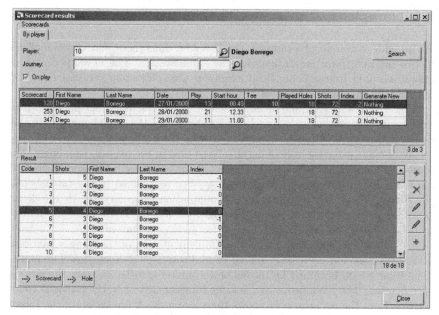

Fig. 4. Example of an implementation for Windows.

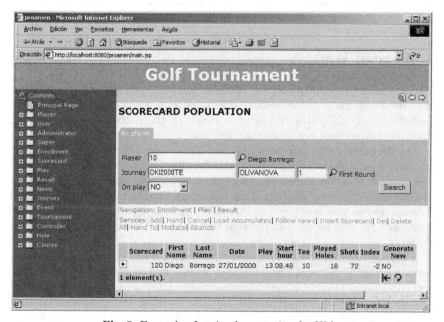

Fig. 5. Example of an implementation for Web.

7   Examples

We provide a couple of examples to show the differences and commonalities of two different implementations for the same system. The developed system manages a golf tournament. Both examples are completely generated and do not contain any manual changes.

Fig. 4 shows an example of implementation for the Windows platform produced automatically using a translator for the Visual Basic 6.0 language. In this figure, a *Master/Detail pattern* can be observed (Scorecards play the role of master and Result plays the role of detail). Note that in the master component, the scorecard number 120 is selected. The detail shows 18 results for such scorecard number 120. In the master component, a *filter* (contained in the tab labeled: 'By Player') is applied to constrain the population of scorecards. In the detail component there are two toolbars. The right vertical bar is used to *offer actions* while the bottom horizontal one is used for additional *navigation*.

On the other hand, Fig. 5 shows an implementation of the same scenario in a Web environment using JSP, HTML, and JavaScript technologies. The implementation is also obtained by means of automatic translation from the system specification. The *filter* provides the same functionality as in the previous counterpart. Here the scenario only shows the scorecards. A limitation in the target platform may discourage the *Master/Detail* presentation, providing a different but equivalent solution: users can *navigate* to Results using the link labeled 'Result' in the navigation bar. *Actions* over objects are accessible from the services bar.

8   Related Work

Martin Fowler [5] has explored the world of analysis patterns and provides lots of examples in his brilliant book. Fowler's patterns are focused on conceptual modelling and the abstraction level is closer to the patterns here presented. However, Fowler does not cover User Interface topics in his book.

On the other hand, van Welie [14] and Trætteberg [12] have developed user interface design patterns collections also focusing in usability issues and Web design. Such collections contain experience accumulated from designers and usability experts. These knowledge sources provides valuable experience and should be employed in the design phase. Accordingly, design patterns collections and languages can also be used as possible reification of Conceptual User Interface Patterns.

Coldewey and Krüger [3] proposed a framework based on a pattern language for developing form-based UIs. They also provide two conceptual patterns: *General Action* and *Dialog Category*. Granlund and Lafrenière [7] have develop the Pattern Supported Approach to cover the User Interface Design Process. In their approach they advocate for using patterns at different phases as medium for collecting experience and document the system. We absolutely agree with them, but we also intent to use patterns for supporting code generation.

Vanderdonckt describes SEGUIA [13,15] as a tool developed for the TRI-DENT environment that provides a semi-automatic generation assisted by the analyst. Implemented as an expert system, SEGUIA assists analysts to transform a TRIDENT specification to source code making questions and suggesting responses to the designer.

Finally, in an excellent article, Bell [1] reviews the Object-Oriented Model-Based Code Generation technologies. He reviews specification approaches, tools support and generation strategies. Such approaches are heavily oriented to develop the system logic and not aboard the problem of User Interfaces.

9   Conclusions

We have presented the kind of patterns we have been using for user interface developing. Such patterns have proven to be useful:

1. *At the analysis phase:* Analysts can employ this kind of patterns as a tool for documenting the user interface requirements. A tool based on such patterns helped to build UI specifications for information systems. The patterns were implemented as constructor concepts in a conceptual modeler tool.
2. *At the design phase:* The specification based in such conceptual patterns can be refined applying design patterns as described in [14] and [12]. Moreover, a design tool can suggest a reduced choice of mappings from each conceptual pattern to design patterns.
3. *At the implementation phase:* The design specification can be automatically transformed to source code to build parts or the complete user interface.
4. *During the entire life-cycle:* The documented specification based in conceptual patterns can be used to exchange ideas or knowledge among the members of the development team. It constitutes a *lingua franca* as stated by Erickson [4]. Therefore, they increase the effectiveness of the communication among developers.

Furthermore, the refining of UI conceptual patterns for different platforms has allowed us to provide a systematic approach for obtaining automatic implementations directly from the analysis models. Thus, it constitutes an excellent method for rapid prototyping and for increasing the productivity of software development.

The approach described is appropriate for resolving the problems presented in ubiquitous computing in a natural way: the development team must invest its effort in the abstract specification, minimizing the manual refinements for a given platform and tuning translators for each desired platform or device. Note that such tuning is done only once (the first project for such a device), the next time, the tuning can be reused. The principle followed is:

"Build one specification, translate it to N implementations".

The work is not over, it is just starting. Patterns should be distilled, reviewed and updated. In the next months we expect to discover new patterns and continuously enrich the pattern language that we employ [8,9]. At the same time, we think that public review is the best method to obtain valuable feedback from the research community to improve the pattern languages.

References

1. Bell R. *"Code Generation from Object Models"*. Embedded Programming Systems Journal, March, 1998.
2. Buschmann F., Meunier R., Rohnert H., Sommerland P., and Stal Michael. *"Pattern-Oriented Software Architecture – A System of Patterns"*. John Wiley & Sons Ltd., Chichester, England, 1996.
3. Coldewey J. and Krüger I. *"Form-Based User Interfaces – A Pattern Language"*, in Buschmann, Riehle (Eds.): Proceedings of the 2nd European Conference on Pattern Languages of Programming, Bad Irsee, 1997.
4. Erickson T. *"Pattern Languages as Languages"*. CHI'2000 Workshop: Pattern Languages for Interaction Design, 2000.
5. Fowler M. *"Analysis Patterns"*. Addison Wesley, 1997.
6. Gamma E., Helm R., Johnson R., and Vlissides J. *"Design Patterns: Elements of Reusable Object-Oriented Software"*. Addison Wesley, 1992.
7. Granlund Å. and Lafrenière D. *"A Pattern-Supported Approach to the User Interface Design"*. In Proceedings of HCI International 2001, 9th International Conference on Human-Computer Interaction, pages 282–286, New Orleans, USA, August, `http://www.sm.luth.se/csee/csn/publications/HCIInt2001Final.pdf`, 2001.
8. Molina P.J., Pastor O., Martí S., Fons J., and Insfrán E. *"Specifying Conceptual Interface Patterns in an Object-Oriented Method with Code Generation"*. In Proceedings of UIDIS'2001, pages 72–79, Zurich, Switzerland, May, IEEE Computer Society, 2001.
9. Molina P.J., Meliá S., and Pastor O. *"JUST-UI: A User Interface Specification Model"*. Computer-Aided Design of User Interfaces III, Ch. Kolski & J. Vanderdonckt (eds.), In Proceedings of the 4th International Conference on Computer-Aided Design of User Interfaces CADUI'2002 (Valenciennes, 15–17 May 2002), Kluwer Academics Publisher, Dordrecht, 2002.
10. Pastor O., Insfrán E., Pelechano V., Romero J., and Merseguer J. *"OO-Method: An OO Software Production Environment Combining Conventional and Formal Methods"*. Proceedings of 9th International Conference, CAiSE97, Lecture Notes in Computer Science 1250, pages 145–159, Barcelona, Spain. June, 1997.
11. Pastor O., Abrahão S., Molina J.C., and Torres I. *"A FPA-like Measure for Object Oriented Systems from Conceptual Models"*. Current Trends in Software Measurment, Ed. Shaker Verlag, pages 51–69, Montreal, Canada, 2001.
12. Trætteberg H. *"Model Based Design Patterns"*. Workshop on User Interface Design Patterns (position paper), CHI'2000, The Netherlands, 2000.
13. Vanderdonckt J. *"Advice-Giving Systems for Selecting Interaction Objects"*. Proc. of UIDIS'99, 1999.
14. van Welie M. *"Web Desing Patterns (The Amsterdam Collection of Patterns)"* `http://www.welie.com/patterns/index.html`, 2000.
15. Vanderdonckt J. *"Assisting Designers in Developing Interactive Bussiness Oriented Applications"*. HCI'99, 1999.

Monitoring Human Faces from Multi-view Image Sequences

Nailja Luth

Fraunhofer Institute for Computer Graphics, Division Rostock
Joachim-Jungius-Str. 11
18059 Rostock nluth@rostock.igd.fhg.de
http://www.rostock.igd.fhg.de

Abstract. The paper proposes a vision-based monitoring of human faces based on the automatic pose-invariant face detection and generation of detailed parametric descriptions of dynamic changes of face mimics. The monitoring approach involves the extraction and the classification of face features. The approach is designed especially for the monitoring of faces which captured directly during the Human Computer Interaction. The use of multi-view images provides sufficient information for the automatic head pose estimation and face mimic changes. The results of the automatic facial image analysis are described by the so-called Face Mimic Graph. The Face Mimic Graph provides the quantitative and qualitative information of face mimic changes captured during the face monitoring.

1 Introduction

The monitoring of human face mimics could be very useful on different applications, e.g. teleconferencing, Human-Computer-Interaction (HCI), virtual avatars. Especially in the HCI, the results of the face expression recognition in direct conjunction with the working environment of the user can lead to a derivation of emotional states of a person. The ability to recognize and to understand facial expression automatically may facilitate communication. Computer Vision community is mainly interested in the tracking of human face and in the recognition of facial expressions. Most automatic expression analysis systems attempt to recognize a small set of prototypic expressions, such as happiness, anger, surprise and fear. In our daily real communication with other persons we seldom deal with isolated face expressions but more often our evaluation of emotional expression is based on the total observable behaviour in a given situation.

1.1 State of the Automatic Face Expression Recognition

The difficulty and complexity of the automatic face expression recognition are reasoned by a variety of facial expressions across human population and context-dependent variety even for the same person [1]. The automatic face expression recognition needs to solve following tasks: detection and location of faces in a scene, facial feature extraction (FFE) and face expression classification (FEC).

P. Forbrig et al. (Eds.): DSV-IS 2002, LNCS 2545, pp. 173–184, 2002.
© Springer-Verlag Berlin Heidelberg 2002

In this paper we address the task of FFE and classification of face feature changes. Compared to research works for face recognition, there is a relatively small amount of work on FFE and FEC. However in the last two years the number of publications is permanently growing. The proceedings [2] of a recent conference on automatic face and gesture recognition presents many papers on face detection. There are mainly two approaches: holistic template-matching systems and geometric feature-based systems. In holistic systems, a template can be a pixel image or a feature vector obtained after processing the face image as a hole. In the latter, principal component analysis and multiplayer Neural Networks are extensively used to obtain a low-dimensional representation. In geometric feature-based systems, major face components and/or feature points are detected in the images. Different methods were developed to automatically recognize facial expressions. In [3] a system uses optical flow within local face regions for recognition. These methods are relatively insensitive to subtle motion because information about small deviations is lost when their flow pattern is removed or thresholds are imposed. As a result, the recognition ability and accuracy of the systems may be reduced. A 3D-face model was used to fit it into an image. Initial adjustment between the 3D-Model and surface images was performed automatically using View-based and Modular Eigenspace methods.

The distances between feature points and the relative sizes of the major face components are computed to form a feature vector. The feature points can also form a geometric graph representation of the faces. Feature-based techniques are usually computationally more expensive than template-based techniques, but are more robust to variation in scale, size, head orientation and location of the face in an image. All works can be divided in two groups: work with static images and with image sequences. Most methods in the first group are based on principal component analysis [4, 5]. In [6] two types of facial features will be extracted: geometrical positions of fiducal points on a face and a set of multiscale and multi-orientation Gabor wavelet coefficients. An architecture based on a two-layer perceptron for the face expression recognition was developed.

1.2   Facial Action Coding System

Over the past decade many research works on face expression recognition are based on the special coding system FACS: Facial Action Coding System, developed by P. Ekman & W. Friesen [7]. FACS has been used extensively also in facial animation to help animators interpret and construct realistic facial expressions. FACS is an anatomically based coding system that enables discrimination between closely related expressions. FACS deals only with what is a clearly visible phenomena. FACS is concerned only about the description of facial motions. In reality, humans are capable of producing thousands of expressions varying in complexity and meaning that are not fully captured with a limited number of expressions and emotion categories. Therefore the systems in [8, 9] are aimed to recognize both subtle feature motion and complex facial expressions. This approach allows to capture the full range of facial expressions. In [8] the approach recognizes upper face expressions in the forehead and brow regions. Initially the feature points will be marked manually. The further automatic tracking of their movements across an image sequence is performed by using special pyramidal optical flow algorithm. The recognition of upper face AUs was developed by applying of Hidden Markov Models (HMM). In [9] the approach was extended to lower face AUs. The further development of the system for automatic face analysis (AFA) [10] involves additionally the extraction of furrows.

2 Monitoring Approach Description

The key features of our approach are shown in Figure 1. It must operate in future under a variety of conditions, such a varying of illumination, backgrounds, it must be able to handle non-frontal facial images of both males and females of different ages and races. We designed the approach for tracking of facial mimic changes based on automatic analysis of image sequences. Every image frame from the sequence will be automatically normalized and decomposed into face feature. We used the definition of Action Units (AU) of Facial Action Coding System FACS [7] for encoding the movements of face features (FFs). To minimize the user assistance we developed special image analysis methods for automatic detection and extraction of FFs from an image. The classification of some FFs was performed using Hidden Markov Models. The results of the face decomposition will be transformed into a face mimic graph (FMG). The visualization of face mimic changes that are recorded in the Face Mimic Graph and evaluation of the FMG are represented in Chapter 6. In the first version we integrated the dual uncalibrated camera system for capture of face expressions. The simultaneous frontal and profile images of a face mimic deliver a sufficient information concerning the movements on a face. The functionalities in rough overview are the following:

- registration and estimation of significant 2D-changes in nearly multi-view images
- automatic face feature extraction and tracking
- creation of a dynamic parametric description of the face mimic graph
- visualization and evaluation of the face mimics dynamics using the Face Mimic Graph

3 Facial Image Analysis

Facial Image Analysis involves both image processing and analysis tools. First, is to detect faces in image sequences. Second, to track the detected faces over consecutive frames and select the frames that will be best for the classification. The final step is the facial mimic detection on the extracted faces.

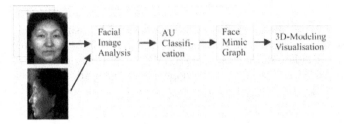

Fig. 1. Functionalities of our approach

3.1   Image Frame Normalization

The first component of the Facial Image Analysis is the image sequence capture. The facial expressions of some persons "on-demand" were recorded as training sequences. The persons sat in front of the first camera, in profile of the second camera. Each facial expression began with neutral face expression. The image sequence is recorded with 20 frames. In the first version every fifth frame is selected as a relevant intermediate one. The captured face feature moving was enough to track their displacement positions. Every intermediate frame represents both the face feature moving and the head moving, that is mostly typical for face expression of an individual. Exact estimation of the head movement from the captured image sequence will be very difficult. When out-of-plane rotation of the head is small, an affine transformation on images can align images so that face position, size and orientation are kept relatively constant across persons, and these factors do not interfere significantly with feature extraction. To estimate the parameters of the affine transformation we used the position of three stable facial points. In our experiments three points were sufficient in most cases. The estimated transformation matrix is used to normalize the image frame relatively to the previous frame and is involved in the face mimic graph. The meaning of the normalization is illustrated in comparing of both subtraction results (Fig.2). The lower right difference image in Fig. 2 shows only relevant displacements that are generated by face mimic changes. On the contrary, the upper right image illustrates difference image that includes face changes as well as head moving. The estimation of real face feature moving can not be done exactly without the consideration of the head moving.

3.2   Face Feature Detection

Automatic detection of changes in a face mimic begins with the detection of the face position in a image and division of the face image into face features, like brows, eyes, lips, and furrows (Fig. 3). Because of face asymmetry we consider structural and expression's asymmetries as important characteristics of faces.

The detection and localization of face features is based on the detection of changes. The main steps of the process are described below.

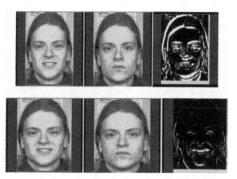

Fig. 2. Example of image normalization. The upper two grey level images show original neutral and smile images without normalization; the third upper image represents the result of subtraction. The lower right image, as a subtraction of normalized images, shows the real moving of face features from neutral to smile state

Fig. 3. Some examples of face features

Fig. 4. Detection of change regions. The right image represents the result of segmentation and closing of the difference image between two left successive images.

1. **Extraction of change regions.** The change regions are face feature changes that are appearing during the face mimic changes. The extraction method is based on the subtraction of two first images and then the segmentation and further filtering of the result difference image using closing operator (Fig. 4).

2. **Finding of face features search regions.** Firstly, all extracted change regions will be transformed into one-pixel-regions, using the skeletonization method. The generated skeleton lines (Fig. 5, left image) characterize the change regions more efficiently. According the general parametric face model (Fig. 5, right image) can be now all search regions for feature candidates defined and consequently processed.

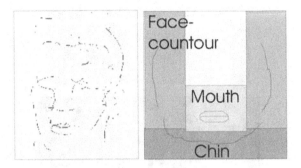

Fig. 5. Skeleton image and the general face

3. **Analysis of every search region** with the aim to extract the chin form, left and right face contour and mouth lines (Fig. 6). Extracted skeleton lines are considered as candidates for face regions.

Fig. 6. Extracted skeleton lines as candidates for chin, eyes and mouth search regions.

4. **The geometry models** of face features will be generated under consideration of the hypothetic suppositions about their positions and the positions of extracted skeleton lines (Fig. 7).
5. **The algorithm for the search of feature points** will be illustrated by example for finding of feature point P1 of the left lip corner. We adapted the main idea of the method in [11] to our application. A trapeze window with short basic line on the left side. A mean value of grey levels mean_grey and minimal value min_grey will be calculated for every column. In case of

$$min\_grey/mean\_grey < threshold \qquad (1)$$

the number of minimal column will be calculated. The left and right corners of lips and eyes are the darkest points in their environment. The value for threshold is equal 0.6. This estimation was done on the basis of calculated diagrams of many experiments (Fig. 8).

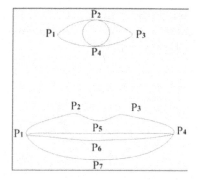

Fig. 7. Parametric geometry form of lips and eyes boundaries. The points Pi represent an approximated polylines of lips and eyes contours. They are called feature points and their displacements are important for the classification of face feature changes.

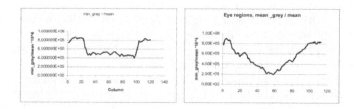

Fig. 8. Statistical quotation between the grey level of the lip or eye corner and direct neighbourhood

The results of lip, eye and brow corner finding are represented in Fig. 9. The left and right corners of lips and eyes are the darkest points in their environment. The value for threshold is equal 0.6.

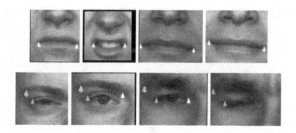

Fig. 9. Results of the detection of mouth and eye & brow corners

6. **The search of other feature points** P2, P3, P5, P6, P7 (Fig. 7) will be detected by using the edge detection. We applied the Deriche's gradient operator modified by Lanser [12] (Fig. 10).

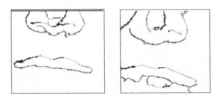

Fig. 10. Example of the edge detection for lip contours

7. **The tracking of feature points** in next image will be done using correspondence analysis. For instance, a detected chin, mouth, brow or eye contours build potential search regions. After the detection of these regions, a more refined model for the face is required in order to determine which of the detected regions correspond to valid faces. The use of the eye detection algorithm in conjunction with the head detection module improves the accuracy of the head model and discards regions corresponding to back views or other regions that do not correspond to a face. The results of the eye detection algorithm are used to estimate the face pose and to determine the image containing the most frontal pose among a sequence of images.

8. **The detection of furrows** is based on the gradient filters. The results of detected furrows are represented in Fig. 11. We consider furrows in forehead, eyes, between brows and cheek regions.

Fig. 11. Detected furrows

4   Facial Action Units Classification

The changes of feature points for every face region could be well coded by FACS [7]. FACS breaks down the face into upper and lower face actions and further subdivides facial actions into small units called Action Units (AUs). Each AU represents an individual muscle action, or an action of muscle group, into a single recognizable facial posture. In total they classify 66 AUs that in combination could generate defined and gradable facial expressions. Example AUs are the inner brow raiser, the outer brow raiser and the lid tightener. Each AU is a minimal action that cannot be divided into smaller actions. The extracted feature positions will represented by feature vector sequence. The classification of feature vectors that we are proposing involves the use of Hidden Markov Model (HMM). The "states" of the HMMs include the movements of feature points of brows, eyes or lips. First the feature vectors will be transformed into a sequence of a finite set of symbols using the quantization function. Our quantization function is developed using the clustering analysis. As an example, we describe the sequences of feature vectors (FV) for brow regions. The FV with length 12 v=(vi), i = 1,..12 will be quantized into 16 clusters: 1, ..., K, K = 16. Every symbol sequence corresponds to an Action Unit, which is modeled by HMM. HMM describes the statistical behaviour of a process that generates time series having certain statistical characteristics. A discrete HMM has N states $\{S_1, S_2, ..., S_N\}$ and M observation symbols $\{O_1, O_2, ..., O_N\}$. We used a 4-state HMM with left-to-right-topology for the classification of brows motions, AU1, AU2, AU4 (Fig. 12).

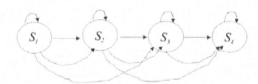

Fig. 12. HMM-topolgy for AU1, AU2, AU4

For every AUs of brow motions was a separate AU-HMM modeled. The classification procedure is following: the observable chain of states of a face feature and will be classified using all AU-HMMs for this face feature. The maximum of the probability defines the corresponding AU (Fig. 13).

5   Face Mimic Graph

Despite some restriction of FACS we decided to use it because of the general character of coding of face expressions. The essential restriction of FACS are following:

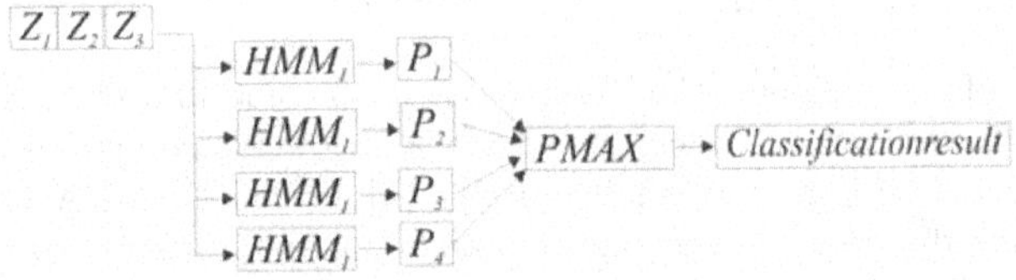

$$Z_1 Z_2 Z_3$$

$HMM_i \rightarrow P_1$
$HMM_i \rightarrow P_2$
$HMM_i \rightarrow P_3$
$HMM_i \rightarrow P_4$

$PMAX \rightarrow Classificationresult$

Fig. 13. Classification procedure

- Real facial motion is almost never completely localized. However Facial Action Units in FACS are purely local spatial patterns. Therefore the detecting of an unique set of action units for a specific expression is not guaranteed.
- The description of AU is qualitative. The subtle motions of eyes, lips or brows can not be described quantitative.

We designed a Face Mimic Graph – FMG, that allows to describe more flexible and dynamical the motions of face feature and to avoid some FACS limitations. The FMG (Fig. 14) involves both permanent face feature – lips, eyes, brows, face contour – and transient feature – furrows.

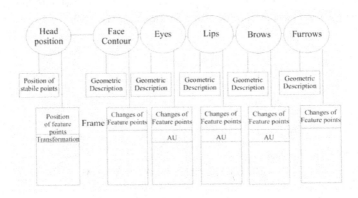

Fig. 14. Face Mimic Graph

The geometric description of every face feature consists of the position of feature points and parameterized curves of feature contours. In the next table "Changes" all the displacements of feature points will be notated for every frame. In case of eyes, lips and brows the AU-classification result will be written. The combination of facial AU for every frame could be used in future for the classification of face mimic.

6   Monitoring of Facial Mimics

The results of the face changes monitoring is registered in the Face Mimic Graph. It involves all information that describes the face feature changes, head moving and results of Action Unit classification. In the first version we developed only the classification of some face feature changes. These registrations of face feature changes are the first step towards the classification of the face mimics. The classification of main important face mimics are our next future tasks. Under main mimics we mean a-priori defined mimics states clusters that are relevant for specific applications, such as positive or negative emotional states. In the current state, the visualization of the Face Mimic Graph is limited by a histogram of changes dynamic. In Fig. 15 is an example histogram on image sequence monitoring over a short time. The person changed his face mimics "on-demand", the captured image sequences was automatically analyzed.

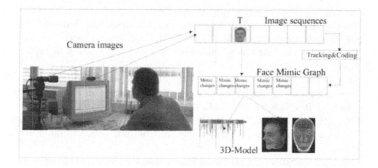

Fig. 15. Histogram of face change dynamic over 3,5 minutes

The corresponding images to a chosen time point can be visualized directly by setting of cursor, e.g. the cursor position is labelled by black color in figure 15. The corresponding images are shown on the right side.

7   Conclusions

In the first version main functionality of the automatic face monitoring is developed. The special methods of the detection of face features and the estimation of their changes are developed. The results of automatic tracking of feature changes and their classification are described in the Face Mimic Graph. Additionally, the 3D-modelling of a face provides the 3D-visualization of the face and the estimation of 3D-changes of face features. There are some significant restrictions in the first version:

- only one face must be represented in a image
- stable background without quick movements behind the observed head
- manual interaction for definition of stable points and sometimes for editing of found coincident feature points
- using HMMs means the training for all Action Units. Alternative classification methods are required in future.

The important future extension of the approach lays in the classification of important face mimics, that describe positive expressions, like smile, as well as non-positive ones, like sadness or unhappiness. Additionally we plan to integrate more alternative methods especially for automatic analysis and classification.

References

[1]   Wierzbicka, A.: Emotions Across Languages and Cultures: Diversity and Universals, Cambridge University Press, 1999

[2]   Proceedings of the fourth international conference on Automatic Face and Gesture Recognition, 28–30 March 2000, Grenoble, France.

[3]   Essa, I.: Coding, Analysis, Interpretation and Recognition of Facial Expressions. IEEE Transaction on PAMI, Volume 19(7), July 1977

[4]   Lanitis, A., Taylor, C., Cootes, T.: Automatic interpretation and coding of face images using flexible models. IEEE Transaction on Pattern Analysis and Machine Intelligence, 19(7):743–756, July 1997

[5]   Padgett, C., Cottrell, G.: Identifying emotion in static images. In Proceedings of the 2nd Joint Symposium on Neural Computation, volume 5: 91–101, La Jolla, CA, 1997

[6]   Zhang, Z.: Feature-Based Facial Expression Recognition: Experiments with a Multi-Layer Perceptron. ISSN 0249-6399, February 1998

[7]   Ekman, P., Friesen W.: Manual for Facial Action Coding system. Consulting Psychologists Press, Inc. Palo Alto, CA, 1978

[8]   Lien, J., Kanade T., Cohn, J., Li Ch-Ch: Automated Facial Expression Recognition Based on FACS Action Units. Proceedings of FG'98, April 14–16, 1998 Nara Japan

[9]   Lien, J., Kanade, T., Li, Ch-Ch.: Detection, Tracking and Classification of Action Units in Facial Expression. Journal of Robotics and Autonomous Systems, 1999

[10]   Tian, Y., Kanade, T., Cohn, J.: Recognizing Action Units for Facial Expression Analysis. IEEE Transaction on Pattern Analysis and Machine Intelligence, Vol. 23, No.2., February 2001

[11]   Gebhard, A., Paulus, D., Suchy, B. Wolf, S., Niemann, H.: System zur Diagnosenunterstuetzung von Patienten mit Gesichtlaehmungen. Bildverarbeitung fuer die Medizin 2000, proceedings of the workshop in Munich. 12.–14. Maerz 2000

[12]   Lanser S., Eckstein W.: A Modification of Deriche's Approach to Edge Detection. Proceedings of the 11 ICPR, IEEE Computer Society Press, 1992, pp. 633–637

Improving Mouse Navigation – A Walk through the "Hilly Screen Landscape"

David Ahlström, Martin Hitz, and Gerhard Leitner

University of Klagenfurt, Department of Informatics-Systems,
Universitätsstraße 65-67, A-9020 Klagenfurt, Austria
{david.ahlstroem, martin.hitz,gerhard.leitner}@uni-klu.ac.at

Abstract. During computer interaction much time is spent navigating the graphical user interface to find and invoke functions through interface controls. If this navigation process could be optimised, users would spend less time searching for and navigating to interface controls. This paper presents a walk through an ongoing research project aimed at developing and assessing a navigation support module for mouse based interaction, which enhances standard screen pointer behaviour with position context sensitive functionality – creating a "hilly screen landscape". The main hypothesis of this work is that a context sensitive screen pointer prevents navigation to and selection of erroneous and inappropriate interface controls, decreases pointing and selection times and contributes to increased overall usability of the application. A description of the navigation support module and hypothetical situations where such a module could prove to be useful are provided together with major implementation and evaluation issues of the project.

1 Introduction

The complexity of a software's functionality is normally reflected in its GUI (Graphical User Interface). Small and simple software products often have simple and easy to understand GUIs. As the complexity of the functionality grows, the GUI becomes more and more complex and for the user harder to understand and to operate. In complex GUIs of modern software with several menus, buttons and other interaction controls, it is hard for the user to know where to navigate, how and when to invoke functions. Moreover, increasing use of mobile computers equipped with pointing devices with questionable ergonomic properties (such as track points, track balls and touch pads) in inappropriate working environments (like planes, trains, or cars) significantly complicates mouse based navigation for most users. Hence, there is an increasing need to explore new methods to support the user in the GUI based interaction dialogue.

Since much of the time spent during interaction is invested in the actual navigation process (visual search of the GUI to localise the appropriate interface control, followed by moving the screen pointer to the control in order to manipulate the control), this seems to be one promising point of attack to tackle the problem of complex GUIs in order to make them easier to operate.

P. Forbrig et al. (Eds.): DSV-IS 2002, LNCS 2545, pp. 185–195, 2002.
© Springer-Verlag Berlin Heidelberg 2002

In this paper we present an ongoing research project which aims to optimise mouse based interaction and navigation. We intend to implement and evaluate a navigation support module which overlays GUIs with simulated gravitation fields, making the screen pointer position context sensitive. The navigation support module defines peaks and valleys within the GUI and thus forms what we call a "hilly screen landscape". Contrary to ordinary GUIs (with totally flat screen landscapes), a GUI enhanced with such a navigation support module exhibits changes in effort required to navigate within certain areas of the screen. Mouse motions within a valley results in faster screen pointer motions, allowing easy and smooth navigation. Whereas moving the screen pointer alongside a valley or "downhill" is easy, moving the mouse "uphill" results in delayed reactions of the screen pointer, making it harder for the user to navigate in that direction.

We hypothesize that in applications enhanced with such a navigation support module and the resulting hilly screen landscape

- navigation will be easier and less error prone compared to applications with standard GUIs,
- cursor targeting and selection task times will be reduced, and
- that the module contributes to an increased overall usability of the application.

The following section points out relevant related work. In Section 3, we present the planned functionality of the navigation support module along with some concrete user situations where the module might be useful. Section 4 describes major implementation issues and Section 5 emphasizes on the planned assessment and evaluation process. The paper concludes by briefly describing the project outline, highlighting important project steps, and sketching the current status of the project.

2   Related Work

Accurate navigation and screen pointer positioning are particular problematic with isometric pointing devices [13] and other pointing devices with similar questionable ergonomic properties [1]. The main remedy approach for navigation problematic has been to introduce new hardware devices.

Previous research done to support the navigation process can roughly be divided in two categories, research and development of new haptic input devices which enhance interaction by tactile and force feedback, and research concentrated on navigation and object manipulation within virtual reality environments. In the first category we find work with the FEELit (Immersion Corporation [8]), a mouse physically attached to a limited workspace and equipped with motors to steer the hand of the user. The produced forces where found to improve steering and targeting tasks [6]. Similar results are reported in [2], where a multi-modal mouse with both force feedback (produced by creating a drag between an electromagnet in the mouse and the iron mouse pad) and tactile feedback (produced by a solenoid-driven pin stimulating the index finger) was used. In [4], Campbell et al. describe a vibrating isometric joystick and stress the importance of synchronization between tactile and visual feedback.

The usage of haptic devices such as the PHANToM (SensAble Technologies Inc. [15]) for object manipulation and navigation in virtual reality environments has been evaluated [3]; research was done also into enhancing the traditional desktop system with the same device [12]. Oakley et al. [14] augment buttons and scrollbars with different haptic effects using the PHANToM. They show that mechanisms which automatically push the screen pointer towards the widget's centre can be helpful in targeting tasks, thus supporting "clear" hits and prohibiting accidental slip offs. Considering size and complexity of the device, the usability in mobile and desktop computing is questionable.

Little work has been done to experiment with **standard input devices** such as the mouse and its derivatives for mobile computers, found in most modern computing environments.

One common drawback of the above mentioned projects is that they all are device centred. For the user to enjoy the extra functionality and the extra feedback, an often clumsy and expensive device has to be purchased and installed. A new way to operate the computer has to be learned and trained. Furthermore, most of the devices are only applicable and usable in the context of special software applications.

Thus, it seems promising to investigate the possibilities of enhancing GUI based navigation in the context of standard hardware equipment and everyday software applications.

3   Description of the Hilly Screen Landscape

We use the metaphor of a hilly landscape to facilitate the understanding of the navigation support module's functionality. In nature, a landscape is a region of land with distinguishing characteristics and features. If one of its characteristics is that of differences in altitude, the landscape is said to be hilly or mountainous.

As a runner in an orienteering competition has to navigate from control station to control station in the landscape, the computer user has to navigate through a screen landscape from widget to widget in order to complete his tasks. Whereas the athlete might have to navigate throughout a hilly landscape, where the control stations are placed on the top of hills, on plateaus and in valleys, the computer user always navigates in a totally flat landscape. On his map, the athlete sees the changes in altitude and he can also notice the changes while running. The effort required to run uphill is greater than the effort required to cover a downhill distance. For the computer user navigating in the screen landscape, the effort required to cover a certain distance is equal anywhere in the landscape.

Our navigation support module transforms the flat screen landscape into a hilly screen landscape. As the orienteering competitor, the computer user can now notice changes in altitude during navigation in the screen landscape. A graphical representation of the screen landscape indicates the locations of hills and valleys on the screen in order to provide further and visual support.

By careful and intelligent placement of peaks and valleys, the resulting hilly landscape can reflect the intended and most optimal navigation paths for the current screen. The screen pointer behaviour is made context sensitive, depending on screen position and widgets at the position. Less frequently used or even dangerous areas, such as delete buttons etc., are placed on top of hills, to keep them out of the natural navigation path. Many screen areas are of no or little interest, containing no interaction elements, and navigation should be focused to the relevant areas.

3.1   Concrete Usage Situations

Fig. 1 depicts a typical data entry form which contains a number of input fields and buttons, often found in e.g. Web applications. The curved line (starting at the top of the form) symbolises a characteristic navigation path through the form. The user navigates from field to field, finally arriving at the lower right hand corner at the submit button.

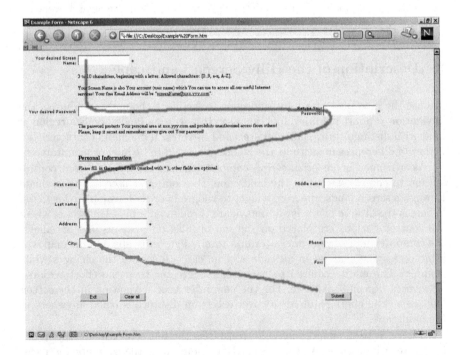

Fig. 1. A typical data entry form with marked characteristic navigation path.

The interesting parts of the form are the areas that contain interaction elements. Empty parts or parts with only text are of low relevance for the navigation process. To support navigation to and within the interesting areas, we put them at low altitude in the hilly screen landscape, making it easy for the user to move the screen pointer to and within these areas. We want to discourage navigation in the direction of the bottom left hand side of the form where the "dangerous" buttons labelled "Exit" and "Delete" are located. In order to make it harder for the user to reach these buttons, we place them upon a hill. Fig. 2 depicts the hilly screen landscape for the data entry form in Fig. 1.

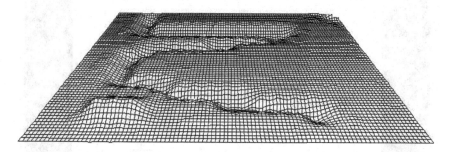

Fig. 2. Graphical representation of the hilly screen landscape for data entry form in Figure 1.

The screen shot in Fig. 3 shows a frequently occurring situation. During a slide show presentation, the main interaction task for the presenter is to step between the slides. The presenter might be using an optical mouse operated with a track ball (as often found in auditoriums) to navigate the GUI and control the computer. Having no stable support for the hand movements, the task of selecting and pressing the back and forward buttons in the bottom part of the screen will most certainly be a difficult task. Using the navigation support module, the bottom part of the screen could be placed in a valley, thus supporting the navigation towards this interaction relevant area. A user that is aware of the landscape, having a mental picture of it and its functionality, can deliberately take advantage of it. With minimal mouse movements he/she can start the motion towards a valley then letting the screen pointer slide down in the valley, towards the target. But a user does not have to be aware of the landscape to take advantage of its functionality, since the screen pointer automatically moves in the "right" direction (i.e., downwards).

In several applications, the user is confronted with very small control elements (e.g. buttons for scrolling up and down in text documents and handles for selection and manipulation of items in drawing application) which require precise and accurate screen pointer positioning. By placing small targets within dimples in the screen landscape the target areas are virtually made larger. As the screen pointer reaches the vicinity of the target, it slides towards the target center, ensuring a hit. The acquiring act, precisely positioning of the screen pointer, and then determine that a successful acquisition has taken place can put great burdens on low vision users [7] and motor disabled users [16], as well as on non-disable users. "Gravity fields" around targets might reduce this burden.

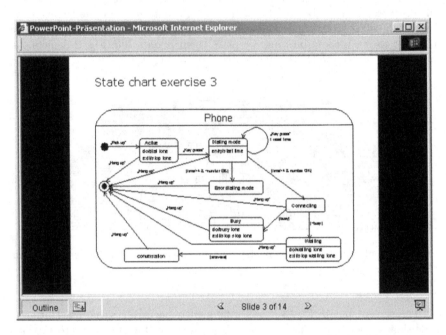

Fig. 3. Example situation where the hilly screen landscape could be useful. By placing the back and forward buttons (bottom) in a valley, navigation is supported towards this relevant area.

3.2 Additional Functionality

Beside the main functionality of the navigation support module, i.e. creating a hilly screen landscape which provides support during navigation, some additional functionality seems to be appropriate and/or required in order to maximize the usefulness, such as

- a visual representation of the hilly screen landscape (such as a map with contour lines or a 3D graphic), which can be activated and deactivated by the user,
- activation and deactivation of the module itself and
- mechanisms that let the user modify and reshape the landscape according to desire and needs.

4   Implementation Issues

The functionality of the hilly screen landscape and the concrete user situations described in previous sections reveal some constraints and issues we have to take into account during the specification and implementation of the navigation support module (called "HSL" in what follows). The most prominent issues concern

- ways to manipulate the screen pointer behaviour (techniques to implement the "gravitation" fields which realise the slopes within the hilly screen landscape),
- the choice of implementation platform and language,
- the level of implementation (device driver level vs. application level),
- portability and operating system independence and
- the possible integration of a 3D environment for visual representation of the hilly screen landscape.

From a broad architectural perspective, the HSL will be injected between the GUI oriented parts of the operating system layer and the application layer, respectively (Fig. 4). The HSL control module can be conceived of as an extension of the respective operating system services, taking into account any screen landscape definitions provided and controlling screen pointer movement accordingly. It offers an API to the application layer, which in turn needs to be augmented by a HSL definition module. The main function provided by the API is the screen landscape definition: The HSL definition module informs the HSL control module about the topography of each affected window employed by the application. The HSL control module will then modify the screen pointer movement characteristics whenever the respective window gains the interaction focus. In addition, the API of the HSL control module encompasses auxiliary functions to control diverse HSL states like enabling/disabling gravity effects, displaying/hiding the landscape representation, etc.

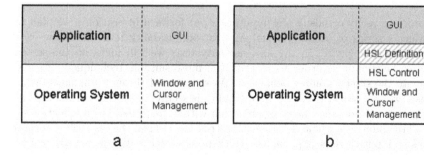

Fig. 4. Conceptual view of a standard architecture (a) and conceptual view of a HSL enabled architecture (b).

We have divided the actual implementation process of the navigation support module into roughly five phases, where each phase is followed by a usability evaluation phase.

1. *Motion manipulation.* The focus of phase one is set on the actual behaviour of the screen pointer. Experimental development is used to identify possible techniques for manipulating the screen pointer motion behaviour under different operating systems and programming languages. This experimental phase is followed by an evaluation process which has as its primary aim to identify the most suitable technique(s) for further implementations, as well as to collect basic and valuable user attitudes to the idea of a navigation support module.
2. *Characteristic application.* Based on the results of the first implementation and evaluation phase, the product of implementation phase two is a small application-like (e.g. a data entry form as such in figure 1) prototype where user navigation tasks can be examined within a realistic setting.
3. *Additional functionality.* The third implementation phase concentrates on additional features of the navigation support module, i.e. functions for run-time modification and visualization of the hilly screen landscape, to be integrated into the prototype from the previous phase.
4. *Example application.* Phase four of the implementation process results in a full scale test application, with all functionality integrated, which allows us to evaluate the implications of the navigation support module on all levels, ranging from execution of user sub-tasks to implications of overall application usability.
5. *Plug-and-play.* The last phase is devoted to implementation of a plug and play functionality, where we explore possible solutions to make the navigation support module executable with arbitrary applications.

For a brief report on the current state of development, we refer the reader to Section 6.

5   Usability Evaluation Issues

In order to verify or falsify our hypotheses put forward in Section 1 we plan to conduct a series of usability tests. At least one usability test will follow each implementation phase. In the first usability tests we will focus on the screen pointer behaviour in order to identify the most suitable technique(s) to manipulate the screen pointer behaviour. As we proceed through implementation phase two and three, the basic functionality is secured and we can evaluate the navigation support module in combination with a "real-life-like" application.

Throughout the whole assessment process, we will run the tests using several types of input devices (e.g. mouse, track point, track ball, touch pad) to find out what devices are most successfully combined with the navigation support module.

The following two subsections describe the usability tests in some more detail.

5.1   Early Usability Tests

Users will be confronted with the functionality of the navigation support module without performing a concrete task. They will be asked to navigate around as they like to for a few minutes. Parameters such as eye movements on the screen and facial expressions will be recorded. Additionally, the subjects will be asked to verbalize their thoughts about the "device" (i.e. the behaviour of the screen pointer), what they think is the difference to other "devices" they are familiar with and what their subjective impression about the "device" is. Different data will be collected in order to find out whether and how subjects are acting and reacting in a subjective as well as in an objectively measurable way on the feedback given from the different input devices and screen pointer manipulation techniques.

Next, the subjects will be asked to perform a small dummy task to collect also data of a real application task. The subjects should be able to complete the task due to the previous habituation phase. Objective measures such as task completion time, error rate, error correction possibilities can be recorded and will serve as an additional criterion for the usability of the different navigation techniques.

Results of the first step should be that we can decide what screen pointer manipulation technique is best for implementation and what features are "musts" and "must nots".

5.2   Later Usability Tests

In later stages of usability testing we will run usability tests of "real-life-like" applications. This could be for instance a comparison of two user-groups using the same application or Web-site. The control group will be confronted with conventional flat screen landscapes, the test group will work with the hilly landscape functionality. The control and test groups again are to be divided in subgroups on the basis of at least two criteria: expert vs. standard user and standard device (mouse) vs. special device (track point, track ball and touch pad). Several parameters will be recorded, such as objective measurements like task completion time, error rates etc., as well as subjective measurements like verbal and non-verbal expressions of the test subjects. Additionally, the observation methods mentioned in the previous subsection, e.g. eye-tracking, will be applied too.

To provide a realistic situation, some auxiliary tasks are to be considered, e.g. installing the device drivers or plug-ins or activation and disabling of the functionality.

These later usability tests will also evaluate the implemented additional functionalities, visualization and modification of the screen landscape and how they influence user behaviour and performance.

Finally, statistical analyses will be used to identify overall and special advantages or disadvantages of the navigation support module.

6   Ongoing Work

In the initial project stage, which can be described as a preliminary investigation and analysis stage, we focused on the desired screen pointer behaviour and motion characteristics. The goal was to find suitable ways to manipulate the standard screen pointer behaviour and to select the most appropriate programming language and platform for implementation. To keep the implementation of the module as portable and flexible as possible, we aimed to find programming solutions for the screen pointer manipulation at the highest possible level, thus avoiding having to work at device driver level. After some exploration and experimental implementations, Java [9] with the Java 3D API [10] turned out to be the most prominent candidate. This alternative meets all requirements extracted from the relevant implementation issues listed at the beginning of Section 4.

At the time of writing, we are working on the implementation of three different screen pointer manipulation techniques which we call *sliding, affixing,* and *friction.* Using the sliding technique, within a gravitation field (i.e. slope) the screen pointer automatically moves in one direction (representing the down hill direction) forcing the user to "work" in the opposite direction to go uphill, or just let the screen pointer "slide" downhill. The affixing technique lets the screen pointer stay still in a slope as long as the input device does not produce any motion events. The gravitation force is first activated when the user starts to move the screen pointer in one or the other direction. The realisation of the friction technique is based on manipulation of the control-display (C-D) gain setting as described in [11]. A low setting represents the uphill direction and a high setting the downhill direction.

The next project step will be the specification of the navigation support module. The description of the navigation support module is rather (and easier) made by the emotions, reactions and behaviour it should awaken and triggered during usage, than by concrete functions. Therefore, the specification and description will be based on two parts, one "emotion" oriented and one function oriented part, as recommended in [5]. We suspect that this division will prove to be helpful when designing and developing such an ease-of-use oriented artifact as the navigation support module. A challenging specification subtask is the modelling of the navigation support module. UML will be used for modelling purposes.

Parallel with the implementation of the navigation support module we will work on the development of the usability process and typical methods. In the first phase we have to consider fundamental research, such as cognitive psychology to evaluate for example whether and how our model is influencing common interaction patterns, familiar action-feedback loops, etc. Perceptual, cognitive and motor aspects will be taken into account. This is important because our module touches different sensing channels in a new way. In distinction to e.g. devices with tactile feedback, our module does not give tactile feedback but aims to simulate motoric effort (going up a hill) by visual feedback. In the case of isometric joysticks, e.g. track points, the required extra pressure needed to go uphill results in a kind of force feedback.

In the later phases more or less standard usability methods such as expert reviews and usability test with users will be performed to prove the costs and benefits of our module. On the basis of a framework of standard methods we probably have to expand the available methods due to the specific questions mentioned above. Development of e.g. special software test tools could be necessary and will be considered in the project plan.

References

1. Accot, J. and Zhai, S. (1999): Performance Evaluation of Input Devices in Trajectory-based Tasks: An Application of The Steering Law. In Conference Proceedings: Conference on Human Factors in Computing Systems, ACM Press, pp. 466–472.
2. Akamatsu, M. and MacKenzie, I.S. (1996): Movement Characteristics Using a Mouse With Tactile and Force Feedback. International Journal of Human-Computer Studies (45), pp. 483–493.
3. Arsenault, R. and Ware, C. (2000): Eye-Hand Co-ordination with Force Feedback. In CHI 2000 Conference Proceedings: Conference on Human Factors in Computing Systems, ACM Press, pp. 408–414.
4. Campbell, C., Zhai, S., May, K. and Maglio, P. (1999): What You Feel Must Be What You See: Adding Tactile Feedback to the Trackpoint. In Human-Computer Interaction – Proceedings of INTERACT '99, IOS Press, pp. 383–390.
5. Cooper, A.(1999): The Inmates Are Running the Asylum: Why High Tech Products Drive Us Crazy and How To Restore The Sanity, Indianapolis, Indiana, SAMS.
6. Dennerlein, J. T., Martin, D. B. and Hasser, C. (2000): Force-Feedback Improves Performance For Steering and Combined Steering-Targeting Tasks. In CHI 2000 Conference Proceedings: Conference on Human Factors in Computing Systems, ACM Press, pp. 423–429.
7. Fraser, J. and Gutwin, C. (2000): A Framework of Assisive Pointers for Low Vision Users. Fourth Annual ACM Conference on Assistive Technologies (ASSETS 2000), ACM Press, pp. 9–16.
8. http://www.immersion.com
9. http://java.sun.com
10. http://java.sun.com/products/java-media/3D/index.html
11. MacKenzie, I. S. (1995): Input Devices and Interaction Techniques for Advanced Computing. In Virtual environments and Advanced Interface Design, pp. 437–470, Oxford University Press, Oxford, UK.
12. Miller, T. and Zeleznik, R. (1998): An Insidious Haptic Invasion: Adding Force Feedback to the X Desktop. In proceedings of the 11th annual ACM symposium on User Interface Software and Technology, ACM Press, pp. 59–64.
13. Mithal, A.K. and Douglas, S.A. (1996): Differences in Movement Microstructure of the Mouse and the Finger-Controlled Isometric Joystic. In CHI 1996 Conference Proceedings: Conference on Human Factors in Computing Systems, ACM Press, pp. 300–307.
14. Oakley, I., McGee, M. R., Brewster, S., and Gray, P. (2000): Putting the Feel in "Look and Feel". In CHI 2000 Conference Proceedings: Conference on Human Factors in Computing Systems, ACM Press, pp. 415–422.
15. http://www.sensable.com
16. Trewin, S. (1996): A Study of Input Device Manipulation Difficulties. 2nd ACM/SIGCAPH Conference on Assistive Technologies, ACM Press, pp. 15–22.

Designing User Interaction for Face Tracking Applications

David Chatting and Jeremy Thorne

Content and Coding Lab, BTexact Technologies, Adastral Park, Ipswich, UK,
{david.chatting,jeremy.thorne}@bt.com

Abstract. Face tracking could potentially become a powerful new technology in the Interaction Designer's arsenal, providing new modes of access to computing and communications. However, such interfaces could be misused in ways that confuse and worse misrepresent users, leading to poor interactions. Careful considerations of the human face, facial expression and the characteristics of tracking systems are required to ensure responsible design. This paper begins to explore this necessary field of study highlighting the need for future experiments. We conclude that due to the imperfect nature of tracking systems, feedback is immensely important and we consider methods of providing this.

1 Introduction

Apparatus for tracking the facial expressions of humans have existed for some years [1][2]. Traditionally these have been captured using markers placed on the face, however using computer vision techniques markerless systems are becoming viable [3][4]. The inconvenience and expense of marker based systems limit their use to specialist applications with large budgets, the markers are quite obtrusive and inhibit performance. Markerless systems enable many to have access to this technology using only an inexpensive camera, in a variety of locations and situations. There are a wide variety of applications including: mobile videophones, animation, broadcast television, accessibility aids and affective computing. Using such technology there is the scope for creating extremely natural computer interfaces and communication systems. However, we present some properties of such applications and argue that these systems require special attention.

Our current work is in the development of a markerless face tracking system for the Prometheus project [5] a three-year collaborative LINK project under the Broadcast Technology Programme funded by the UK DTI and EPSRC. The project includes markerless face and body tracking, actor and clothing model animation, scene construction and three-dimensional display technologies. It is seeking to build a virtual production chain for 3D television to encapsulate these technologies.

The Prometheus face tracker uses a single camera to capture the actor's performance in real-time, using a tracking algorithm derived from [6] and described by [7] from which it derives the head's orientation and the facial expression.

P. Forbrig et al. (Eds.): DSV-IS 2002, LNCS 2545, pp. 196–207, 2002.
© Springer-Verlag Berlin Heidelberg 2002

This can be encoded as an MPEG-4 stream [8] and be used to animate a photo-realistic head.

The thoughts presented in this paper are the result of our own experience using markerless face trackers over the past three years and the application of research from other areas to this new field. As yet we have not verified our hypotheses by experiment. Our hope is to open up this area for further study.

2   Characteristics of Face Tracking Systems

It is important to understand the nature of face tracking systems in order to design responsible user interfaces.

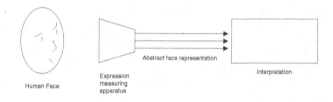

Fig. 1. A minimal face tracking system

Figure 1 shows the minimal set of components required for a face tracking system: the human face, expression measuring apparatus generating an abstract representation of that face and an interpretation stage, where that representation is manipulated. Arising from these components any face tracking system will exhibit the combination of their characteristics, regardless of its form. We also consider there to be two broad system classes; Facial Human-Computer Interaction (FHCI) and Human-Human Computer Mediated Facial Communication (CMFC). This section considers the general characteristics and those of the two classes.

2.1   Characteristics of a Minimal Face Tracking System

The human face is an extremely mobile and flexible device. There are enough muscles in the face to distort the face into over 7,000 unique facial actions [9]. The face can move fast too: the smallest perceptible expression exists for as little as one twenty fifth of a second [10]. However the features and their placement on the human face are universal and in addition Darwin [11] claimed that there are universal expressions that are recognised cross-culturally.

The expression measuring apparatus transforms the motion of the face into some abstract representation of the expression. There will inevitably be some optimal operating conditions e.g. the actor is within the field view of the camera, the lighting is correct, and some constraints on the range of facial motion detectable.

We will only consider here computer-based systems where the representation of expression will exist as a digital sequence. The sampling process required to convert continuous facial motion to a discrete digital sequence will necessarily introduce quantisation noise and have a limited frequency response.

The effects of digital representation are also dependent on the specific representation we use for expression. There are many existing schemes including: FACS (Facial Action Coding System) [12], MPEG-4 FAP (Facial Animation Parameter) [8], AMA (Abstract Muscle Action) [13] and FAML (Facial Animation Markup Language) [14]. Any conceivable scheme is an abstraction of reality and as such will be more or less suitable for some applications. For instance, systems implementing the original FACS scheme can not represent asymmetric expressions, but FACS can provide a high-level description suitable for machine classification of emotion [12]. The MPEG-4 FAP coding gives a lower level representation defining the displacement of known control points on the face along significant axes. Associated displacements along other axes must be interpreted and cannot be represented explicitly in the coding. Since MPEG-4 does not prescribe how the interpretation should proceed, expression reconstruction will vary between implementations.

Inevitably there is delay between the expression being posed and its complete interpretation. There will be a trade-off between accuracy and system performance, which will be made according to the application; be it real-time or off-line.

Given the mobility of the face, the issues of representation, and the current state of the art, it seems likely that any tracking system will remain 'blind' to some classes of expression in the foreseeable future. The tracking equipment and representation of expression should be chosen to match the requirements of the ultimate application.

2.2   Characteristics of Facial Human-Computer Interaction (FHCI)

We consider computer interfaces driven by human face tracking as belonging to a class of interaction that Nielsen calls "Non-command User Interfaces" [15]. These interfaces are those which do not rely on formal commands and syntax, such as command lines and WIMP (windows, icons, menus and pointer) paradigms. Examples of such are gesture recognition systems [16], eye tracking [17] and ubiquitous computing scenarios [26].

Eye tracking systems are cited as an example of a non-command style interface and many of the issues surrounding eye tracking are also common to face tracking. For example, care must be taken with the interpretation of eye tracking data, since the movement of the eye is far more complex than the viewer is consciously aware. The eye makes frequent saccades and even when fixated there is significant jitter. Also the distinction between exploratory and intentional eye fixations must be made to avoid the 'Midas touch' effect where everything the user looks at is selected, for instance every folder is automatically opened even when the user is merely reading its name [17].

Similarly with facial expression we are generally not directly aware of our current expression and many of the movements we make are not necessarily intentional. It is impossible to disengage the face, it is 'always on' even when distracted by something else. Jacob [17] suggests the use of a 'clutch', pressing a key or making some other form of input to release the face.

While the eyes have a clear mapping as a pointing mechanism, the face is much more flexible and the high level concepts expressed are less easily mapped to computing tasks. More "natural" input modes does not necessarily lead to more intuitive interfaces.

2.3   Characteristics of Human-Human Computer Mediated Facial Communication (CMFC)

Human-Human Computer Mediated Communication is concerned with enabling real-time communication between two or more people via computers and networks.

We seek face to face communication as it facilitates non-verbal communication, which helps us gauge the attitude of the other party with more confidence. The generation of facial expressions is in part at a subconscious level, it is difficult to have conscious control of the expression on the face all the time. For instance, few people can artificially pose a convincing smile, as they are unaware of the spontaneous timings that occur. Our true emotions are hard to suppress and professional actors are considered skilful, so we tend to trust the facial cues we see.

However, where facial expression is represented digitally, it can be duplicated, stored and modified; as with any other binary sequence. We can imagine a face tracking system where dishonest faces are caught by the system and replaced with amiable expressions. It becomes possible to manipulate consciously something that was largely out of control and digital facial expression no longer naturally reflects our true emotions. There is clearly much scope for deceit. We should therefore question whether there is any basis for trust in this scenario. Will this devalue this means of communication in virtual environments?

Donath [18] discusses many implications of using representations of a human face in the design of computer-mediated human interactions; including the perception of identity, social identity and expression.

In certain circumstances it might become desirable to hide our facial identity or only selectively reveal different attributes to different people [19] due to the large number of social assumptions inferred from the appearance of a face.

3   Feedback in Face Tracking Applications

From our previous analysis, face tracking applications necessarily have limited capabilities. The user should be informed of these by a responsible application, allowing them to adjust their behaviour with predictable and so learnable results. We introduce here three feedback mechanisms through which the user can become aware of an application's capabilities: Reviewable, Reflective and Indirect.

3.1 Reviewable (Non-real-Time Feedback)

An application is Reviewable if it allows the user to review how the machine has interpreted the face, before it is committed. This essentially allows the "undo" function with which we are familiar in the desktop paradigm. Making the actions of the user reversible inspires confidence and promotes the exploration of the systems. Examples of this include animation applications where face tracking data can be iteratively reviewed and tweaked by the artist until the desired character manipulation is achieved.

However, there are some classes of face tracking applications where this review is impossible. For instance in real-time telecommunication, where the machine must interpret the face and reconstruct a rendering of it at the far end instantaneously.

3.2 Reflective (Real-Time Feedback)

An application is Reflective if it presents to the user a real-time view of the machine's interpretation of their face. This should allow the user to learn the cause and effect relationships and the degree of expression that stimulates large or small responses. Most face tracking systems today incorporate some augmented self-view indicating the computer's interpretation [3][4].

However, there are some applications where feedback in this way is difficult. Consider a machine where a display (optical, aural or haptic) can not be physically incorporated into the device due to the small size, or other operating constraints.

3.3 Indirect

In everyday social situations we can not see our own facial expression, only gauge them indirectly via the response of others. Applications may be designed using a similar feedback approach.

For example consider Figure 2 which illustrates a communication system. Participant 1 only sees a reconstruction of Participant 2's face and vice-versa; hence each is aware of the other's reactions. However as we have previously discussed, any system will have capabilities and limitations, being blind to some faces and misinterpreting others. There are two stages of interpretation in this loop, each potentially having a different set of characteristics, both of which can manipulate the reconstructed face in unintended ways. This may result in misunderstanding and confusions, especially where each participant is unaware of the limitations of the underlying system. With necessarily imperfect interpretation stages this style of feedback may prove to be hazardous.

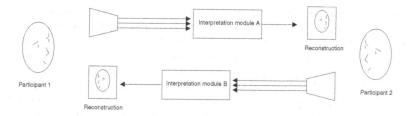

Fig. 2. Indirect Feedback Example

4   Face Tracking Applications

We present here a set of scenario applications and discuss their properties and design challenges with reference to the application classes and possible feedback mechanisms that could be employed.

4.1   Mobile Videophone (CMFC)

The problem of reliable translation of facial expression is of particular importance in telecommunications applications; for instance a mobile videophone arrangement where the participants' faces are tracked and drive virtual masks visible to the other. The most obvious advantage of tracking and virtual masks over coding the video is the reduced bandwidth requirement for high level descriptions of facial motion. In this scenario the expression must be interpreted in real-time and sent immediately to the receiver, so this can not be made a reviewable system. We would discourage designing an indirect system for the reasons discussed. However it may also be difficult to implement a reflective system using video due to small screen sizes for handheld devices, and alternative output modes should be investigated.

Here the system has an obligation not to misrepresent. Given this situation there must be overwhelming evidence before a "dangerous face" is pulled. A dangerous face is one that expresses an extreme emotion, for example an angry snarl or a suggestive wink; these may differ between cultures. Human translators of conversation face a similar problem, although in most circumstances they are able to verify the speaker's intention. For these reasons it would seem likely that such systems would tend to be used for relatively passive exchanges.

4.2   Animation (CMFC)

In this scenario the goal is to create a stream of data that can be applied to the head of an animated character to recreate a believable sequence of facial expressions, emotions and lip synchronisation. The quality of the data is of the greatest importance; in terms of frame-rate, range and smoothness of expressions. Thus the priority of the tracking application is to capture the raw data with as much precision as possible, so that post processing to determine facial motion has the greatest chance of success. That is to say capturing uncompressed frames of video from high quality cameras at a high frame rate, that can be analysed by the computer at its leisure after capture has completed. Gleicher discusses the challenges of using vision techniques to drive animation in [20].

We feel a degree of real-time feedback is important to demonstrate to the user that the video input is acceptable. The system should also be reviewable to enable the user to determine and correct (by re-recording or manual editing) any misinterpretations made in the processing.

4.3   Broadcast Television (CMFC)

Using face tracking to code video or drive 3D facial models as part of a virtual production chain such as Prometheus [5] provides advantages for broadcast (e.g. news or chat shows) in that the output can be scaled more intelligently for different transport networks and end devices.

As with animation, quality is the main priority, and a delay while processing occurs is acceptable. However if the broadcast is "live" then there is no opportunity to review the computer's interpretation before broadcast. The real-time reflective interface must show sufficient detail to allow the producer to make quick decisions whether to trust the output of the computer. Particularly with news broadcasts it is again important not to pull dangerous faces with extreme emotion that might put a different slant on the content. Hence a fairly emotion-less, cautious approach is required in the tracking.

4.4   Accessibility Aids (FHCI)

Non-intrusive facial tracking provides obvious advantages for users who find traditional input devices - keyboard and mouse - difficult or inconvenient to use. Jacob [17] suggests that for quadriplegics or for users whose hands are occupied (e.g. pilots) eye or face tracking interfaces provide significant benefit, even if they perform only minimally well because the users have no other available method of input.

If face tracking is to be used for controlling user interfaces, the tracking algorithm must run in real-time but not absorb a major share of computational resources, since other tasks must be able to run concurrently [21].

This scenario provides some inherent feedback since the user can see how the interface has responded to their actions through menu option choosing, or navigation through virtual worlds. However, because of the potentially dangerous consequences of some of these actions, the interface should also be at least partly reviewable with the options to confirm actions or undo mistakes.

Existing techniques have focused on gross head movements or eye tracking, but as techniques and computing power improves the ability to detect and process more subtle gestures and expressions will become possible. This will lead to richer interaction and an increased bandwidth flow into the computer [22]. However the gestures must be natural to avoid fatigue through repeated actions.

4.5   Affective Computing (FHCI)

Affective computing is concerned with responding appropriately and sensitively to user's emotions. For example MIT [23] have developed a CD player that plays music based on the listener's current mood and listening preferences. There are applications of affective face tracking in ubiquitous computing environments, where the aim is to make many computers available throughout the physical environment, while being effectively invisible to the user.

Emotions and mood changes are generally gradual and the computer will only become 'aware' of a user's mood over time. Hence continuous real-time feedback is inappropriate, as is occupation of a large portion of the available display space. A small visual token (e.g. icon, light, flag) or ambient change may be more useful. Existing research has already addressed classification of emotion in faces [10][24] and real-time systems that combine this with face tracking are feasible in the near term.

5   Discussion

Having presented our views on the classes of face tracking applications, some mechanisms for providing feedback and some sample applications we now discuss some of the specific issues that arise for interaction design.

5.1   Manifested Interfaces

We observe that the interaction may be constrained and not fully natural. Consequently face tracking applications must expose the system's capabilities and make them apparent to the user so as to allow their actions and the reaction to be predictable and learnable. The interface mustn't suggest too much or too little functionality.

It has been suggested that "Face-to-Face Implies no Interface" [25]. Ideally this would be the case, but practically given the imperfect nature of the tracking and representation, we consider a manifested interface to be essential. We must prevent failures in the system being responsible for escalating failures in the communication. In their description of Ubiquitous Computing, Mynatt and Nguyen [26] note that, "...systems rely on implicit sensing that is naturally ambiguous or error-prone, it is up to the designer to help users comprehend the, sometimes variable, limitations of the system."

In dealing with error, there are two ways in which the tracking can fail: the system can lose track of the subject (system failure), or it can misinterpret a facial expression (false reading). In the first, the computer is aware of its failure and alerting the user can be straightforward. In the second, the computer makes a mistake on a single frame, but doesn't realise it. In addition the user may also not spot that the fed back interpretation is incorrect. That is, we suspect that if in general the tracking is perceived to be correct, quick aberrations will go unnoticed. However in CMFC systems, the recipient may notice the mistake, particularly if the expression posed was "dangerous". Therefore if the system is to allow dangerous faces and not cautiously filter them out, then feedback must specifically alert the user to their creation.

In situations where a reflective interface is appropriate a 'Magic Mirroring' metaphor provides a useful tool. The user can see themselves on the screen as they face it; it appears like a mirror which augments the view with computer generated markers. For this metaphor to be apparent the screen and camera must be collocated and the image must be flipped horizontally in order to maintain the illusion. This is the interface currently employed in the Prometheus tracker.

The choice of markers is important. Some existing systems [3] overlay the face with spots that reflect the image features being tracked. The augmented face appears as if physical markers had been stuck to the skin. This interface seems appropriate if the captured data is used to reconstruct the same feature motions on a remote model of the face, however no clue is given as to the computer's understanding of the expression. For example in lip tracking enough information could be inferred from the points around the lips to correctly reconstruct the face, but the unseen classification as happy or sad could be incorrect. Here, more iconic markers may provide an advantage by giving the user a pictorial representation of the computer's understanding - for example a symbol depicting creased lines overlaid on the brow to represent the detection of a frown. It is possible to use multiple reflective interfaces to give the user feedback pre and post interpretation. For example displaying of both the feature detection and the 3D puppet.

If a true reflective interface is not appropriate - because the display is occupied by something else, or there is no display - subtle feedback is still possible through the use of colour, sound or other modes.

5.2   Interface Paradigms

As we have demonstrated there are a number of application scenarios in which we feel it is desirable to have face tracking based interfaces. In these circumstances the expression capture equipment (for instance camera) may be the primary or sole input. The traditional interface paradigms of pull down menus and windows have been designed for mouse and keyboard operations and a new set of primitives may be needed for face tracking based interfaces. The use of face tracking, or any other "natural" communications mode, does not necessarily result in intuitive interaction and requires careful design, as we discussed in relation to the problems of eye tracking.

5.3   Initialisation

Attention must be given to the design of the initialisation stage in which the face is first acquired. The delay and impositions of this stage must be endured by the user each time the interface is used. Here the face cannot be augmented or labeled as the system is not yet aware of it. Practically since the computer is still searching for the face a greater amount of processing is taking place that will inevitably lead to lower frame rates and an increased latency in the feedback. In a more ubiquitous scenario where the user is not directly aware of the interface, the initialisation becomes hidden and this acquisition stage becomes even more complex, as there can be no dialogue between human and machine.

5.4   Expression Representation

The internal representation for the interpreted facial expression should be chosen to match the target application. For instances where reconstruction or playback of the face is required low-level prescriptive representations are good since this reduces the requirements on the player to understand or interpolate the data. If understanding is required then progressively higher level representations and the tools to convert between these interpretations are crucial. High level representations are also key to reducing bandwidth requirements.

5.5   Trust in CMFC Systems

Trust is a fundamental notion a communications system, that the message sent matches the message received. In a CMFC system we have considered the dangers of the system pulling "dangerous" faces unintended by the user and the consequences for the discourse.

Additionally we highlighted the responsibility of the system to have overwhelming evidence before such a face is sent. Additionally, where the sampling rate of the face acquisition is below that of the speed at which an expression can pass over the face we observe that brief expressions can become unobserved. Ekman finds "micro-expressions" of approximately 25th of a second to often disclose dishonest behaviour, where normal "macro-expressions" often last between half and a few seconds [10]. In such a system the recipient could not perceive these micro-expressions and would not be given the opportunity to judge the other as dishonest. However, Ekman showed visual lie detecting to be a difficult task at which many of us are poor.

All these factors mean that a CMFC user should be prepared for the representation of the other to deviate from reality. A responsible application should endeavour to match the users' perception of the systems trustworthiness, with reality. It is our hypothesis that too much trust will be attributed to the system, leading to communication difficulties. Assuming that to be true, we would need to introduce an element of mistrust in the user's mind.

There are many ways in which we build trust relationships and there has been work to extend these notions to computer interfaces [27][28]. We are considering promoting a little mistrust in the interface, which requires that many of these principles are actively broken. In a face interface there are a number of ways in which we might change the user's perception of trust, mainly through the appearance of the head, it's animation and the voice. One approach may be to deliberately make the face unrealistic in ways that prompts the user to reassess it, perhaps inserting strange (although not deliberately disturbing) animation. Continuing studies are required to investigate these ideas further.

6   Conclusion

Face tracking technology is available now. With advances in markerless techniques there are many situations in which it can be valuably applied. We do not believe that these "natural" interfaces inherently provide natural and intuitive interaction, considering there to be serious design challenges that must be addressed in responsible systems. We have sought to identify a number of these challenges and further work is required to test our hypotheses.

We have considered how the limitations of these systems necessitate feedback, to provide the user with a view of the machine's understanding and interpretation of the scene, aiding learning of its capabilities. We have discussed three possible feedback mechanisms; Reflective, Reviewable and Indirect. We consider that a Reflective or Reviewable interface should be implemented whenever possible. Additionally, we have described a set of scenarios where face tracking may be applied with reference to these concepts.

Given the human face as an extremely subtle communications mode, we have highlighted some means in which it can be distorted through a FHCI and considered how we might design such applications to promote a little mistrust to prevent communication problems.

Acknowledgements. We are grateful to Anna Haywood, Daniel Ballin, the members of Content and Coding Lab and the Future Content Group of BTexact Technologies for their advice and comments.

References

1. Bergeron P and Lachapelle P: 'Controlling facial expressions and body movements', in Advanced Computer Animation, SIGGRAPH 1985 Tutorials, ACM, New York, Vol. 2, pp. 61–79 (1985)
2. SimGraphics: Virtual Actor System (1994).
3. Eyematic Interfaces: FaceStation – http://www.eyematic.com
4. Seeing Machines: FaceLAB – http://www.seeingmachines.com/
5. Price M and Thomas G A: '3D virtual production and delivery using MPEG-4', International Broadcasting Convention (IBC 2000), Amsterdam, IEE Conference Publication (2000) – http://www.bbc.co.uk/rd/pubs/papers/pdffiles/ibc00mp.pdf
6. Machin D J: 'Real-time facial motion analysis for virtual n teleconferencing', Proc. of the Second Int. Conf. on Automatic Face and Gesture Recognition, IEEE Comput. Soc. Press, pp. 340–344 (October 1996).
7. Mortlock A N, Machin D, McConnell S and Sheppard P J: 'Virtual Conferencing', in Sheppard P J and Walker G R (Eds.): 'Telepresence', Kluwer Academic Publishers, Boston, pp. 208–226 (1999).
8. MPEG-4 – http://www.cselt.it/mpeg/standards/mpeg-4/mpeg-4.htm

9. Scherer K and Ekman P: 'Handbook of Methods in Nonverbal Behavior Research', Cambridge University Press, Cambridge, UK (1982).
10. Ekman P: 'Why don't we catch liars?' Social Research, Vol. 63, No. 3, pp. 801–817 (1996).
11. Darwin C (edited by Ekman P): 'The Expression Of The Emotions In Man And Animals', Oxford University Press, ISBN 0195112717 (1998).
12. Ekman P and Friesen W V: 'Facial action coding system: A technique for the measurement of facial movement', Consulting Psychologists Press, Palo Alto, California (1978).
13. Magnenat-Thalmann N, Primeau E and Thalmann D: 'Abstract Muscle Action Procedures for Human Face Animation', The Visual Computer, Vol. 3, No. 5, pp. 290–297 (1988).
14. Facial Animation Markup Language – http://www.vhml.org/
15. Nielsen J: 'Noncommand User Interfaces', Communications of the ACM Vol. 36, No. 4 pp. 83–99 (April 1993).
16. Sato Y, Kobayashi Y and Koike H: 'Fast tracking of hands and fingertips in infrared images for augmented desk interface', Proc. IEEE FG2000, pp. 462–467 (2000).
17. Jacob R J K: 'Eye Tracking in Advanced Interface Design', in Barfield W and Furness T (Eds.): 'Advanced Interface Design and Virtual Environments', Oxford University Press, Oxford, pp. 258–288 (1995).
18. Donath J: 'Mediated Faces', in Beynon M, Nehaniv C L and Dautenhahn K (Eds.): 'Cognitive Technology: Instruments of Mind Proceedings of the 4th International Conference', CI 2001, Warwick, UK (August 2001).
19. Coutaz J, Crowley J and Bérard F: 'Eigen-Space Coding as a Means to Support Privacy in Computer Mediated Communication', Proc. of INTERACT'97, Chapman & Hall (1997).
20. Gleicher M, 'Animation From Observation: Motion Capture and Motion Editing', Computer Graphics 33(4), pp 51–54 (1999).
21. Bradski G R: 'Computer Vision Face Tracking For Use in a Perceptual User Interface', Intel Technology Journal, 2nd Quarter '98 (1998).
22. MIT AI Lab Vision Interfaces – http://www.ai.mit.edu/projects/vip/index.htm
23. Healey J, Picard R and Dabek F: 'A New Affect-Perceiving Interface and Its Application to Personalized Music Selection', Proc. of the 1998 Workshop on Perceptual User Interfaces San Fransisco, CA (November 1998).
24. Essa I and Pentland A: 'Facial Expression Recognition Using Image Motion', in Shah M and Jain R (Eds.): 'Motion Based Recognition', Kluwer Academic Publishers, Computational Imaging and Vision Series (1997).
25. Burford D and Blake E: 'Face-to-Face Implies no Interface', 2nd South African Conference on Human-Computer Interaction (CHI-SA2001) (September 2001).
26. Mynatt E D and Nguyen D H: 'Making Ubiquitous Computing Visible', position paper at ACM CHI 2001 Conference Workshop: 'Building the Ubiquitous Computing User Experience' (2001).
27. Cassell J and Bickmore T: 'External Manifestations of Trustworthiness in the Interface', Communications of the ACM, Vol. 43, No. 12 (2000).
28. Riegelsberger J and Sasse A: 'Face it-Photos don't make a Web Site Trustworthy', Extended Abstracts of CHI2002 (2002).

Performance Evaluation as a Tool for Quantitative Assessment of Complexity of Interactive Systems

Xavier Lacaze, Philippe Palanque, David Navarre, and Rémi Bastide

LIIHS-IRIT, University of Toulouse III
118, route de Narbonne
31062 Toulouse Cedex 4, France
{lacaze, palanque, navarre, bastide}@irit.fr

Abstract. While research in the field of HCI seems to focus on usability issues real-time safety critical systems deals with specific requirements that make usability only one of the main factors that designers of such systems have to deal with. Indeed, reliability and efficiency are also to be taken into account. This paper presents extensions to previous work done in the field of formal description techniques for interactive systems by adding temporal elements to the ICO formalisms. These temporal elements are used for evaluating in a quantitative way the relative efficiency of different designs. Such results are aimed at supporting design decisions in the design process of safety critical interactive systems.

1 Introduction

Interactive systems development process promotes iterative user centred design allowing for testing and evaluating the usability of the system with users. This kind of approach leads to usable systems that meet user needs and user activity. The primary factor favoured by such approaches is usability and it is well agreed upon that this is at the detriment of other factors such as reliability, safety or efficiency.

It is reasonable and even desirable to have usability as the primary factor when business-oriented applications are considered. Indeed, such applications target routine tasks and a large number of potential users. Considering usability as a primary concern allows reducing training costs that could be prohibitive due to the large number of users. Those applications generally present the property of reversibility i.e. that most actions can be reversed in order to put the application back to its previous state.

In this paper we present a set of temporal extension to the ICO formal description technique allowing for quantitative modelling of time in order to assess the complexity of several designs. These extensions are exploited within a methodological framework that provides guidelines on where temporal elements should be embedded in the models.

P. Forbrig et al. (Eds.): DSV-IS 2002, LNCS 2545, pp. 208–222, 2002.
© Springer-Verlag Berlin Heidelberg 2002

The content of this paper has been developed within a military-funded research project on command and control interactive systems for drones (UAV[1]) for which the three factors usability, reliability and efficiency are of equivalent concerns. However, due to confidentiality concerns and by sake of simplicity we will present the use of the temporal extensions and its related framework on a simple case study.

Section 2 briefly recall the basic principles of the ICO formal description technique and its case tool PetShop.

Section 3 describes the case study based on currency converters which aims at presenting how the temporal extensions introduced in the ICO formal description technique are integrated into models.

Section 4 is dedicated to performance evaluation and present how ICOs temporal extensions allow for quantitative and objective assessment of complexity and efficiency between two different designs.

Section 5 presents conclusions and perspectives for future work.

2   Interactive Cooperative Objects

This section is dedicated to the ICO formal description technique First an informal presentation of the formalism is given. Temporal aspects that have been added to the ICO formalism are then presented.

2.1   Informal Description

The Interactive Cooperative Objects (ICOs) formalism is a formal description technique dedicated to the specification of interactive systems [3]. It uses concepts borrowed from the object-oriented approach (dynamic instantiation, classification, encapsulation, inheritance, client/server relationship) to describe the structural or static aspects of systems, and uses high-level Petri nets [9] to describe their dynamic or behavioural aspects.

In the ICO formalism, an object is an entity featuring four components: a cooperative object with user services, a presentation part, and two functions (the activation function and the rendering function) that make the link between the cooperative object and the presentation part.

Cooperative Object(CO): a cooperative object models the behaviour of an ICO. It states how the object reacts to external stimuli according to its inner state. This behaviour, called Object Control Structure (ObCS) is described by means of high-level Petri net. A CO offers two kinds of services to its environment. The first one, described with CORBA-IDL [16], concerns the services (in the programming language terminology) offered to other objects in the environment. The second one, called user services, provides a description of the elementary actions offered to a user, but for which availability depends on the internal state of the cooperative object (this state is represented by the distribution and the value of the tokens (called marking) in the places of the ObCS).

---

[1] Unmanned aerial vehicle

Presentation part: the Presentation of an object states its external appearance. This Presentation is a structured set of widgets organized in a set of windows. Each widget may be a way to interact with the interactive system (user → system interaction) and/or a way to display information from this interactive system (system → user interaction).

Activation function: the user → system interaction (inputs) only takes place through widgets. Each user action on a widget may trigger one of the ICO's user services. The relation between user services and widgets is fully stated by the activation function that associates to each couple (widget, user action) the user service to be triggered.

Rendering function: the system → user interaction (outputs) aims at presenting to the user the state changes that occurs in the system. The rendering function maintains the consistency between the internal state of the system and its external appearance by reflecting system states changes.

ICO are used to provide a formal description of the dynamic behaviour of an interactive application. An ICO specification fully describes the potential interactions that users may have with the application. The specification encompasses both the "input" aspects of the interaction (i.e. how user actions impact on the inner state of the application, and which actions are enabled at any given time) and its "output" aspects (i.e. when and how the application displays information relevant to the user). Time-out transitions are specials transitions that do not belong to the categories above. They are associated with a timer that automatically triggers the transition when a dedicated amount of time has elapsed. When included in a system model such transition is considered as a system transition. They can also be included in a user model representing spontaneous user's activity. Such modelling is presented in section 4.2.

An ICO specification is fully executable, which gives the possibility to prototype and test an application before it is fully implemented [14]. The specification can also be validated using analysis and proof tools developed within the Petri nets community and extended in order to take into account the specificities of the Petri net dialect used in the ICO formal description technique.

2.2   Temporal Aspects

One of the advantages of Petri nets with respect to other formal description techniques is their possibility to handled in a very efficient way both qualitative temporal aspects (before, after, meanwhile, ...) and quantitative temporal aspects (seconds, dates, stochastic durations, ...).

Quantitative time is what is used for performance analysis. Several temporal extensions to basic Petri nets have been proposed in order to deal with it.

Adding Time to Transitions. Adding time to transitions is the first extension that has been proposed. The basic idea in this work is that firing of a transition can take time. This has been used, for instance, in the field of flexible manufacturing systems in which an action performed can take some time.

First work described in [19] proposed timed transitions. For each transition of this type in a Petri net, a predefined firing time (d_i) added. Tokens used for firing are reserved by the transition and when time has elapsed the transition is fired removing the reserved tokens.

Other work such as [11] proposed to add indeterminism in duration. For each transition an interval $[t_{min}, t_{max}]$ is added to each timed transition. In this temporal model the models tells that the firing of the transition takes more than t_{min} and less than t_{max}. The precise amount of time taken for the firing is unknown at first.

Adding Time to Places. The main problem of this temporal extension is that it requires managing two different markings for the Petri net: available marking and reserved marking. This makes most of the analysis techniques not available for these Petri nets dialects, and this is the reason why we do not use it.

Stochastic Time. Generalized Stochastic Petri Nets [1] associate time to transitions. However, GSPN feature two main differences with respects to the Petri nets presented above. The first one is the stochastic nature of duration i.e. duration follows a distribution of random variables. The second one is the fact that time is associated with tokens. When a transition is fireable a timer is set with each token that makes this transition fireable. The timer goes on until the duration associated to the transition has elapsed. If the tokens are still available then the transition is fired. Meanwhile the tokens may have been used by other conflicting transitions that would prevent the timed transition for being fired when the time has elapsed.

The work presented in this paper exploits this kind of time modelling in Petri nets. We have already used temporal extensions for performance evaluation in previous work [17] and this work builds upon it and goes further by embedding values coming from human factors studies and by providing a framework for going from a system model to a extended system model dedicated to performance evaluation.

3   Currency Converters Case Study

Prior to the arrival of the Euro (1st January 2002) and its apparition as a real currency in the wallets of most citizens in the Euro zone, banks and other organisms distributed to their clients various currency converters. As quite a lot of people have been using extensively these systems recently, we have decided to take them as the basis for the description of how performance evaluation techniques could help in evaluating the complexity of interactive systems.

3.1   Informal Presentation of Currency Converters

As a basis for the performance evaluation we have taken two currency converters provided by the same bank. The first one was issued by the bank before about one year prior to the deployment of the Euro while the second one was issued in late fall 2001. The first one is on the left-hand side of Fig. 1 while the second one is on the right-hand side.

Fig. 1. Two-currency converters

The first one is a basic currency converter. It is made up of buttons for inter-action and one display. A button labelled "rate " is also available for changing the rate between Franc and Euro (this offers the opportunity to use this con-verter for other currencies than Euro). The use of the converter is quite trivial and can be guessed after few trials. A new rate can be set by first entering the digits for the rate and then pressing the button "Taux[2]". A conversion can be made by entering the digits corresponding to the amount you want to convert and then pressing either the red button with the € (for Euros) symbol or the red button with the F (for Francs) symbol.

The second convertor offers more user services than the first one. Some but-tons appear both on the first and the second system but four main features make it significantly different: (1) it proposes two displays, (2) it is impossible to change rate, (3) it allows for basic arithmetic operations, (4) it provides a function calculating the change to be given back to customers (with the buttons labelled "Paie[3]" and "Chg[4]".

The second converter is modeless as both displays are used at the same time. The user only has to select which one is the input as the upper display is dedicated to Euros and the lower one to the national currency (actually French Francs). To use this converter, your first action is to choose the currency for which you need to enter an amount. Pressing the button labelled "€ /F" switch the input to the currently unselected display.

3.2 Tasks Models

Tasks models are used in this paper to represent possible activities from the user that will be used for comparing the respective efficiency of the converters.

We use ConcurTaskTree notation to represent tasks [18]. CTT represents hierarchical level and temporal relation between elementary tasks. CTT defines four types of tasks: abstract task (represented by a cloud), system task (rep-resented by a computer), interaction task (represented by a user in front of a

---

[2] "Taux" is the French word for rate
[3] "Paie" is the French word for pay
[4] "Chg" stands for change

computer), and a cognitive task (depicted as a user). These tasks are organised hierarchically from abstract to concrete levels. The temporal relationships between tasks of the same level are described by means of temporal operators. $T1|||T2$ indicates the tasks can be performed in concurrent way. $T1[]T2$ describes a choice between two tasks. $T1 >> T2$ is used for describing a sequence of tasks i.e. $T2$ only starts when $T1$ is completed. $T1[] >> T2$ expresses a sequence between tasks and that some information from the task $T1$ are transmitted to task $T2$. $T1[> T2$, when $T2$ starts the task $T1$ is disabled. $[T1]$ models the fact that task $T1$ is optional while $T1^*$ model iteration.

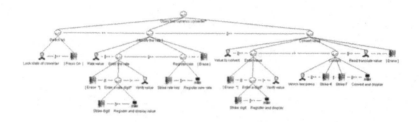

Fig. 2. A task model for the first currency converter

Task Models for the Currency Converters. We construct the task model with the CTT graphical editor called CTTE. We decomposed the task model of the first convertor in two major subtasks: change rate and convert a value, see Fig. 2. A task model for the second currency converter is presented in Fig. 3. This task model is divided into two subtasks: verify the mode and convert a value.

These two task models feature commonalities and discrepancies. Both task models contain the subtask "convert a value" whereas the other subtasks are specific for each currency converters ("change the rate" and "verify the mode").

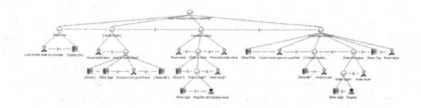

Fig. 3. A task model for the second currency converter

Scenarios. Using CTT Environment it is possible to extract scenarios from the simulation of task models. We have extracted the same scenario (convert 10 Euros) from these two tasks models. In order to take into account the values the scenario is transformed into a high level Petri net (the same dialect as the one used for modelling the ObCS of the objects). As the tasks are not supported in the same way by both currency converters two Petri nets have been built. These two Petri nets are presented in Fig. 4.

Fig. 4. On the left, Petri net model of the scenario (convert 10 Francs): first converter. On the right, Petri net model of the scenario (convert 10 Francs): second converter

Common actions between scenarios are: switch on the converter, read the value, press_1 and verify press_0 and verify, read the converted value. For the first scenario we suppose that the correct rate has been already set. If this is not the case the user will have to test the converter for instance by entering a basic value (one Euro for instance) and checking it with respect of some knowledge he/she has or some external material. Such considerations make a huge difference between the two devices under consideration but for space reasons we do not report them here.

3.3   System Model

In this section we describe, using high-level Petri Nets, the system model of each currency converter. We do not use all the features of the ICO formalism as performance is mainly based on sequences of actions rather than on presentation aspects (even though the layout of the converters will also be used). Input is also not considered as for both converters inputs only occur through similar press buttons.

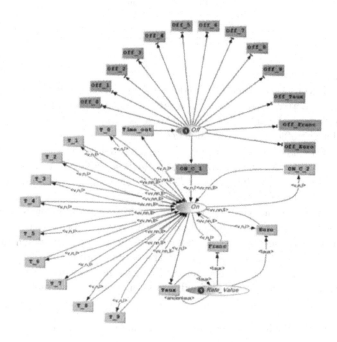

Fig. 5. The system model of the first convertor

First System Model. As introduced in section 2.1 the model of the system integrates external and behavioural aspects. Fig. 5 presents the behaviour of the first currency converter. For sake of simplicity the dot button is not represented. Table 1 presents an excerpt of the activation function of the first currency converter. First column of the activation function represents the interface element (widget), second column the event corresponding to user action on the widget. And the last column represents user services and its related transition in the ObCS.

Table 2 presents the rendering function i.e. how internal state of the system is presented to the user. The first column contains the name of the place in the ObCS, the second column describes the state change (for instance a token has been removed from a place or has entered a place) and the last column the method triggered when the state change occurred.

Table 1. Excerpt of the activation function of the first currency converter

Widget	Event	User Service (transitions)
Button ON/C	Press	On (ON_C_1, ON_C_2)
Button F	Press	Francs (Franc)
Button €	Press	Euros (Euro)
Button 0	Press	Zero (T_0, Off_0)
All buttons	Press	...
Button Taux	Press	Taux

In the initial state place Off holds a token representing the fact that the system is not active. Place *Rate_value* holds a token too and this token is not of a basic type as it contains a value (the actual value of the rate). By default we consider the official rate 1€= 6,55957 FF.

Places *Off* is of basic type i.e. the tokens in the place are simple token carrying no value. At the contrary place *On* is a triplet $< v, n, l >$, where v represents the current value presented on the calculator, n the number of digits and l the last button pressed.

Whatever state the system is in, at least one transition for each user service is always available. This is typical of non software systems where it is impossible to disable interactive objects. In classical interactive systems when no transition related to a user service is available the corresponding interactive object is disabled. Transition *Time_out* is not related to a user service. It is a temporal transition that fires after a predefined period of time after becoming available.

Table 2. The rendering function for the first currency converter

ObCS Element	Feature	Rendering method
Place *Off*	token entered	Show(off)
Place *On*	token entered	Show(token)
Place *Rate_Value*	token entered	No rendering

Second System. In order to take a common ground for comparing the converters, in system model of the second converter we do not take into account new functions with respect to the first one (+, -, * and /). Activation function rendering functions and system model of the second converter are not presented here for space reason, but can be found on a larger version at the page http://lihs.univ-tlse1.fr/lacaze.

A significant difference in the behaviour of the second converter is related to button € /F. Indeed, according to the state of the system pressing this button changes mode from Euro to French Francs and vice versa (if there is no value entered) or plays as a backspace key removing the last digit (if a value has already been entered).

The system model of the second converter is more complex in terms of number of Petri net components. Place Off models the same behaviour as for the first converter. Places Euro and Franc models the two input modes for the system. Indeed, user can choose to enter either Euros or Francs. When the system is switched on the token in place Off moves to place Euro (default input mode). Tokens that can be stored in places Euro and Franc are not of Basic type. Type of the tokens is a 5-uplet $< f, e, n, p, l >$. f (resp. e) contains the amount in French Francs (resp. Euro), n represents the number of digits in the zone entered, p the value typed-in by the user after pressing Paie button, and l the last button pressed by the user. This variable is dedicated to performance evaluation activity as it stores the last position of user's finger on the converter.

4   Performance Evaluation

This section is dedicated to performance analysis. This analysis aims at evaluating among several designs which one is the most efficient. In this work, efficiency is measured according to the time needed for a user to perform a scenario which is extracted from a task model. Therefore, hereafter, we use the tasks models, the scenarios and the system models presented above.

4.1   Performance Analysis Framework

In order to be able to make some performance analysis, it is necessary to add temporal information to the models. With respect to previous work we proposed in this field [17] this paper presents a framework describing how such temporal information should be added to the models and present precisely how accurate information could be calculated using human factors results on human performance.

4.2   Temporal Information Modelling

Main user model like for instance ACT-R [2], EPIC [10], and the human model processor [7] promote decomposition of user's behaviour in three main components. According to terminology used in [7] these three components are: Motor processor, Perceptual Processor and Cognitive Processor.

Motor Activity. Human factors' resources we have been investigating two approaches: the keystroke-level model [6] and Fitt's law [8]. The first approach has not been used in this study as it is more suitable for interaction with keyboard and mouse and only provides average values. We decided to use Fitt's law is more accurate and its application to motor movements can be directly exploited. Fitt's law is presented in Formula (1) and is more general as it represents an index of difficulty for reaching a target (of a given size) from a given distance.

Movement time for a user to access a target depends on width of the target (W) and the distance between the start point of the pointer and the center of target (A).

$$MT = a + b * \log_2(2A/W) \tag{1}$$

For predicting movement time on the systems under consideration constant are set as follows: $a = 0$ and $b = 100ms$ (mean value for users).

Table 3. Temporal values (in ms) for user interaction using Fitt's law (first converter)

	0	1	2	3	4	5	6	7	8	9	On	Frans	Buro	Rate
0	100	151	236	319	251	234	340	310	324	365	210	322	350	389
1	151	100	219	319	151	236	328	251	234	344	244	283	332	366
2	236	219	100	219	244	151	244	289	251	289	161	300	300	309
3	319	319	219	100	328	236	151	344	234	251	244	332	283	366
4	251	151	244	328	100	228	328	151	244	332	289	222	315	320
6	234	236	151	236	228	100	228	251	151	251	251	268	258	234
8	340	328	244	151	328	228	100	332	244	151	228	315	222	320
7	310	251	289	344	151	251	332	100	228	228	332	142	300	277
8	324	234	251	234	244	151	244	228	100	228	310	215	215	194
9	365	344	289	251	332	251	151	328	228	100	332	300	142	277
On	210	244	151	244	289	251	289	332	310	332	100	332	332	379
Frans	258	319	336	368	258	256	351	178	251	336	368	100	292	246
Buro	389	368	336	319	361	256	258	336	251	178	368	292	100	246
Tau	367	304	317	304	297	262	297	255	172	255	367	187	187	100

According to the restrictions made of the second converter (not taking into account +, -, *, /, .) each converter is made up of 14 buttons as modelled in Fig. 5. Fig. 6 presents the system model extended in order to embed temporal information for Table 3. For sake of simplicity we do not present the complete system model but only an excerpt with the first four numerical buttons. The entire Petri net contains all the interactive buttons.

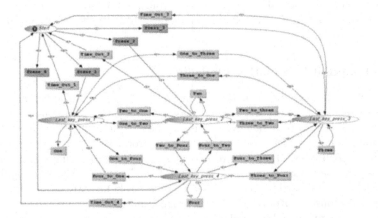

Fig. 6. System model extended to incorporate physical time values

In order to be able to calculate time movement using Fitt's Law, we have to know where the movement starts and where it finishes. This is the reason why we have added transitions for representing all the possible movement on the currency converter as time, for instance, is different when pressing button 1 immediately after pressing button 9 or 2 (the figures are shown in Table 3). For instance time needed for pressing button 1 after button Franc is 283ms. For reading the value from table in Table 3 first find the "from" button in first row (here button 1) then read value corresponding to the "to" button (here button Franc). It is interesting to note that the order in which buttons are pressed is of importance value for first Franc the button 1 is 319ms). This is due to the different size of the physical buttons (see Fig. 1).

However, as some buttons are of identical size, simplifications could be made. For instance as buttons 2 and 4 are similar, in Petri net model in Fig. 6 transition Four_to_Two and Two_to_Four could be merged, but in order to keep models consistent and more understandable we keep them distinct. This is an architectural consideration making models independent from temporal values. This is mandatory for software user interfaces as presentation part is subject to frequent modifications during development.

Cognitive Time. Fig. 7 presents the Petri net model for users' cognitive activity embedding temporal information. As for system model important information is associated to transitions. The model is very simple as cognitive activity is quite limited for using the devices. However, more complex models could be considered for modelling information that must be remembered as in [13]. Temporal information in the Petri net presented in Fig. 7 comes from work presented in [7]. In this work mean cycle time for cognitive activity is set at 100ms [25~170ms] and this temporal value is associated to transition Generic_cognitive_activity. Another parameter that is also taken into account in the model is the comparison of values. Russo [20] estimates that time needed for comparing two numbers is about 33ms. In this paper, the exact temporal values are not very important as the aim of performance evaluation is to compare two existing devices. In the development process of those systems the accuracy of values is usually much more important as it might drive design decisions.

As stated above, some transitions in a cognitive model can be of type Time-out. For instance, as introduced in [12] due to memory overload some information might be lost in short term memory. This would be modeled (in a user cognitive model) using a Time-out transition automatically removing information from the place representing information in short term memory.

Fig. 7. On the left, cognitive model. On the right, perceptual model

Perceptual Time. As for cognitive activities, temporal information for perceptual activity is added to a dedicated Petri net model (see Fig. 7). Here again temporal value comes from work described in [7] and is associated to the transition. Average time needed for the eye to capture information is about 100ms but is subject to users' variability [50~200ms]

System Time. The work presented here does not take into account time related to system execution. Indeed for such systems we can consider that the with respect to user's time frame system time is not significant. This is a more general problem of including time in models and both simulating and computing performance evaluation on those models. However, in classical interactive systems such as the ones we are considering in the project, the system is distributed and time plays a significant role with respect to user's interactions. O'Donnell, in [15], shows that user's strategy depends on machine's response time. In order to deal with these temporal issues we use the temporal policy proposed in generalised stochastic Petri nets [1]. Another advantage of this approach is that is allows for modelling temporal unpredictability in distributed systems by using the stochastic capabilities of this Petri net model.

4.3 Exploiting Temporal Information

Temporal information that has been added to models is exploited through scenarios. Indeed, each action appearing in a scenario can be related to a transition is one of the models.

Table 4. Table describing effective time for each action or transition (First scenario)

Scenario 1	Type of transition	Time
Verify_state_converter	Cognitive	100 ms
Press_on	Physical	251 ms
Read_10_Francs	Perceptual	100 ms
Press_1	Physical	244 ms
Verify_value	Cognitive	100 ms
Press_0	Physical	151 ms
Verify_value_1	Cognitive	100 ms
Choose_key_to_press	Cognitive	100 ms
Press_E	Physical	353 ms
Read_value	Perceptual	100 ms
	TOTAL	1599 ms

Table 4 describes the mean time needed by a user for performing the selected scenario using the first device. The mean time needed to perform the scenario with the second device (not presented here) is 1699 ms.

It can be easily seen that there is not a huge difference in performance of the selected scenario between both devices. Other scenarios might have been impossible to perform (for instance convert 10 francs into British pound) with second device but easily performed with the first one. Scenarios including more complex activities such as giving change back in a different currency can only be performed using second converter.

This is why we have been using task models as a basis for scenarios description. The idea is to extract interactively scenarios from task models and to use temporal extensions added to system, cognitive and perceptual models to perform, in an automatic way, performance evaluation. This phase requires a bridge between task model and system model as presented in [14] and the extension of PetShop in order to process models extended with temporal information.

5 Conclusion

Work presented in this paper deals with performance evaluation techniques for interactive systems evaluation. We have presented a generic framework for adding temporal information to models and for relating tasks models to system models through scenarios. This work has been presented through a simple case study allowing us to show how such temporal information can be added in a systematic way and how it can be used for assessing designs.

The framework proposed is currently used more thoroughly by taking into account more complex user's cognitive and perceptual models. For instance we take into account the impact of practice using stochastic time. Such information is extracted from [7] and called power law of practice in which time T_n to perform a task on the nth trial is $T_n = T1_n^{-r}$, where $r = .4 \ [.2 \sim .6]$.

Similarly, time needed for a user to choose between different alternatives is not constant and increases with the judgement or decision to be made function of probabilities of different alternatives. Decision time T increases with uncertainly about the judgments or decision to be made as described in [7]. We are currently working on integrating these temporal elements in PetShop in order to integrate performance evaluation as a interactive assessment technique for helping designers to rationally and quantitatively select design options.

Acknowledgements. The work presented here is fully funded by French defence agency (Direction Générale pour l'Armement) under contract #00.70.624.00.470.75.96. Special thanks to Didier Bazalgette for precise information about the field of command and control systems in military field.

References

1. Ajmone Marsan, M., Balbo, G., Conte, C., Donatelli, S., Franceschinis, G.: "Modelling with generalized stochastic Petri nets." Wiley 1995.
2. Anderson, J.R.: "Rules of the Mind." Lawrence Erlbaum Associate 1993.
3. Bastide, R., Palanque, P., Le, D.H., Muñoz, J.: "Integrating Rendering Specifications into a Formalism for the Design of Interactive Systems." In *Proceedings of 5th Eurographics workshop on "design, specification and verification of Interactive systems", DSV-IS'98, Abdington, U.K., 3–5 june 1998*, Springer Verlag 1998.

4. Bastide, R., Sy, O., Palanque, P., Navarre, D.: "Formal specification of CORBA services: experience and lessons learned." In *Proceedings of ACM Conference on Object-Oriented Programming, Systems, Languages, and Applications (OOP-SLA'2000); Minneapolis, Minnesota USA.*, ACM Press; 2000: 105–117. ACM SIG-PLAN Notices. v. 35 (10)).

5. Bastide, R., Navarre, D., Palanque, P.: "A model based tool for interactive proto-typing of Highly Interactive Environement." Demonstration paper in *Proceedings of ACM CHI 2002*, conference companion, ACM Press.

6. Card, S.K., Moran, T.P., Newell, A.: "The Keystroke-Level Model for User Per-formance Time with Interactive Systems." In *Communications of the ACM*, 1980; 23(7): pp. 396–410.

7. Card, S.K., Moran, T.P., Newell, A.: "The Model Human Processor: An Engi-neering Model of Human Performance." In *Handbook of Perception and Human Performance*, 1986: pp. 1–35.

8. Fitt, P.M.: "The information capacity of the human motor system in controlling the amplitude of movement." In *Journal of Experimental Psychology*, 1954; 47: pp. 381–391.

9. Genrich, H.J.: "Predicate/Transition Nets." In K. Jensen and G. Rozenberg (Eds.) *High-Level Petri Nets: Theory and Application.*, Springer Verlag, Berlin, pp. 3-43.

10. Kieras, D., Meyer, D.: "An Overview of the EPIC Architecture for Cognition and Performance with Apllication to Human-Computer Interaction." In Human Com-puter Interaction 1997, 12, pp. 391–438.

11. Merlin, P., Farber, D.J.: "Recoverability of communication protocols-Implications of a theoretical study." 1976; 24, (9).

12. Miller, G.A.: "The Magic Number Seven Plus or Minus Two.", 1956, 63, pp. 81–97.

13. Moher, T., Dirda, V., Bastide, R., Palanque, P.: "Monolingual, Articulated Mod-eling of Devices, Users, and Interfaces." In *Proceedings of DSV-IS'96, Namur, Belgium*, Springer Verlag; 1996: pp. 312–329.

14. Navarre, D., Palanque, P., Bastide, R., Sy, O.: "Structuring Interactive Systems Specifications for Executability and Prototypability." In *Proceedings of 7th Eu-rographics Workshop on Design, Specification and Verification of Interactive Sys-tems, DSV-IS'2000, Limerick, Ireland, 2000*, Lecture notes in Computer Science n° 1946, Springer Verlag 1996.

15. O'Donnel, P., Draper, S.W.: "How machine delays change user strategies.", ACM SIGCHI Bulletin. 1996; 28(2): pp. 39–42.

16. OMG: "The Common Object Request Broker: Architecture and Specification." In *CORBA IIOP 2.2 /98-02-01*, Framingham, MA (1998).

17. Palanque, P., Bastide, R.: "Performance evaluation as a tool for the design of inter-active systems." In *Proceedings of Conférence internationale IEEE SMC CESA'96*, IEEE Press Université de Lille, 9-12 July 1996. p. 328–333.

18. Paternò, F.: "Model-Based Design and Evaluation of Interactive Application.", Springer Verlag 1999.

19. Ramchandani, C.: "Analysis of asynchrounous concurrent systems, an Overview.", Ph.D. Thesis, MIT, Project MAC TR-120, 1974.

20. Russo, J.E.: "Adaptation of Cognitive Processes to Eye Movements. Eye Move-ments and Higher Psychological Functions.", Lawrence Erlbaum; 1978.

Blending Descriptive and Numeric Analysis in Human Reliability Design

Shamus P. Smith and Michael D. Harrison

The Dependability Interdisciplinary Research Collaboration
Department of Computer Science, The University of York
York YO10 5DD, United Kingdom
{Shamus.Smith, Michael.Harrison}@cs.york.ac.uk

Abstract. Scenario based design allows for the early elicitation of requirements and can be helpful in the design phase of system development. It is typical for cycles of iteration to be used to refine a design so that it more closely meets its requirements. Such refinements are in terms of the original requirements specification and any new requirements that have been identified. However, not all defined requirements are equally essential. Although descriptive methods for scenario analysis can be used to highlight new requirements, it can be difficult to evaluate the impact of these new requirements.

In this paper, we exemplify this problem and investigate how numeric methods can be used to highlight the impact of consequences identified by descriptive scenario analysis. An example from the context of human reliability analysis is presented.

1 Introduction

Iterative methods are common in the development of computer systems. Within software system life-cycles, such methods are used to refine the current state of the design of a system so that it more closely meets its requirements. This is particularly evident in the design and prototyping phases of a system's development. In this paper we are concerned with the design phase and with the step preceding a new iteration being applied to a design. By design iteration we mean the process of applying newly identified or refined requirements to an existing design. In the literature there are many candidate methods for design analysis (for examples see [15]) that provide mechanisms for identifying the requirements for alternative and/or new designs. These methods need to provide two components: the new requirements and the rationale for the application of the new requirements.

Typically, design analysis techniques evaluate the current design and look for problems (for example usability issues [8]). The identified problems are used to construct recommendations to solve design problems. However, before these recommendations can be considered and applied as new requirements, it is necessary for some rationale to be provided. Therefore after the application of a design analysis technique, there are three issues that need to be addressed:

P. Forbrig et al. (Eds.): DSV-IS 2002, LNCS 2545, pp. 223–237, 2002.
© Springer-Verlag Berlin Heidelberg 2002

1. Does the analysis technique provide a structure, for the identified problems, to allow the designer to successfully argue/defend the recommendations for redesign?
2. Which of these recommendations are *most* important, i.e. preferred requirements, for the new design?
3. Is it possible to optimise the work effort for the redesign by using the two issues above to focus on the critical new requirements?

These three issues are at the core of the work that is discussed in this paper. We are particularly interested in the arguments that can be developed through this process to support the identification of new requirements and to focus the redesign process.

In this paper we investigate a simplified example in the domain of designing for human reliability. However, we consider that the issues involved are scalable to larger problems and over other domains. The format for the remainder of this paper is as follows. Section 2 introduces the work described in this paper in the context of system design and the application of new requirements. Next we define the example context, human reliability analysis (HRA), and the design analysis technique we have applied (Technique for Human Error Assessment – THEA [10]) including a small example. This will be followed, in Section 4, by a discussion of the descriptive arguments that can be developed from the THEA analysis. A treatment of statement belief, expert judgement and requirement impact will then be presented. Section 5 will introduce a numeric approach (Human Error Assessment and Reduction Technique – HEART [17]) and demonstrate its application to the issues raised by the THEA analysis. In Section 6, we investigate how the descriptive and numeric approaches we have considered can be generalised and briefly describe their application in an alternative domain. The paper concludes with a summary of conclusions.

2   System Design and New Requirements

In this paper we are interested in the use of scenario based design, where cycles of scenario descriptions can be used to refine the current state of a system design so that it more closely meets its requirements and potential faults are eliminated in this context. We have been investigating the choice of requirements to integrate into a design before the next iterative cycle of design evaluation is attempted.

At this stage of the design process problems leading to faults will have been identified. These may be viewed as new requirements for a redesign. However, not all requirements are equal and whether these requirements must be addressed first is a matter for expert judgement. Some requirements may be considered essential to any redesign and others may have only minor consequences for the development [13]. It is common for the consideration of these issues to be approached in an ad hoc manner. For example, the use of problem clusters, as part of change analysis, to identify change needs [16, pg 96]. This is problematic as traceability for the design decisions can be lost in the subjective nature of such techniques.

In this paper we explore how quantification of new design requirements may be used to reinforce descriptive scenario analysis and will discuss its limitations. In order to have a demonstrable example, we have scoped our work to one area of interest for system dependability: human reliability analysis (HRA). One part of the design phase where human reliability analysis is of interest is where analysis is applied so that new design requirements can be identified. When functional deficiencies are found in a design, their correction leads directly from the design specification. However, a design that is complete in terms of functionality may still have problems in terms of human reliability. Human actions are inherently more difficult to regulate and predict than the functions of the technological components [6]. What we are interested in is identifying how vulnerable a system is.

3   Human Reliability Analysis

Kirwan [7] observes that one of the primary goals of human reliability analysis is to provide a means of properly assessing the risks attributable to human error and for identifying ways of reducing system vulnerability to human error impact. He notes that this is achieved through three processes:

- Identifying *what* errors can occur (Human Error Identification)
- Deciding *how likely* the errors are to occur (Human Error Quantification)
- Enhancing human reliability by *reducing* this error likelihood (Human Error Reduction)

We have investigated how descriptive methods for human error identification can be augmented by techniques that generate numeric values for human error quantification. The aim is to enhance human reliability through the reduction of human errors that these processes facilitate. In Section 5 we investigate a technique for human error quantification but before this can happen, we need to explore the process of human error identification. For this we are using a scenario based technique developed at The University of York called THEA [3,10].

3.1   THEA

THEA (Technique for Human Error Assessment) [3,10] is a technique developed to help designers of interactive systems to anticipate interaction failures or human errors that may be problematic once their designs become operational. The technique is intended for use early in the development life-cycle, as design concepts and requirements concerned with safety and usability, as well as functionality, are emerging [3]. Fields, Harrison and Wright [3] note that errors in human reliability can be regarded as failures in cognitive processing. They present an outline of a variant of Norman's [9] execution-evaluation model of human information processing (see Figure 1).

Five components from Norman's cyclic model are used as the basis for identifying ways in which human information can potentially fail. THEA consists of

Fig. 1. Cyclic model of human information processing

a checklist of questions about the performance of each of the cognitive components in relation to the use of the system with the aim of anticipating where cognitive failures might occur which lead to behavioural errors. These questions are applied to a scenario in order to help uncover places in the scenario where cognitive failure modes may occur. The steps used in this process are shown in Figure 2 (from [3]).

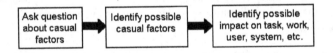

Fig. 2. Identification of potential errors

Pocock et al. [10] observe that "THEA explicitly takes contextual and cultural issues into consideration by means of usage scenarios. In this way it is hoped to elicit the way work is *actually* practised and not simply how designers *envisage* it as being practised." This scenario oriented approach distinguishes THEA from techniques that begin by generating error producing scenarios from models of users and domains (for example [4]). Due to space constraint, full coverage of THEA is not possible and the reader is directed to [3,10]. A THEA example for this paper will be presented in Section 3.3 but before we can apply this technique, we must specify the domain, and more specifically the scenario where this analysis is focused. Although the example we present is based in the physical world, the principles of the treatment apply over a broad range to environments including software systems.

3.2   The Domain and Scenario

The problem domain is in safety dependency issues on-board an oil tanker. In the scenario we are considering, the vessel has entered into some stormy conditions and the crew are preparing a lifeboat in case there is a need to abandon the vessel. Although the lifeboat can be launched from the ship's bridge, it must be manually primed beforehand. This involves a crew-member going on deck with a key to unlock the storage constraints/handles on the lifeboat. The key used in this task is also the key that is used to initiate the lifeboat launch from the ship's bridge.

3.3   Fragment of the THEA Analysis

Part of the THEA analysis from the scenario described in Section 3.2 can be seen in Figure 3. A THEA analysis is roughly split into eight components. Four sets of rows associated with the four cognitive failure areas discussed in Section 3.1 and four columns that make up the structure of THEA. These consist of the checklist questions, the causal issues, the consequences and any design issues. The questions column is the same for every THEA analysis and the other spaces are completed by the domain expert doing the analysis. For our example, we have only included a selection of questions taken from each of the four failure areas. In a full analysis, there are four *goals* questions, four *plans* questions, four *actions* questions and eight *perception, interpretation and evaluation* questions.

4   Qualifying the Issues

Analysis of a proposed design provides a set of identified issues/problems with the design. This may also be accompanied with some suggested solutions to deal with the identified issues. These recommendations have differing *force* as requirements for any redesign. Also there may be varying degrees of rigour in the specification of these recommendations that may affect any justification of their use as requirements. This rigour may influence the nature of the argument that can be constructed from the recommendations to support their implementation.

For each answered question, THEA produces a triple structure from design analysis comprising of the causal issues, associated consequences and suggested design issues. These triples can be presented as binary statements (either present or absent). Although the output of the THEA process is a set of recommended design decisions this is not an argument for design. THEA provides subjective declarations of possible design needs with an associated rationale that may be subject to external scrutiny. This can be problematic as the statements are constructed by experts and are summary statements and as a result bias can be introduced into the description. Also the level of detail that is described and the number of alternative solutions proposed is determined on a case by case basis at the expert's discretion.

Analysis of THEA, as a descriptive approach, raises two main issues. Firstly, what level of belief can be associated with the expert judgement and the structure provided by the technique? Secondly, how can we decide which recommendations are most important in the context of a redesign, i.e. what is the *impact* on the redesign process? These two issues will be considered in Sections 4.1 and 4.2 respectively.

Questions	Causal Issues	Consequences	Design Issues
GOALS, TRIGGERING & INITIATION			
G1: *(Is the task triggered by stimuli in the interface, the environment or the) task itself?)*	No, on command of the Captain.	The Captain may fail to trigger the crew-member to remove the handles on the lifeboat.	Some form of interlock should exist to prevent lifeboat launch if handles are not removed.
G4a: *(Can a goal be achieved without all its 'subgoals' being correctly achieved?)*	No, crew-member must return key to the Captain before the lifeboat can be initialised.	If the crew-member is disabled deck-side, the lifeboat can not be initialised.	Alternative method of initialisation.
G4b: *(Can a goal be achieved without all its 'subgoals' being correctly achieved?)*	No, crew-member must return key to the Captain before the lifeboat can be initialised.	Crew-member may lose the key.	Secure key to crew-member.
PLANS			
P2: *(Are there well practised and pre-determined plans?)*	Yes, crew training.	-	-
ACTIONS			
A3: *(Is the correct action dependent on the current mode?)*	Yes, crew-member must ensure they have key with them while on deck.	Potential danger from: 1) Bad weather 2) Premature attempt to launch lifeboat	Some means whereby crew-member must remove key from bridge before going on deck.
PERCEPTION, INTERPRETATION & EVALUATION			
I1: *(Are changes to the system resulting from user action clearly perceivable?)*	Yes, crew-member can see the removed handles from the lifeboat.	-	-

Fig. 3. THEA Fragment

4.1 Belief, Expert Judgement, and Structure

There is evidence of the questionable value of expert judgement [1] and the associated belief in those judgements. Hollnagel [5] notes that expert judgements are an uncertain and imprecise source of information. What THEA does provide is a structure for documenting the issues that have been elicited via the analysis. On an individual THEA question basis, the triples in the structure could be used to build an argument for the identified issue. For example, a dialectical argument (see Figure 4) could be constructed for the design issue "An alternative initialisation mechanism is needed" from entry G4a in Figure 3.

THEA does not provide a mechanism to show the dependence of individual statements. Therefore, if the statements are changed at a local level in the THEA structure, any global consequences are not necessarily evident. The filtering of any associated changes in the other THEA entries is completely at the whim of the expert and their knowledge of these consequences. Inconsistencies in the *issue, consequence* and *design issue* statements could easily be introduced that would then cast doubt on the validity of any associated design based arguments. Also there is no weighting on any of the statements in such arguments. Therefore all statements may be considered to be of equal importance. This is clearly not the case for most sets of requirements.

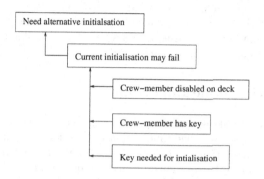

Fig. 4. Example dialectical argument from a THEA design issue (G4a)

4.2   Design Issue Impact

When there is a large set of requirements the challenge of determining the most appropriate requirements for a redesign is difficult. If a technique like THEA is used, its output is a set of design recommendations/issues. As noted by Pocock et al. [10] the design issues identified by THEA are "intended to assist designers reason about about errors at the early stages of a design before it becomes impractical or prohibitively expensive to effect a longer term design change or implement shorter term procedural 'fixes' or limitations."

Unfortunately, there is typically no indication of the worth of the design issues to any redesign. This worth must be determined by the reader of the recommendations. This can easily lead to an ad hoc approach to redesign and the selection of new requirements for a redesign. However, one approach to measuring worth is to examine the *impact* of applying candidate recommendations. Dearden and Harrison [2, pg 161] provide an informal definition of impact as:

the effect that an action or sequence of actions has on the safe and successful operation of a system.

Although THEA based analysis identifies the consequences of actions, it does not explicitly identify the impact on the new design. A notion of impact provides a means of discussing the consequences of possible human-errors, independent of the probability of these errors occurring within a particular design [2]. Not considering impact can be problematic when there are limited resources available. If there is only a limited budget, in terms of time, person power, money etc., then it may not be possible to implement all the recommendations. Also if new requirements are in conflict, which of them should be given priority when conflict resolution is attempted? Unfortunately, the use of ad hoc criteria to select new requirements may lead to the absence of possibly essential recommendations, in the analysis expert's judgement, not being selected. Ideally, it would benefit the redesign process to be able to get an objective view of the design recommendations. Hopefully, this would allow informed decisions to be made in terms of the scope of the design and the consequences for the system. The use of a numeric approach to this problem will be considered in the next section.

5   Quantifying Issue Importance

In this section the ranking of descriptive design recommendations provided by THEA is discussed through one candidate approach for HRA probability generation, namely HEART (Human Error Assessment and Reduction Technique) [7, 17]. Our aim is to investigate the addition of numerical precision to reinforce or highlight a notion of impact for the new requirements.

5.1   HEART Overview

HEART [17] is a quick technique for the quantification of human reliability. It is based on a review, by its author, of both literature on human factors and of experimental evidence showing the effects of various parameters on human performance. The technique defines a set of generic human error probabilities (HEPs) for different types of tasks. These are used as the starting point for HEART quantification. After a task has been classified, an analyst then determines whether any error-producing conditions (EPCs) are evident in the scenario under consideration. For each error-producing condition, the generic human error probabilities are multiplied by the error-producing condition which increases the human error probability. An example of HEART will be described in Section 5.2. The reader is directed to [7] for an overview of HEART and other techniques for human reliability analysis. They will not be discussed in detail here as our motivation for using HEART in our example is threefold. Firstly, HEART is based in human reliability analysis. This considerably eases the task of combining the data from the approaches and simplifies the job of our domain expert. Secondly, both techniques have been developed using the same rationale, that is, to be quickly applied methods to identify the "big" problems in a target domain. Thirdly, in the human reliability analysis community, HEART is readily understandable by all interested parties and is a way of supporting dialogue about human reliability estimates [10].

5.2   HEART Application to THEA

The descriptive approach, as discussed in Section 3.3, is suggestive of problems in our design. When applying human reliability analysis to high consequence systems, such problems are of particular concern. For the example in this paper, we have applied a HEART analysis to the THEA material presented in Figure 3 to refine any justifications for the redesign recommendations. In the scenario analysis four design issues were identified by the descriptive method, namely:

1. Interlock to prevent the launch of the lifeboat if the handles are not removed (G1 from Figure 3)
2. Alternative method of initialisation (G4a from Figure 3)
3. Secure the key to crew-member (G4b from Figure 3)
4. Some means whereby crew-member must remove key from bridge before going on deck (A3 from Figure 3)

The scenario is one of pre-evaluation preparation and the task is to remove the locks from the lifeboat. As a starting point for HEART analysis, the expert has identified that this task is one that is a routine, highly practised, rapid task involving relatively low levels of skill. HEART provides sets of generic categories [17] and for this example a starting value of human unreliability of 0.02 is defined. The next stage of a HEART analysis is the identification of error-producing conditions (EPCs) that are evident in the scenario and would have a negative influence on human performance. The domain expert examined the causal and consequence issues defined in the THEA analysis and identified three HEART EPCs that range over the design issues.

1. Little or no independent checking or testing of output
2. No obvious way to keep track of process during an activity
3. Hostile environment

Each EPC has an associated value (from [17]) that indicates the predicted effect and the extent to which unreliability will change due to the EPC. However, there are different levels of significance for any EPC. As the EPC values are general, an assessed proportion of effect significance is used to customise the specific relevance to the unreliability calculation. In this example, the domain expert has determined that the crew are highly trained and this includes training for bad weather. Hence, low significance values have been associated with the EPC effects. A summary of these values[1] can be seen in Figure 5.

Error Producing Condition	HEART effect	Assessed significance
Little or no independent checking or testing of output	*3	0.12
No obvious way to keep track of process during an activity	*1.4	0.25
Hostile environment	*1.15	0.12

Fig. 5. HEART EPCs and significance effects

HEART provides a formula to determine the final assessed effect for an error-producing condition:

---

[1] The HEART EPC effects are determined from [17] while the significance values were assessed by the domain expert.

((HEART effect $-$ 1) $*$ assessed significance) $+ 1 =$ final EPC assessed effect

The nominal likelihood of failure for a scenario based task is calculated by the product of the initial starting value of human unreliability (in our example, as noted above, 0.02) and the assessed effects of the relevant[2] error producing conditions. For example, take the design issue G1 from Figure 3 "Interlock to prevent the launch of the lifeboat if the handles are not removed". This issue is associated with two of the identified EPCs, firstly that as it is a solo self verified task *there is little or no independent checking or testing of output* (e.g. the Captain can forget to tell the crew-member to remove the handles) and secondly, the task is taking place in a hostile, stormy, environment. The product of assessed effects[3] of these two EPCs and the starting value of reliability is:

$$(1.24 * 1.018 * 0.02) = 0.025246 \text{ or } 2.52\%$$

This number is an absolute probability and is not of interest to us as such. However, the application of the HEART analysis to all the design issues provides us with a ranking for the problems identified by the descriptive method. The ranked design issues can be seen in Figure 6.

5.3   Numeric Impact

The priority listing can be used as part of the justification process for arguing about implementing redesign options in terms of maximising the reduction of negative consequences in a scenario. Hence, the ranking can be seen as a numeric measure for consequence impact.

From our scenario, having the crew-member remove the key from the bridge before going on deck is a critical action in terms of the task we have examined. A number of dangerous consequences can result if this is not carried out, for example the lifeboat may be launched while the handles are still in place. This would have a number of dangerous results including damage to the ship, the lifeboat and possibly a crew-member who was on deck. As the example is only a fragment of a full THEA analysis, the analysis of this action, and the resulting consequences if it is not carried out may have been lost in the documentation that results from a full descriptive analysis. The HEART analysis identifies this as the most important design issue in the sense that it is the most likely where human reliability is a contributing factor. What the HEART analysis provides is an indication of likelihood on the design problems but not any level of severity. Expert judgement is required to define any tradeoffs between the likelihood of a consequence (as indicated by the HEART analysis) and the severity impact

---

[2] Not all EPCs, and their associated assessed effects, are necessarily applicable for all design issues. For instance, in the following example only two EPCs are used to calculate the probability of failure.

[3] Each EPC assessed effect was calculated via the HEART formula ((HEART effect $-$ 1) $*$ assessed significance) $+ 1$ from [17].

the consequence has in the scenario context. However, the numeric method has refined the process of recommending design issues to allow the designers to make better, informed, decisions in the context of the redesign of the system.

Design issue	Likelihood of failure (%)
A3: Crew-member must remove key from bridge before going on deck	2.78
G1: Interlock to prevent the launch if the handles are not removed	2.52
G4a: Alternative method of initialisation	2.24
G4b: Secure key to crew-member	2.04

Fig. 6. Design issue rankings based on the HEART analysis

6   Discussion

In this paper, we have demonstrated how a descriptive analysis can be augmented by the use of a numeric technique to refine a measure of impact for identified problems in a design. In an example, numeric probabilities of human reliability are used to determine the significance of the descriptive recommendations. While we have been using THEA and HEART as examples of descriptive and numeric methods, to a certain degree, the use of these methods is arbitrary. There is a host of alternative methods that could be substituted in the current examples. What is of more importance is the process that is involved and the role that probabilities play. In our examples we have investigated the development/evaluation of new requirements for a design. This has involved two levels of refinement of the issues identified from example scenarios.

The first refinement is after the initial application of the descriptive method. Initially, the descriptive method identifies areas of concern, and/or issues that require attention, in the current design. The severity of these issues can be identified by impact analysis on the consequence of such issues. Although, as noted in Section 4.1, issues are commonly defined as *being of concern* without differentiation, in practice, expert judgement would be used to rate the severity of the issues, at least informally, based on the consequences of the issues. This informality, and therefore lack of credibility, is what we wish to reduce by the application of a numeric technique.

The second level of impact refinement is in the use of a numeric method to indicate probabilities that can be used to highlight the severity of a design deficiency. In our example we have been using HEART to identify the likelihood of failure due to human unreliability. As we are interested in dependable systems, the level of reliability can be used as an assessment criterion, e.g. if some component is very unreliable then this could be seen as having a higher justification for redesign.

The process we have described is focused on the initial use of a descriptive method and later refinement with a numeric method to provide quantitative precision. There are several advantages to this approach. Numeric methods commonly require specialised knowledge for their application. However, descriptive methods, by their informal nature, can be used by a larger user base. For example, THEA has been developed so that the causal model of human error and the questionnaire can guide a non human factors expert with domain expertise. Secondly, the application of numeric methods is notoriously time consuming and error prone. The use of descriptive methods to rank identified issues can reduce the need to apply numeric methods over all cases. Thirdly, methods that use generic probabilities or weighting factors (e.g. error producing conditions) are difficult to apply without bias. Changes in the generic variables chosen [2, pg 162], and changes in the environment or human performance data, can drastically alter the final probabilities. Numeric precision can easily be lost through inaccuracy. Although descriptive methods may not provide exact values, the ranking of issues may be all that is required.

Another advantage of the initial use of descriptive methods is the focus of work in context. The use of scenario based descriptive methods allows the elicitation of problem issues to be identified in the actual work context. This can be particularly useful if domain experts (with limited time commitment) are to be involved in the early stages of the development of a causal model.

An alternative approach is that presented by Galliers, Sutcliffe and Minocha [4]. Their approach is built around the construction of a Bayesian Belief Network (BBN) as a means of combining a set of generic influencing factors into a more formal and predictive model of human error. Their method comprises of ten stages:

1. Analyse domain to list key safety critical properties for the domain
2. Select influencing factors and build BBN as a causal model
3. Calibrate BBN and node probability tables
4. Select domain scenarios
5. Measure and estimate scenario variables
6. Input scenario variables into BBN
7. Analyse user's task
8. Input sub-goal complexity assessment
9. Run BBN model
10. Walkthrough sub-goals with design guidelines

For Gallier et al. [4], the application of BBN affords numeric precision early in the analysis process. As such, they can generate human error probabilities, in terms of *slips* and *mistakes* (see [12]), as part of the causal analysis process (Steps 1–9 in the list above). Step 10, the sub-goal walkthrough, combines the error probabilities with descriptive safety critical user interface guidelines to provide either generic requirement recommendations for new designs or evaluations of existing designs. Galliers et al. [4] summarise this process as "the BBN analysis first highlights particular scenarios where errors may occur due to a certain combination of operators and the task environment, then given a set of tasks, how the BBN predictions of mistake or slip-errors can be interpreted in a walkthrough of the user's task to consider which safety-critical guidelines might be recruited to the design."

Although BBNs can be difficult to build from scratch, Gallier et al. propose that generic BBN models can be calibrated and customised for individual domain analysis. This reuse of the BBN structures can considerably reduce the time needed to generate the error probabilities. Unfortunately, the development of the BBN causal model does require a large commitment on the part of the domain experts and users liasing with the BBN developers. Also much of the data for the BBN is derived from historical data, expert knowledge and user experience. These are subjective sources and it can be difficult to determine their accuracy. This is problematic when their input becomes an integral part of a process that promotes numeric precision, i.e. the use of probabilities.

Also one of the advantages of starting with a descriptive approach is that it can reduce the numeric calculations that are required. The output of Galliers et al's BBN is numeric data that is then reconciled with general design guidelines, task by task, in the context of a design. Although this may provide ample coverage of possible error scenarios, it may require more work on the part of the analyst to relate the results back to actual likely situations.

Where Gallier et al's process becomes descriptive, in the application of the numeric probabilities via the walkthrough process, the descriptive method we have investigated begins. While their numeric precision is blended through the descriptive analysis, ours is used to reinforce and refine the conclusions that are informally defined in the early stages of consequence analysis. However, the scope of the examples presented in this paper are relatively small and grounded in one domain, human reliability assessment. We propose that the issues raised in our analysis are of a broader appeal to other domains and systems. For example, in terms of generalising these issues, consider an alternative example in the design of a security software system.

A descriptive approach similar to the THEA checklist could be used to elicit issues in terms of security concerns, for example password validation, encryption schemes or access to physical systems. Scenario analysis could then be used to identify the consequences of failure in these issues and possible countermeasures defined as recommendations for a redesign. Ideally, we would expect that the descriptive checklist would identify areas of failure in the current design (for example, over Randell's classification of *errors*, *faults* and *failures* [11]) and encourage a dialogue for designers to develop problem solutions. Identifying the issues is the first step. Ranking the issues provides us with quantifiable rationale to proceed with a certain redesign solution.

When investigating the ranked security issues in terms of impact (which may identify "high risk" security concerns), a descriptive measure of their contribution to system failure goes hand in hand with determining more traditional numeric measures, i.e. probabilities to determine how often an event will happen or determining the *likelihood* that the event will not be dealt with. A combination of these measures affects the overall classification of the consequences to the system under analysis. For example, designers may not be concerned with the impact of issues that have a very low frequency (i.e. the ever present 10^{-9} of avionics and nuclear industry safety cases) or a low likelihood that the issue will be problematic (i.e. issues that may be easily detected and fixed).

However, notions of impact, frequency and likelihood provide a currency for negotiation for trade-off arguments and can be used to highlight issues where further consideration is required in design analysis (for example reuse [14]). This allows a richer view of the design requirements to be developed particularly in terms of known analysis technique problems such as expert judgement, issue dependence and the debatable value of numbers.

7   Conclusions

The elicitation of new requirements in an iterative design process is an important part of system development. The construction of arguments to support the rationale for using new requirements is also valuable. In this paper we have examined use of descriptive methods to build initial recommendations for redesign requirements and have investigated the use of numeric methods to enrich the justification for these requirements.

Although we have applied two particular techniques (THEA and HEART) in a single domain (human reliability analysis), we feel that this type of analysis process is applicable over other techniques and domains. The approach supports the redesign process and provides a mechanism to increase developer confidence that the work is progressing in a cost, e.g. time or effort, effective way.

However, the work presented in this paper is only an initial step. The numbers that are generated, and the associated descriptive statements, are all subjective measures and are influenced by expert judgement bias. Also any arguments that are developed from this process have only a limited notion of structure and are presented in a non-rigorous form. If an approach is to become useful in industry then a more formal structure and defined blending of the descriptive to the numeric will be required. These are issues that the authors are currently investigating.

Acknowledgements. This work was supported in part by the UK EPSRC DIRC project, Grant GR/N13999.

References

1. Peter Ayton. How bad is human judgement? In G. Wright and P. Goodwin, editors, *Forecasting with Judgement*. Wiley, Chichester, England, 1998.
2. A. M. Dearden and M. D. Harrison. Impact and the design of the human-machine interface. In *Eleventh Annual Conference on Computer Assurance: Compass'96*, pages 161–170. IEEE, 1996.

3. Bob Fields, Michael Harrison, and Peter Wright. THEA: Human error analysis for requirements definition. Technical Report YCS-97-294, The University of York, Department of Computer Science, 1997. UK.
4. Julia Galliers, Alistair Sutcliffe, and Shailey Minocha. An impact analysis method for safety-critical user interface design. *ACM Transactions on Computer-Human Interaction*, 6(4):341–369, December 1999.
5. Erik Hollnagel. *Human Reliability Analysis: Context and Control.* Computers and People Series. Academic Press, London, 1993.
6. Erik Hollnagel. *Cognitive Reliability and Error Analysis Method (CREAM).* Elsevier Science Ltd, Oxford, UK, 1998.
7. Barry Kirwan. *A Guide to Practical Human Reliability Assessment.* Taylor and Francis, London, 1994.
8. William M. Newman and Michael G. Lamming. *Interactive System Design.* Addison-Wesley, Harlow, UK, 1995.
9. D. A. Norman. *The Psychology of Everyday Things.* Basic Books, 1988.
10. Steven Pocock, Michael Harrison, Peter Wright, and Paul Johnson. THEA – a technique for human error assessment early in design. In Michitaka Hirose, editor, *Human-Computer Interaction: INTERACT'01*, pages 247–254. IOS Press, 2001.
11. Brian Randell. Facing up to faults (Turing Memorial Lecture). *Computer Journal*, 43(2):95–106, 2000.
12. James Reason. *Human Error.* Cambridge University Press, Cambridge, 1990.
13. Shamus P. Smith and Michael D. Harrison. Augmenting descriptive scenario analysis for improvements in human reliability design. In Gary B. Lamont, editor, *Applied Computing 2002: Proceedings of the 2002 ACM Symposium on Applied Computing*, pages 739–743, New York, 2002. ACM.
14. Shamus P. Smith and Michael D. Harrison. Improving hazard classification through the reuse of descriptive arguments. In Cristina Gacek, editor, *Software Reuse: Methods, Techniques, and Tools*, volume 2319 of *Lecture Notes in Computer Science (LNCS)*, pages 255–268, Berlin Heidelberg New York, 2002. Springer.
15. Ian Sommerville. *Software Engineering.* Addison-Wesley, Harlow, England, fifth edition, 1995.
16. R. J. Wieringa. *Requirements engineering: Frameworks for understanding.* John Wiley and Sons, Chichester, England, 1996.
17. J. C. Williams. HEART – a proposed method for assessing and reducing human error. In *9th Advances in Reliability Technology Symposium.* University of Bradford, 1986.

Towards a Ubiquitous Semantics of Interaction: Phenomenology, Scenarios, and Traces

Alan Dix

Lancaster University, Lancaster UK
alan@hcibook.com
http://www.hcibook.com/alan/papers/dsvis2002/

Abstract. This paper begins a process of building a semantic framework to link the many diverse interface notations that are used in more formal communities of HCI. The focus in this paper is on scenarios – single traces of user behaviour. These form a point of contact between approaches with very different models of interface abstractions or mechanisms. The paper looks first at discrete time models as these are more prevalent. Even here there are substantive issues to be addressed concerning different interpretations of timing that become apparent when you relate behaviour from different models/notations. Ubiquitous interaction, virtual reality and rich media all involve aspects of more continuous interaction and the relevant models are briefly reviewed. Because of their closer match to the real world, they differ less in terms of ontological features of behaviour.

1   Introduction

In the formal HCI literature, notations and modes of description seem to proliferate without limit, both system-oriented dialogue notations and more user-oriented goal and task descriptions. This paper aims to start a process of uncovering common semantic models for user interaction. There are several reasons for taking on this task:

Practical so that we can confidently use multiple notations applied to real systems and have a basis for interchange between support tools

Theoretical so that we can give common semantics to diverse notations, and so understand their overlaps and differences

Philosophical in grappling with these semantic roots, we begin to have a better grasp of the meaning of interaction

Furthermore, HCI is changing from the 1980's "one man and his machine" to a situation with many people and many devices embedded in a rich environment. Dourish calls this 'embodied interaction' and describes it as "interaction in real time in the real world" [16]. There is comparatively little formal work on these new devices and modes of interaction. Extending existing techniques is going to be a major challenge of the next few years and revisiting our semantic roots, one way to make sense of these multiplying computational phenomena

So this semantics aims to be ubiquitous in two senses:

P. Forbrig et al. (Eds.): DSV-IS 2002, LNCS 2545, pp. 238–252, 2002.
© Springer-Verlag Berlin Heidelberg 2002

- applicable to notations addressing different aspects of the user interface: task, goal, dialogue behaviour, system state, informal and formal
- applicable to types of interaction: GUI, wearable, mobile, ubiquitous, continuous and discrete

Saying "start process of uncovering common semantic models" does not mean there are no existing semantic frameworks. Indeed, many formal papers are based on semantic models rather than notations (e.g. the PIE model [11,12], the template model [36], LADA [15], status-event analysis [13,14]) and many notations have their own semantic models (e.g. trace semantics of process algebras).

However, as a discipline we have few common points to anchor our diverse activities, in contrast to, say, architecture, where the intended physical building links diverse representations (scale models, service schematics, artist's impressions, plans). This paper proposes that such anchor points are valuable and starts an explicit process of addressing the resulting agenda.

To some extent both the original PIE model and, in a different way, the syndetic modelling framework [6] purport to be universal models of interaction. In the current work the aim is to be less normative and more inclusive, setting up a framework for linking multi-paradigmatic analyses rather than proposing a single multi-faceted analysis.

This is potentially a huge task, so this paper focuses on a part, the phenomenological semantics of scenarios and traces of activity. Observable phenomena are often the easiest point of contact between different descriptions (as in the case of architecture). Furthermore, they are the point of contact between systems and people and so can relate user and system descriptions.

The next section revisits this rationale in greater detail, looking at why diverse notations exist (and should exist), the need for common semantics and the power and complexity of scenarios. Section 3 looks at discrete traces of activity, as are found in most formal approaches, and Section 4 considers continuous phenomena, which cannot be characterised in simple state transition schemes. In both cases we will be interested in the way that different levels and different kinds of description may be related to one another.

Note that this paper differs slightly from the version issued at DSVIS 2002. Some details have been removed from this version and the original did not incorporate the happening–instance distinction in the meta-model. The original paper can be obtained from the web address at the top of this paper.

2   Rationale

2.1   Bewildering Diversity

There is something about computing that encourages the proliferation of notations and the more formal the area the more different notations we find. This is certainly true in the more formal aspects of user interaction. There are good reasons for this:

- we need to state things precisely, whether we are talking about system states or user tasks, hence notations
- we have different concerns and so want to discuss easily various significant aspects, hence diversity

However, there are downsides:

- a danger of focusing on notations themselves as significant ('I can do this with mine' papers)
- a confusing plethora of incompatible notations understood only by their particular cognoscenti

The latter problem is especially clear in systems specification notations (pick up a previous DSVIS proceedings - do any two papers share a notation?), because they tend to be more detailed and differ in the formal expression of those details. In contrast user-focused notations (e.g. task/goal descriptions) often have 'fuzzy' boxes at the lower levels and allow annotation for complex interactions, making them easier to understand and employ by those outside the notation's cabal.

So, despite the strengths of diversity, there are problems both within the community of those who accept the importance of formalisation and even more so outside.

2.2   Common Semantics

This paper aims to address these problems in part by starting the process of producing a common semantic framework for user interaction notations.

Note this is not a 'unified notation' or even 'unified method' involving multiple notations, but instead a means of understanding and relating existing and new notations. Neither does this paper contain an extensive review of UI notations, although a common semantics certainly aids the process of comparing and selecting appropriate notations.

Semantic models have proved invaluable in many areas of computing. For example, denotational semantics not only produced a common framework for expressing semantics of programming languages, but led to a common vocabulary for describing them (binding environment, continuations etc.). Although not usually linked to theory, we see a similar 'coming together' at a practical level when modules written in different programming languages are compiled into linkable object files – a common semantic form – allowing multi-language programming.

The need for this common semantics is evident in several areas of UI modelling. For example, CTT and ICO have been linked using scenarios [25], which effectively established a *de facto* common semantics between them. Also in model checking, researchers always find themselves manipulating the UI notation to translate it into the notation for the model checker – is this the 'right' manipulation, would a different 'translation' give different results? As interaction becomes more rich and diverse the need for common underpinnings will increase.

Although semantic models are in some ways more abstract than notations, they are often easier to 'ground' in reality and easier to reach common agreement. This is because notations have many concerns over and above 'meaning': tractability, clarity of expression, maintenance etc.

Although we look for a common semantic framework, this does not mean a single unified model. Instead we will find a collection of complementary descriptions that map on to one another, following the pattern of many mathematical formalisms, with several complementary descriptions for 'the same' type of thing. For example, in topology we can start off with open and closed sets or with 'neighbourhoods' of points and from each derive the other. There is even a 'pointless topology' that has neighbourhoods as the primary objects and then 'recovers' points.

This pattern of multiple related formulations exists within several specific methods. Cognitive complexity theory [20] had a production rule description of goal driven user activity and a system description and verified that the goals can be achieved using the system. This was possible because the lowest levels of goal description involved explicit user actions which could be mapped to system commands. In Abowd's thesis [4] he used both an internal CSP-like process algebra description and also an external 'set of traces' description. These were not duals of one another, but instead specified different aspects of the required behaviour. The overall agent behaviour was constrained to satisfy both requirements. Again the linkage was possible because both descriptions share a common event vocabulary. In syndetic theory different interactors are described in their own 'microtheories' then linked by 'macrotheory' [6].

The linking between different semantic models is complicated by the fact that the concrete semantics of a description in a particular notation is governed not just by the formal semantics (where it exists) of the notation, but also the 'binding' of the constructs in the description to phenomena in the real world.

For example, consider, a two state toggle (figure 1.i) with two states, S1 and S2, and a single action, A, that moves back and forth between the states. This has a very clear formal semantics (figure 1.ii shows one behaviour assuming start state is S1).

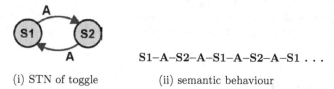

(i) STN of toggle   (ii) semantic behaviour

Fig. 1. Formal semantics of two state toggle

However, it makes a big difference whether we 'bind' this to the on-off state of a computer (S1=off, S2=on, A=on/off button). In this case all other activity in the computer is enabled/disabled by this state. In contrast, if we 'bind' this to a bold character format tick box in a word-processor dialogue box (S1=bold-off, S2=bold-on, A=click the tick box), the network is only enabled while the dialogue box is visible and may be operated concurrently with other parts of the interface.

Some of this binding may be specified within the formalism, but some level of binding is always outside the formal system itself.

2.3   Scenarios and Phenomena

Although notations differ markedly in the way in which they describe and structure interaction, they 'come together' at the surface level of user and system actions. This is inevitable as in the end an expert in the notation should be able to look at an actual trace of observable interface behaviour and say 'yes' or 'no' that is or is not valid with respect to this specification. In addition, internal structural elements, such as states, goals, tasks, internal events, can often be associated with points or portions of the trace – 'this happens then'.

This use of scenarios as lingua franca can be seen in various places. In the CTTE tool, rich scenarios are mapped onto ConcurTaskTrees (CTT) [31], which have then been used to generate more formal traces of actions to validate ICO user interface specifications in PetShop [25]. Model checking has been used or several UI notations including LOTOS and CTT [28,30], propositional production systems [2] and State Charts [22]. The advantage of model checkers over theorem proovers is that when they fail they give a counter example, in the form of a trace of actions – a scenario.

Looking further than UI notations and formalisms, scenarios have been used as a common focus for diverse design techniques [8], in the form of stories, incidents or snippets of interaction, they are part of the common language of more sociological descriptions of human behaviour, and several 'soft' descriptions such as patterns or cases involve some sort of scenario. So, focusing on 'what happened' or 'what might happen' also puts us in a better position to relate to this level of description.

Note that the focus on phenomenological semantics is not because it is the only level of valid description, as has become a common philosophical position in many areas of HCI. Instead, it is the focus as a practical point of 'agreement' between diverse descriptions, including those involving motivation, intentions and cognitive process of human agents and the mechanisms and abstractions of computational components ... and even descriptions which deny the validity of either!

3   Discrete Behaviour

This section is about discrete behaviour in the sense of behaviour that takes place in discrete time. The issue about whether the value domains for phenomena are discrete or continuous is not really relevant, as it makes no difference to our models. (Although more detailed models of continuous time do require differences).

At first discrete models seem as if they are simpler. They are certainly far more common. For example, in Palanque and Paternó's collection [26] no paper deals with continuous phenomena and in recent DSVIS only three papers in total. However, in some ways discrete models are also more complex. The real world exists in continuous time and so we have a touchstone with which to compare our semantics. In contrast, with discrete behaviours we have to choose which moments we deem significant and the way in which we relate phenomena, which take place over finite times into momentary measures.

3.1   Trace as Event Time Series

As a first model of discrete behaviour consider a simple stream of events:

$event1 - event2 - event3...$

This is precisely the model used for grammars such as BNF [35] or TAG [34] and for process algebras such as LOTOS [27] and CSP [3]. For example a potential behaviour of the process description $P \rightarrow abP \,|\, acP$ would be:

$a - b - a - b - a - c - a - b - ...$

One way to model this is as a function from some time domain Time to events:

$trace : Time \rightarrow EventKind$

Although this 'works' as a representation of event traces, it puts too much emphasis on the arbitrary time domain. The most common choice of Time is an interval of the integers, but this suggests uniformity of the time steps, which is rarely the case. So will adopt a slightly richer model of traces.

3.2   A Meta-model – Instances and Happenings

In order to better model traces we tear them into two major parts:

happenings a collection (often sequence) of moments or periods of time when things happen
instances the instantiation of kinds of events (or other phenomena) from the model

These are related to one another. Happenings have a temporal relation with one another given by a *when* relation. At any happening one or more instances may 'happen'. This is denoted by the *at* function. Finally instances are related to particular kinds of events in the original model (the different instances of 'a's in the trace above) and this is denoted by the *what* function.

$Behaviour =< happenings, instances, when, at, what >$
$where \quad happenings : \quad set\,of\,Happening$
$\qquad\quad instances : \quad set\,of\,EventInstance$
$\qquad\quad when : \quad happenings \times happenings \rightarrow TimeOrder$
$\qquad\quad at : \quad instances \rightarrow happenings$
$\qquad\quad what : \quad instances \rightarrow EventKind\,\{\times Value\}$

Note that the *Happening* and *EventInstance* sets are merely unique labels, the semantics is given by the relations.

The optional value in the *what* function is to allow for models where the general type of event (e.g. channel in process algebras) may also allow some form of value passing. However, this is not just a feature of process algebras. If we were analysing a trace of user interface events we might say something like "the user clicked the mouse" – this is a recognisable kind of event which has an associated value "at pixel location 517, 323".

The *TimeOrder* may be a total order for some models, but others, such as LADA [15], represent truly concurrent, as opposed to interleaved, events, and require a partial order. Further, some notations deal with things that have duration (e.g. tasks in task analysis) and in these cases a richer set of interval relationship such as 'starts before' 'overlaps beginning of' may be needed (e.g. those in [1]).

Optionally, we can then add actual times (or periods of time) to the happenings (consistent of course with the *when* relation).

$$at : Happening \rightarrow Time\{\times Time\}$$

Although we shall use this framework as a touchstone it is not intended to be a final point, merely of sufficient richness to discuss various issues and flexibility to allow the necessary extensions to produce a truly ubiquitous semantics. Note especially that this differs from the model in the paper proceedings at the conference, which did not distinguish the happenings from the instances.

3.3   Relating Behaviours

We can relate behaviours of this kind to one to another by introducing a partial mapping between happenings:

$$B_{XY} : partial\,mapping\ X.happenings \leftrightarrow Y.happenings$$

A relationship of this kind can arise in two ways:

- a particular trace of activity is captured and the actual simultaneity of particular related events in the two models recorded automatically or annotated by hand
- a binding is defined between models, which then gives rise to an induced binding between instances within the behaviours of models and thus to the happenings

Of course, the binding mustn't introduce an inconsistent temporal ordering. In the case when the *when* relations are partial orders this is:

$$\forall xi_1, xi_2 \in X.instances,\ yi_1, yi_2 \in Y.instances \bullet$$
$$B_{XY}(xi_1, yi_1) \wedge B_{XY}(xi_2, yi_2) \Rightarrow$$
$$\neg(xi_1 < xi_2 \wedge yi_2 < yi_1) \wedge \neg(xi_2 < xi_1 \wedge yi_1 < yi_2)$$

This weak ordering preservation is to allow things such as one event in one model to correspond to several in another.

3.4   Turn-Taking and States

Some models, for example the PIE and related models [12] and action–effect rules [23] have a series of user-action – system-response turns. In the PIE this is modelled as an interpretation function (I) between traces of user commands (from $P = seq\,C$) to system effects (E):

$$I : seq\,C \to E$$

The unfolding of the system can then be thought of as a turn-taking sequence:

$$e_0 - c_1 - e_1 - c_2 - e_2 - c_3 - e_3 - c_4 - e_4 - \ldots$$
$$where: \quad e_0 = I(<>), e_1 = I(< c1 >), e_2 = I(< c_1, c_2 >), \ldots$$

State-transition diagrams and related formalisms have states with transitions labelled by the action that caused them and any system response. That is the formal model they represent is:

$$trans : \ (old)\,State \times Action \to Response \times (new)\,State$$

This gives rise to sequences of the form:

$$s_0 - a_1 - r_1 - s_1 - a_2 - r_2 - s_2 - a_3 - r_3 - s_3 - \ldots$$
$$where: \quad s_0 = initial\,state, \ r_i, s_i = trans(a_i, s_{i-1})$$

Note, a new state may be reached 'before' the response, but persists hence the trace order. If we look only at the externally observable phenomena, this then reduces to an action–response trace

$$a_1 - r_1 - a_2 - r_2 - a_3 - r_3 - a_4 - r_4 - \ldots$$

This can be viewed as an event behaviour in two ways. The first way, which is probably the most natural semantics for the STN is to regard the action and response as being facets of the same event (instances that happen *at* the same happening). Call this the 'X' semantics. The second is to regard the action and response as separate events, which is what we would get if we 'translated' the STN into an 'equivalent' process algebra specification. Call this the 'Y' semantics. In this case the instances happen *at* separate happenings. Happily these two semantics can be related to one another by a binding in the obvious way.

If the process algebra had been derived from the STN, or if we were attempting to demonstrate equivalence, we would have some sort of binding relating the STN as a model and the process algebra as a model. In such cases the binding between behaviours would be able to be derived from the model binding (figure 2).

3.5   Interstitial Behaviour

If we choose to retain the states in our semantics of the STN we would get a third semantics obtained from the X semantics by inserting extra state instances between the action-response instances (like the original trace above). Call this

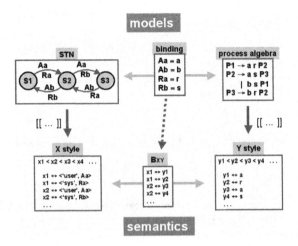

Fig. 2. Behaviour bindings derived from model binding

the 'Z' semantics. Again it is easy to create an X–Z binding between these semantics. However in the relationship between the X and Y semantics we have several instances in the Y behaviour mapping onto a single instance in the X behaviour. In this case, some of the instances in the Z behaviour (the states) have no correspondence at all in the X behaviour, they fall in the gaps between events – the interstice (figure 3).

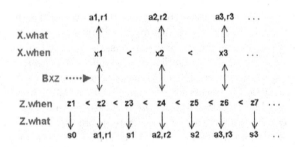

Fig. 3. Binding between X and Z semantics 'leaves out' states

There are two reasons for instances in one behaviour to fall in the interstice of the other. Consider again a process algebra used to specify the interface. Some of the events would correspond to user actions and observable system responses, others would be purely internal. If we wanted to relate the full trace of events with the externally observable one, the hidden internal events would fall in the interstice between the user actions and system responses. These correspond to specific events that happen between the observable events, a form of trace refinement.

In contrast, states are not things that 'happen', but represent something that has a value *throughout* the interval between the events. That is there is a fundamental ontological distinction between the STN states and events. The former are status phenomena – things which have a continuing value over a period of time as opposed to events which occur at an instant. This status–event distinction and the importance of interstitial behaviour was originally proposed in order to deal with continuous behaviour such as mouse movement [13], but as we see, it makes a difference even to the way we regard discrete phenomena.

3.6   Hierarchical and Layered Models

It can be useful to consider some of the internal or structural parts of a model as 'observable' phenomena as we have shown with STN states or hidden events.

Many task or cognitive models are based on hierarchies (e.g. GOMS [7], HTA [37], CTT [29]). We can simply construct traces of unit actions forming a bridge with internal system descriptions, but it is also good to represent the higher-level tasks or goals. In task models higher level tasks 'happen' over a period incorporating instances of lower level tasks and this is reflected in the 'happenings' of the formal semantics.

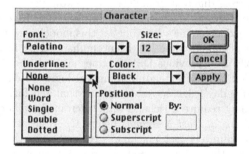

Fig. 4. Simple dialogue box

Slightly different considerations apply to layered architectural models such as Seeheim [33], Arch-Slinky [39] or PAC hierarchies [9]. Consider the dialogue box in figure 4. The user interacts with the pull-down menu in series of lexical-level events, probably managed by the platform widget toolkit. Only at the end of this series of lexical events will there be a dialogue level event 'new underline style is word'. There may then follow further lexical and dialogue events (select position, menu selection of size), before finally the user clicks on 'OK' which gives rise to an application-level event and the selection format is changed (figure 5).

Note the difference. In task analysis the user is 'selecting the underline mode' *throughout* the menu interaction, but when considered in architectural terms the

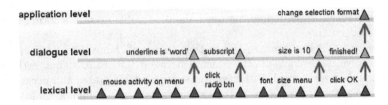

Fig. 5. Levels and interaction points

dialogue event happens *at the end* of the menu interaction. Dialogue events can be seen as coinciding or possibly being 'just after' the final lexical level event of the sequence (the mouse release). These points of synchronisation between different architectural levels are called interaction points [17]. We can regard this either as multiple behaviours with bindings between them at the interaction points, or as a single behaviour with event instances at different levels related by 'coincident with' or 'just after' relations.

3.7   Temporal Granularity and Real Time

This problem of 'coincident' vs. 'just after' when considering interaction points is because different models operate at different temporal granularities. Some relations make sense across different granularities – it would be wrong to have event A be before event B in one model and after in another. However, coincidence should always be read as 'at the same time' at this model's temporal granularity. This fuzzy nature of human time has been emphasised by Payne in his study of calendar use [32]. In a previous DSVIS paper and her thesis [21], Kutar addressed the complex issue of extending temporal logics to express statements, such as 'on the same day', that have both contextual and fuzzy semantics.

Some models may require a richer *TimeOrder* in the *when* relation to say things like B happens *at least 3 seconds* before C. Alternatively, the τ-PIE in "The myth of the infinitely fast machine" [10] embodies the external flow of time very directly in the use of 'ticks' to represent moments where there is no user activity, that is a semantics where happenings may have no corresponding instances. These two semantics can be mapped to one another, so the choice is a matter of convenience.

4   Continuous Behaviour

Although many of the systems and interfaces studied in rich-media and in novel interfaces embody continuous real-time interaction, there are few models of this in the HCI literature. Possibly this is because of the conceptual dominance of discrete models.

Probably the earliest continuous time models in the formal UI literature are the variants of status–event analysis [13,14], and we have already seen a hint of this in discrete systems. Status–event analysis (S–E) distinguishes events that occur at specific moments of time from status phenomena that have (typically changing) values over a period of time. Examples of events include keystrokes, beeps, and the stroke of midnight in Cinderella. Examples of status phenomena include the current display, the location of the mouse pointer, the internal state of the computer and the weather.

Perhaps one of the most significant features of S–E is its treatment of interstitial behaviour. Whereas discrete models focus on the moments when events occur, S-E puts equal emphasis on the more fluid interaction between events. In many GUI systems this is what gives the 'feel' of interaction: dragging, scrolling etc., and in rich media this is likely to be the main purpose of interaction!

Another crucial aspect of S–E, not apparent in discrete system, are status-change events. These occur when status phenomena cross some trigger threshold, for example, when temperature reaches some value or at a certain time (on the clock). The nature of threshold is application dependent and may be dynamic. Furthermore there are issues concerning how status–change events become system-level events: polling, active sensors, etc. At an abstract level of specification one would just say "when this happens ...", but as this becomes operationalised issues of mechanism surface.

In modelling virtual reality systems, Wüthrich [41] made use of cybernetic systems theory using formulae of the form:

$$state_t = \phi(t, t_0, state_{t_0}, inputs\_during[t_0, t)), \quad output_t = \eta(state_t)$$

This treats events on a par with status phenomena, both are merely part of 'inputs at time t', similar to Dirac delta functions in dynamics and signal theory. However, in practice Wüthrich finds it more convenient to describe event phenomena as time-stamped values.

The TACIT project [38] studied a variety of continuous time interactive systems and also considered modelling using hybrid high-level Petri-Nets [24]. In common with many models from the hybrid systems community [19], this takes a largely dualist model of the world with discrete computer systems interfacing with a continuous environment defined by differential equations. The formal expression of this involves 'continuous transitions' – a form of interstitial behaviour.

A component/interactor model based on a similar variant of hybrid Petrinets is proposed in [40] to deal with objects in virtual environments. Its 'world object state' has both discrete and continuous output and input and a threshold on continuous input, producing status-change events. Note that it is quite easy to describe these models in similar terms because they sit closer to the real world than in the discrete case. For behaviour modelling we need only extend the EventInstances to include values that are functions of time (no longer 'EventInstances', just Instances). This can then represent periods where the mouse position moved over a trajectory, or the window tracked the mouse position.

Granularity effects resurface in continuous time and are perhaps more perplexing. We still want to be able to talk about events: the button was clicked, the computer beeps, I had a meeting. It is right to represent these as events, but clearly when looked at closely they take some duration. We can allow many-to-one bindings just as we do in the discrete case. However, this appears a little odd where 'many' is a period with continuous motion (for example, if select menu item at one level became the actual mouse movements at another). In fact, this is not uncommon in applied mathematics where solutions of equations with slow time-varying parameters or small non-linearities are managed by imagining two timescales, one infinitely fast with respect to the other. A technique called two-timing.

The issues of hierarchy and architectural levels are also similar in the continuous case to the discrete one. However, continuous media exhibit a special case of the lexical–dialogue interaction points – temporal gestalt phenomena. Consider gesture recognition – the movement only has meaning once completed, music – the melody is only a melody whilst being played, and even graphics get meaning through movement [5]. This is rather like the fact the typed characters "d", "i", "r", carriage-return only mean "list directory" when considered as a whole. The main difference is that the boundaries are less clear than those of discrete phenomena – the gesture has no definitive start or end although an endpoint would be operationalised by actual recognition software.

5   Summary

This paper has considered the semantics of traces of user-system activities in both discrete and continuous interaction. One might have thought that this would have been a trivial task as all models in some sense are describing 'the same thing', but as we have seen the multiplicity of viewpoints and levels of analysis mean that even establishing commonality at the level of sequences of actions is surprisingly complex.

We have also seen a number of problematic issues for formal treatment of scenarios, especially when we try to align scenarios corresponding to different complementary models. This is because notations differ in which events and actions they regard as atomic, or instantaneous and much of our discussion has been about how to establish bindings between these different accounts.

Another issue that has arisen in both discrete and continuous models is the ontological distinction between status and event phenomena and the important role of interstitial behaviour.

The word 'theory' comes from two Greek words *thea*, "outward appearance", and horao, "to look closely" [18]. This paper has been examining closely the surface of interaction. It has not presented a final or complete semantics, but has shown how common behavioural semantics may be possible for a range of common notations. It is hoped that this will lead towards a rich theory of multi-paradigm interaction modelling.

Acknowledgements. This work was supported by the EPSRC funded project DIRC.

References

[1] G. Abowd. *Formal aspects of human computer interaction*, PhD Thesis, University of Oxford, 1991.

[2] G. Abowd, H. Wang, and A. Monk. *A formal technique for automated dialogue development.* In Proc. DIS'95. ACM Press, 1995. pp. 219–226.

[3] H. Alexander, *Formally-based tools and techniques for human-computer dialogues.* Ellis Horwood, 1987.

[4] J. Allen. *Planning as Temporal Reasoning.* In Proc., 2nd Principles of Knowledge Representation and Reasoning, Morgan Kaufmann, 1991.

[5] M. Bacigalupi. *Designing movement in interactive multimedia: making it meaningful.* Interfaces 44, Autumn 2000, pp. 12–15.

[6] P. Barnard, J. May, D. Duke and D. Duce. *Systems, Interactions, and Macrotheory.* ACM Transactions on Computer-Human Interaction, 2000. **7**(2):222–262.

[7] S. Card, T. Moran, and A. Newell (1993). *The Psychology of Human Computer Interaction.* 1983, Lawrence Erlbaum.

[8] J. Carroll (ed). *Scenario-Based Design: envisioning work and technology in system development.* Wiley, 1995.

[9] J. Coutaz. *PAC, an object oriented model for dialogue design.* In: H-J Bullinger B. Shackel (eds) In INTERACT'87. Elsevier 1987. pp 431–436.

[10] A. Dix. *The myth of the infinitely fast machine.* In Proc. HCI'87, D. Diaper and R. Winder (eds.). Cambridge University Press, 1987. pp. 215–228.

[11] A. Dix and C. Runciman. *Abstract models of interactive systems.* In Proc. HCI'85. Cambridge University Press, 1985. pp. 13–22.

[12] A. Dix. *Formal Methods for Interactive Systems.* Academic Press, 1991.

[13] A. Dix. *Status and events: static and dynamic properties of interactive systems.* in Proceedings of the Eurographics Seminar: Formal Methods in Computer Graphics. Marina di Carrara, Italy. 1991.

[14] A. Dix and G. Abowd, *Modelling status and event behaviour of interactive systems.* Software Engineering Journal, 1996. **11**(6):334–346.

[15] A. Dix. *LADA - A logic for the analysis of distributed action,* in Interactive Systems: Design, Specification and Verification (1st Eurographics Workshop, Bocca di Magra, Italy, June 1994), F. Paternó (ed). Springer Verlag, 1995. pp. 317–332.

[16] P. Dourish. *Embodied Interaction.* ACM Press, 2001.

[17] C. Gram and G. Cockton (eds.). *Design Principles for Interactive Software.* Chapman and Hall, 1996.

[18] D. Gregory. *Geographical Imaginations.* Blackwell, 1994.

[19] R. Grossman *et al.* (eds). *Hybrid Systems.* LNCS 736, Springer Verlag, 1993.

[20] D. Kieras and P. Polson, *An approach to the formal analysis of user complexity.* International Journal of Man-Machine Studies, 1985. **22**:365–394.

[21] M. Kutar, C. Britton and C. Nehaniv. *Specifiying multiple time granularities in interactive systems.* In DSV-IS'2000. P. Palanque and F. Paternó (eds). LNCS 1946, Springer, 2001, pp. 169–190.

[22] K. Loer and M. Harrison. *Formal interactive systems analysis and usability inspection methods: two incompatible worlds?* In DSV-IS'2000. P. Palanque and F. Paternó (eds). LNCS 1946, Springer, 2001, pp. 169–190.

[23] A. Monk. *Action-effect rules: a technique for evaluating an informal specification against principles.* Behaviour and Information Technology, 1990. **9**(2):147–155.

[24] M. Massink, D. Duke and S. Smith. *Towards hybrid interface specification for virtual environments.* In DSV-IS'99. D. Duke and A. Puerta (eds). Springer, 1999, pp. 30–51.

[25] D. Navarre. P. Palanque, F. Paternó, C. Santoro and R. Bastide. *A tool suite for integrating task and system models through scenarios.* In DSV-IS'2001. C. Johnson (ed). LNCS 2220, Springer, 2001, pp. 88–113.

[26] P. Palanque and F. Paternó (eds). *Formal Methods in Human Computer Interaction.* Springer-Verlag, 1997.

[27] F. Paternó and G. Faconti. *On the use of LOTOS to describe graphical interaction.* in Proceedings of HCI'92. Cambridge University Press, 1992. p. 155–173.

[28] F. Paternó. *Formal reasoning about dialogue properties with automatic support.* Interacting with Computers. August 1997, pp. 173–196.

[29] F. Paternó. *Model-based design and evaluation of interactive applications.* Springer, 1999.

[30] F. Paternó and C. Santoro. *Integrating model checking and HCI tools to help designers verify user interface properties.* In DSV-IS'2000. P. Palanque and F. Paternó (eds). LNCS 1946, Springer, 2001, pp. 135–150.

[31] F. Paternó, G. Mori and R. Galimberti. *CTTE: an environment for analysis and development of task models of cooperative applications.* In Proceedings of CHI'01, Vol 2, ACM Press, 2001.

[32] S. Payne. *Understanding Calendar Use.* Human-Computer Interaction, 1993, 8(2):83–100.

[33] G. Pfaff, and P. Hagen (eds). *Seeheim Workshop on User Interface Management Systems.* Springer-Verlag, 1985.

[34] S. Payne and T. Green, *Task action grammars: a model of mental representation of task language.* Human-Computer Interaction, 1986, 2(2):93–133.

[35] P. Reisner. *Formal grammar and human factors design of an interactive graphics system.* IEE Transactions on Software Engineering, 1981. 7(2):229–240.

[36] C. Roast and J. Siddiqi. *Using the template model to analyse directory visualisation.* Interacting with Computers. 1997, 9(2):155–172.

[37] A. Shepherd. *Task analysis as a framework for examining HCI tasks, in Perspectives on HCI: Diverse Approaches,* A. Monk and N. Gilbert (eds). Academic Press, 1995, pp. 145–174.

[38] TACIT: *Theory and Applications of Continuous Interaction Techniques,* http://kazan.cnuce.cnr.it/TACIT/TACIThome.html

[39] *The UIMS tool developers workshop: A metamodel for the runtime architecture of an interactive system.* In SIGCHI Bulletin, 1992, 24(1):32–37.

[40] J. Willans and M. Harrison. *Verifying the behaviour of virtual world objects.* In DSV-IS'2000. P. Palanque and F. Paternó (eds). Springer, 2001, pp. 65–77.

[41] C. Wüthrich. *An analysis and model of 3D interaction methods and devices for virtual reality.* In DSV-IS'99. D. Duke and A. Puerta (eds). Springer, 1999, pp. 18–29.

Architecture Considerations for Interoperable Multi-modal Assistant Systems

Thomas Heider and Thomas Kirste

Fraunhofer-Institut für Graphische Datenverarbeitung Rostock
{Thomas.Heider,Thomas.Kirste}@rostock.igd.fhg.de

Abstract. Creating multimodal assistant systems supporting the intuitive interaction with technical infrastructures of the everyday life is one important goal of
current HCI research.

Building such systems is a substantial challenge – not only with respect to the individual concepts and algorithms that are required at the various levels of multimodal
interaction processing, but also with respect to the overall system architecture. Especially, when we try to address systems that can be extended dynamically and
that are not built by a single vendor.

We will look at some the challenges of creating architectures for such systems and
we will outline the solution approach our research group is currently developing.
The work we present is part of the EMBASSI-project, a joint project with 19 partners
from industry and academia that aims at establishing an interoperable system
infrastructure for multimodal and multimedia assistance systems.

1 Overview: The EMBASSI Project

EMBASSI[1] [7,6] is a focus project supported by the German Ministry of Education and
Research (Bundesministerium für Bildung und Forschung, BMBF) within the strategic
research area Man-Technology-Interaction. With 19 partners from industry and academia
and a time scope of four years, EMBASSI intends to provide an integrated approach to the
development of assistants for our everyday technologies.

The primary application area for EMBASSI are technical infrastructures of the non-
professional everyday life – in particular, application scenarios are being developed in
the home, automotive, and public terminals environments.

EMBASSI is conceptually based on two important paradigm shifts:

- Transition from essentially unimodal, menu-based dialogue structures (with a fixed
  interaction vocabulary provided by the system) to polymodal, conversational dialogue structures (with an unrestricted interaction vocabulary provided by the user).
- Transition from a function-oriented interaction with devices to a goal-oriented interaction with systems.

While these paradigm shifts are being discussed in the research community for some
time now, it is a substantial challenge to make these results accessible to the user of, *e.g.*,
home entertainment infrastructures. This is the goal of EMBASSI.

---

[1] "EMBASSI" is a German acronym for "Multimodal Assistance for Infotainment & Service Infrastructures"

P. Forbrig et al. (Eds.): DSV-IS 2002, LNCS 2545, pp. 253–267, 2002.
© Springer-Verlag Berlin Heidelberg 2002

Building such systems is a substantial challenge – not only with respect to the individual concepts and algorithms that are required at the various levels of multimodal interaction processing, but also with respect to the overall system architecture. Especially, when we try to address systems that can be extended dynamically and that are not built by a single vendor.

In this paper, we will look the challenges of creating architectures for such systems and we will outline the solution approach we are using and developing within the EMBASSI project.

The paper is further structured as follows: Section 2 gives an overview over the challenges of self-organizing multi-modal multi-agent systems. In Section 3, we outline the architectural framework used in EMBASSI. In Section 4, we describe the underlying concepts of the middleware currently being developed in EMBASSI. We relate our work to other approaches in Section 5 and look at future work in Section 6.

2   Middleware Challenges

A central requirement for an EMBASSI architecture is that it should support technical infrastructures that are built from individual components in an ad hoc fashion by the end user. This situation is for instance common in the area of home entertainment infrastructures, where users liberally mix components from different vendors. Also, it is not possible to assume a central controller – any component must be able to operate stand-alone. Furthermore, some infrastructures may change over time – due to hardware components entering or leaving the infrastructure or due to changes in the quality-of-service available for some infrastructure services, such as bandwidth in the case of wireless channels.

Therefore, such an architecture should meet the following objectives:

- Ensure independence of components,
- Allow dynamic extensibility by new components,
- Avoid central components (single point of failures, bottlenecks),
- Support a distributed implementation,
- Allow flexible re-use of components,
- Enable exchangeability of components,
- Provide transparent service arbitration.

When interacting with their personal environment, users may be driving car, enjoying a TV show at home, calling a colleague over the mobile phone, etc. These very different situations do not only influence the assistance strategies provided by the conceptual architecture's components – they also have a strong impact on the hardware infrastructure available for implementing the assistant system. It becomes clear that a broad range of different hardware infrastructures has to be considered as implementation platform – for example:

- mobile personal communicators with wireless access to stationary servers,
- wearable computers using augmented reality displays for interaction,
- a set of networked consumer electronic components, without a central controller,

- the local information network of modern cars,
- the user's PC at home, communicating with globally distributed information servers,
- public terminals, etc.

From these considerations, substantial challenges arise with respect to the software infrastructure that is required for implementing the conceptual architecture. It needs to support functions such as:

- Distributed implementation of components. As soon as more than one host is available (or required) for implementing the architecture, a distribution scheme must be developed. The distribution scheme may either simply allocate different functional components on different hosts (relying on the assumption that inter-component communication is less frequent than intra-component communication) or it may distribute individual components across multiple hosts (making each component virtually available everywhere, but creating challenges with respect to managing a consistent internal state). Clearly, the right choice depends on the concrete infrastructure that is available.
- Communication mechanisms. Once a distributed implementation is considered, the choice of communication concept is no longer a matter of taste. Distributed shared memories or distributed blackboards for example are a much more heavyweight communication scheme than message passing and bus architectures – but simplify communication design for knowledge based systems. Again, the right choice cannot be made without considering the concrete infrastructure, the specific communication needs of the components in question, and the distribution model.
- Ad-hoc discovery of system components. In some infrastructures, new components may join an existing system in an ad-hoc fashion. Consider, e.g., a personal communicator establishing contact to a point of sales terminal, where both components are equipped with their own version of the assistance system. Both systems must be able to integrate with each other and discover each other's components and functionalities, in order to provide an interoperable service (such as using the mobile communicator's input and output devices for the stationary terminal's analysers and dialogue management).
- Ad-hoc (re-) distribution of software components. In case the infrastructure changes during system life, it may become necessary to adapt the distribution scheme towards the new resources. It may even be of interest to change the allocation of software components in an ad-hoc fashion – e.g., by using mobile agents.

3   The EMBASSI Architecture

The generic architecture that we have developed within EMBASSI (Fig. 1) is a pipeline approach to the problem of mapping user utterances to environment changes. Each "level" in the architecture represents one function within this pipeline, while the level interfaces have been introduced at "meaningful" places, separating different ontologies. These "ontologies" (the sets of objects that are discussed at a level) become visible at the level interfaces. The level interfaces make up the EMBASSI protocol suite.

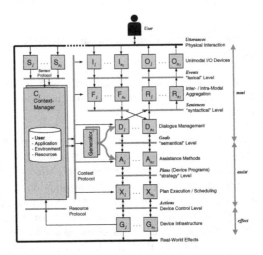

Fig. 1. Generic EMBASSI architecture

Each level consists of a number of processes ("components") that co-operatively implement the level's function. Processes can be added or removed dynamically: suitable co-ordination mechanisms at each level are responsible for managing the interactions between the processes at this level. There is deliberately *no* central co-ordination component (see Section 4 for further details on component co-ordination).

The use of this rather fine-grained level-model in conjunction with the feature of dynamically adding or removing processes at each level allows us to create systems that can be incrementally built and extended in an *ad hoc* fashion, using modular components. Specifically, it allows us to build interoperable systems, where different components are provided by different vendors and where components are added and removed over time by the end-user.

Also, this allows us to collect components in a "technology toolkit", from which specific assistant systems can be built by simply "plugging" these components together.

3.1   The MMI Levels

An EMBASSI system has to accept multimodal utterances which it needs to translate into goals before it can begin to think about changing the environment. According to the architecture in Fig. 1, this translation process can be broken down into three distinct steps[2]:

1. First we translate physical interactions into atomic interaction events (lexical level). The transformation of physical user interactions into unimodal atomic events is done by the *I* components (I = Input).

---

[2] The reader should note that this three-level approach is a rather straightforward adoption of the LANGUAGE model described by Foley and Van Dam [3].

2. The stream of atomic interaction events is then sent via the *Event* interface to the F components (F = Filter). These components are responsible for inter- and intra-modal aggregation of atomic events into amodal *sentences* (syntactical level).
3. The stream of sentences arrives at the D components (D = Dialogue manager). D components are responsible for translating sentences into goals denoted by these sentences (semantical level). Also, D is responsible for managing inter-sentence relations (dialogue memory) and dialogue dynamics (such as turn-taking).

The process is reversed when producing output: D sends amodal output "sentences" to the R components (R = Renderer) which in turn map these sentences to multiple atomic output events for the available output channels, the O components.

3.2   The Assistance Levels

The assistance levels operate on goals which are identified by the MMI levels. The process of mapping goals to changes of the environment consists of the following steps:

1. A components (A = Assistant) take goals (which specify state changes of the environment) and try to develop strategies for fulfilling these goals (strategy level). These strategies are called *plans*.
   There is no predefined way to produce a plan. Some A components may use hard-wired plans, others could use decision trees or even complete inference systems.
2. The plans are sent to the X components (X = eXecution control), which are responsible for the (distributed) scheduling and execution of the plans. (This means, the EMBASSI-architecture advocates a two step planning policy, as described *e.g.* in [15], where strategy planning (A-level) and execution scheduling (X-level) are distinct processes.)
   The scheduling-components ensure the correct sequential processing of the individual steps in a plan. Also, they are responsible for managing the parallel execution of multiple plans and for the management of execution resources needed by the plan.
3. Finally, individual action requests are sent to the (abstract) devices (device control level), the G components (G = Gerät – German for "device"). The G components execute the action request by employing the physical device they control, thus changing the state of the environment and causing an effect as intended by the user.

The **Context Manager** C is responsible for managing the system's view of the world – information about the user, resource profiles, the environment, and also the availability and state of the individual EMBASSI components. Attached to the context manager, we have sensors to obtain biometrics and environmental information – such as the current position of the user or the ambient light level. The context manager supports both pull interface (queries) and a push interface (notifications) to the information it stores.

Finally, based on a self-description deposited by a G-component in the context manager, a *Generator* may be able to automatically create simple A and D components for it. See [7] for further details on this concept.

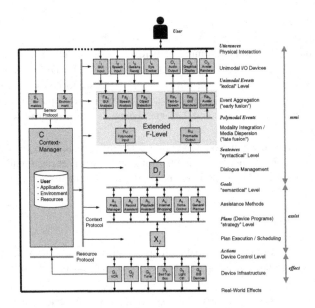

Fig. 2. EMBASSI architecture – Home Control Instance

3.3   Additional Notes on the Generic Architecture

Before addressing the main point of this paper – the middleware infrastructure that is required for building dynamically extensible interactive assistance systems based on the EMBASSI architecture – a few additional aspects of this architecture should be noted:

- The above generic architecture has been instantiated for the various application scenarios investigated in EMBASSI – home control, car infotainment, and point-of-sales / point-of-information terminals. The instance architecture for home control is shown as example in Fig. 2.
- Conventional widget-based user interfaces are quite easily mapped to the EMBASSI architecture: within the Home Control scenario, they correspond to the GUI Analysis / GUI Renderer components.
- The feedback loops *within* an EMBASSI level – *e.g.*, the connection between GUI Input and GUI Renderer are *not* explicitly shown in our architecture. Such feedback loops cleary do exist – but we have not yet ventured into designing a *generic ontology* for these them. Hence, they are not yet part of the EMBASSI protocol suite.
- It is of course possible to map the EMBASSI architecture to existing architecture models for man-machine interfaces such as the ARCH model [1,9]. In ARCH, the levels that map user interaction to system actions are: Interaction Toolkit, Presentation Component, Dialogue Component, Domain Adaptor Component, and Domain-specific Component. Without going too much into the details, one possible mapping of EMBASSI to ARCH would be: I/O-Level = Interaction Toolkit, F/R-Level = Pre-

sentation Component, D-Level = Dialogue Component, A-Level = Domain Adaptor Component, X & G-Level = Domain-specific Components.

In this context, the reader should be aware of the fact that it is *not* the primary goal of EMBASSI to present yet another model for interactive architectures. Rather, we try to build an infrastructure that allows the *dynamic composition* of interactive systems from components in an ad hoc fashion. It is the dynamic composition functionality that is the "interesting" aspect in EMBASSI – at least at the architectural level.

Next, we will look at the middleware model that we use for implementing the dynamically extensible architecture of EMBASSI.

4   The Middleware Model

The goal of our middleware-work is to develop a system model that provides the essential communication patterns of a data-flow based multi-component architectures such as EMBASSI. At the same time, we also want to have an experimental platform implementing this model (a reference implementation) that allows to quickly build and empirically verify experimental applications – specifically with respect to functions such as service arbitration.

Here, the focus of empirical studies is the way *systems* can be build dynamically from individual components and how the mechanisms provided by the model are used for building such systems – a software engineering focus.

The model should have the following properties:

- Support data-flow based event processing topologies.
- Support conventional remote procedure calls.
- Support self-organization of system components.
- Support decentralized problem decomposition and conflict resolution (service arbitration).
- Support dynamic extension by new components.
- Support unification / partitioning of complete system topologies.

The model we have developed so far is called SODA-POP (for: **S**elf-**O**rganizing **D**ata-flow Architectures su**P**porting **O**ntology-based problem decom**P**osition.). Following, we give a brief overview over the salient features of this model.

4.1   Component Types

The SODA-POP model [8] introduces two fundamental organization levels:

- Coarse-grained self-organization based on a data-flow partitioning.
- Fine-grained self-organization for functionally *similar* components based on a kind of "Pattern Matching" approach.

Consequently, a SODA-POP system consists of two types of components:

Channels, which read a single message at time *point* and map them to multiple messages which are delivered to components (conceptually, *without delay*). Channels have no memory, may be distributed, and they have to accept *every* message.

Channels provide for *spatial distribution* of a single event to multiple transducers. The interface buses of the EMBASSI architecture are channels.

Transducers, which read one or more messages during a time *interval* and map them to one (or more) output messages. Transducers are *not* distributed, they may have a memory and they do not have to accept every message.

Transducers provide for *temporal aggregation* of multiple events to a single output. Note that a transducer may have *multiple* input and output channels ($m : n$, rather than just $1 : 1$). The I, F, ... components of EMBASSI are transducers.

The criterion for discriminating between transducers and channels is the amount of memory they may employ for processing a message – *i.e.*, the complexity they create when trying to implement them in a distributed fashion: Channels may use no memory. This requirement clearly makes sense when considering that we may want to use channels as "cutting points" for distributing a system: Implementing distributed shared memory is expensive. Communication primitives for potentially distributed systems therefore should not provide such a facility "for free". In addition, the "'No Memory" Constraint provides a *hard* criterion for discriminating between the functions a channel is allowed to provide and functions that require a transducer.

Finally, it becomes obvious that persistence functionality (such as provided by blackboard-based communication infrastructures, *e.g.* LINDA [4] or FLiPSiDE [13]) shall not be part of a channel, as persistence clearly violates the concept of memory-free channels.

4.2   Channels & Systems

Channels accept (and deliver) messages of a certain type t, Transducers map messages from a type t to a type t'. A system is defined by a set of channels and a set of transducers connecting these channels. So, a system is a graph where channels represent points (nodes) and transducers represent edges[3]. Channels and transducers are equally important in defining a system – a minimal complete EMBASSI system for example consists of 10 channels and 10 transducers (9 and 9 if sensors are omitted).

Channels are identified via *Channel Descriptors*. Conceptually, channel descriptors encode the channel's ontology (the meaning of the messages), so that transducers can be automatically connected to channels that speak the languages they understand.

4.3   Communication Patterns

The middleware for multimodal event processing and multi agent approaches should support at least the following two communication patterns:

- *Events* that travel in a data-flow fashion through the different transducers. When an event e is posted by a transducer t, it (t) does not expect a reply. Rather it expects

---

[3] Rather: a multigraph, because we may have several edges connecting the same two nodes.

that other system components (*i.e.*, the *called* transducer) know how to continue with processing the event.

- *RPCs* that resemble normal remote procedure calls. When a RPC is called by a transducer, it expects a result. Here, the *calling* transducer determines the further processing of the result.

Events and RPCs describe different routing semantics with respect to result processing. When considering the EMBASSI architecture, the flow from I to G is a typical event processing pipeline, where at each level we have a set of transducers that cooperate in order to translate an event received at the input (upper) level into an event posted at the output (lower) level.

Event- and RPC-like result routing semantics correspond to different types of channels, a transducer may subscribe to. Event- and RPC-Channels are the two basic channel types provided by SODA-POP.

With respect to events, there is one important additional requirement: In the normal course of action, events are delivered by a *push* mechanism, initiated by the producer. However, there are also situations when the consumers need to *pull* events – here, event delivery is initiated by the consumers. One specific instance of this pull situation arises when the transducers receiving an event need to *ask back* to the producing level for further information that may be needed to understand the event (*e.g.*: D may ask back to F for further multimodal event information it may need to disambiguate a given user utterance). So each event channel implicitly contains an inverse RPC channel on which an event-pull can be performed.

4.4 Subscriptions

Events and RPCs are (in general) posted *without* specific addressing information: in a dynamic system, a sender never can be sure, which receivers are currently able to process a message. It is up to the channel on which the message is posted to identify a suitable message decomposition and receiver set (service arbitration).

A channel basically consists of a pipe into which event generators push messages (events or RPCs) which are then transmitted to the consumers (transducers) subscribing this channel. When subscribing to a channel, an event consumer declares:

- the set of messages it is able to process,
- how well it is suited for processing a certain message,
- wether it is able to run in parallel to other message consumers on the same message,
- wether it is able to cooperate with other consumers in processing the message.

These aspects are described by the subscribing consumer's *utility*. A *utility* is a function that maps a message to a *utility value*, which encodes the subscribers' handling capabilities for the specific message. A transducer's utility may depend on the transducer's state.

The definition for Utility values in SODA-POP is[4]:

---

[4] The current version of SODA-POP is defined in Haskell [12], the current "standard" functional language

```
type Quality = Int              -- just as example
data UtVal = NotApplicable       -- Can't handle msg
           | Exclusive Quality   -- Expect to handle it exclusive
           | Nonexclusive Quality -- Don't mind if others are involved
           | Cooperative [(Quality,Msg)] -- Can do some parts, but need help
```

And a simple transducer that is able to handle only a single kind of message m0 might provide a utility function such as

```
isForMe :: Msg -> UtVal
isForMe m | m == m0 = Nonexclusive 0  -- if m is m0
          | True    = NotApplicable   -- otherwise
```

The Cooperative value needs further explanation: with this utility value, a transducer may return a list of partial messages it is able to handle, together with a quality value for each sub-message. This gives the Channel the opportunity to select the best tradeoff for decomposing a message across multiple transducers[5].

4.5 Message Handling

Receiver selection & message decomposition. When a channel processes a message, it evaluates the subscribing consumers' handling capabilities and then decides which consumers will effectively receive the message (receiver set). Also, the channel may decide to *decompose* the message into multiple (presumably simpler) messages which can be handled better by the subscribing consumers. (Obviously, the consumers then solve the original message in cooperation.) The basic process of message handling is shown in Fig. 3.

How a channel determines the effective message decomposition and how it chooses the set of receiving consumers is defined by the channel's *decomposition strategy*.

Both the transducers' utility and the channel's strategy are eventually based on the channel's ontology – the semantics of the messages that are communicated across the channel.

For some channels, the concept of cooperative message processing may already be a part of the channel's ontology. This means that the channel's language contains a means for embedding synchronization statements into a (presumably compound) message – such as "wait for completion of sub-request i" and "announce completion of sub-request j". The channel's strategy then embeds suitable synchronization statements into the messages it creates for the receiver set. Corresponding announcements are to be exchanged over a synchronization channel that needs to be established between the receiver set. This mechanism is used in EMBASSI for distributing the execution of strategies computed by the A level across multiple scheduling components at the X-level. (Note in this context that *temporal scheduling* is *not* a channel function as it clearly requires memory in the channel.)

Reply recombination. A channel's strategy may also describe the method for how to assemble the reply messages created by cooperating (or parallel) message consumers into a single aggregated reply. This strategy describes how to wait for the different transducers

---

[5] This is a rather experimental feature.

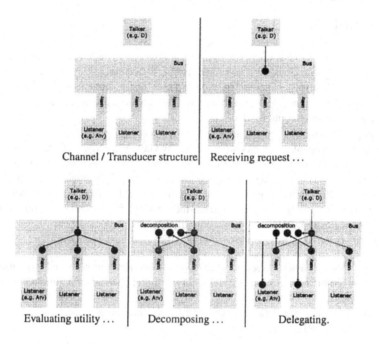

Fig. 3. Basic message handling process in SODA-POP

that have received (partial) messages and what algorithm to use for aggregating these replies. The most simple approach is to just return the first reply that is received. Another simple approach is to wait for all results, put them into a list, and return this list.

Unfortunately, it requires memory to perform this reply recombination: the component responsible for recombination has to remember from whom it can expect replies and which replies it already has received. Therefore, this component can not be handled by a channel. Instead, the channel creates an *implicit transducer* that performs the reply recombination strategy. By factoring reply recombination out of the channel, the design choice of *where* to do recombination in a distributed environment (at the receiver side? at the processing side?) becomes explicit, while at the same time keeping channel functionality lean: The channel may decice *where* to place the recombination transducer – but it does not have to implement its memory functionality.

Note that by putting decomposition and recombination into the channel rather than leaving this to the requesting component, we ensure that message decomposition and reply recombination is *transparent* to a component. This has two effects:

– Component designers are relieved from the task of doing receiver selection and reply recombination, this greatly simplifies implementation.
– The danger of misbehaved components that always select the same kind of receivers (*i.e.*, only receivers from the same vendor . . .) is minimized.

5   Related Work

SODA-POP is not the first concept for addressing the problem of dynamic, self organizing systems. Other approaches are for example HAVi [5] and Jini [17], the Galaxy Communicator Architecture [14,11], and SRI's OAA (Open Agent Architecture) [16,10], where specifically Galaxy and OAA intend to provide architectures for multi-agent systems supporting multi-modal interaction.

Compared to the state of the art, the pattern-matching approach in SODA-POP itself is not new. Comparable concepts are provided by Galaxy, by SRI's OAA, as well as by earlier work on Prolog [2] and the Pattern-Matching Lambda Calculus [18]. Here, SODA-POP simply intends to provide a certain refinement at the conceptual level by replacing language-specific syntactic pattern-matching functionality (such as the Prolog-based pattern matching of OAA) by a language-independent facility based on utility value computation functions that are provided by transducers.

The *important* differences of SODA-POP to the above approaches are

- SODA-POP uses a *two-stage* approach to system decomposition and self organization. Coarse-grained structuring is provided by defining channels, fine grained structure is supported by "pattern matching".
- SODA-POP supports data-flow architectures by providing event channels besides conventional RPC channels.

The *combination* of these two approaches is an important extension over the above systems.

HAVi, Jini, OAA, and Galaxy all provide a *single* mechanism for message routing. In HAVi and Jini, we have a simple event subscription mechanism on a global bus. Furthermore, Havi and Jini both do not provide transparent service service arbitration. OAA basically provides a single SODA-POP RPC channel with a Prolog-based decomposition and recombination strategy. Galaxy provides a centralized hub-component, which uses routing rules for modeling how messages are transferred between different system components. Galaxy too can be modeled by a single SODA-POP RPC channel that uses a decomposition approach built on top of Galaxy's frame language.

On the other hand, both Galaxy and OAA could be used to model SODA-POP – simply by representing channles with *message tags*. (Galaxy and OAA both use heavyweight routing components that incorporate arbitrary memory and are therefore not suited for a distributed implementation – but this is a different issue.)

So the question is not so much which approach is more powerful, but rather: which approach provides those abstractions that best help to structure a system architecture. Specifically, SODA-POP aims at supporting systems that are created by multiple (*e.g.*, 19) partners in parallel.

To our experience it is dangerous to provide only a single granularity for decomposing a complex system structure such as EMBASSI. The single granularity necessarily has to be fine in order to provide the required flexibility. When trying to fix the overal structure of the system, such a fine granularity provides too much detail and quickly leads to a proliferation of interfaces that are shared by only a few components. This danger specifically exists, when the interface discussion is carried out by several project partners in parallel[6]. However, the proliferation of interfaces is a Bad Thing, because it obstructs the interoperability of system components – a prime goal of EMBASSI.

The SODA-POP approach provides abstractions that allow a top-down structuring of the system (channels) *as well as* a bottom-up structuring (within-channel decomposition). In addition, it explicitly includes a data-flow based mechanism for constructing systems out of components, based on SODA-POP Event Channels. As a design paradigm, the SODA-POP approach has already been used successfully in implementing the EMBASSI demonstrator systems.

6   Summary and Outlook

6.1   What Has Been Achieved So Far

In this paper, we have outlined the architecture of a multi-agent system that supports multimodal interaction with technical infrastructures of the everyday life – the EMBASSI architecture. Furthermore, we have outlined the underlying middlware mechanisms, the SODA-POP model, that provides the essential communication patterns of a data-flow based multi-component architectures such as EMBASSI.

The SODA-POP model defined so far contains the following properties:

- Support data-flow based event processing topologies.
- Support conventional remote procedure calls.
- Support self-organization of system components.
- Support decentralized problem decomposition and conflict resolution (transparent service arbitration).
- Support dynamic extension by new components.

The aspect of dynamic unification / partitioning of complete system topologies has not yet been integrated, but should be comparatively straightforward based on the current definitions.

The SODA-POP infrastructure is currently implemented using the functional language Haskell [12]. This implementation[7] serves as a proof of concept of SODA-POP, as well as a testbed for experimenting with different data-flow topologies and alternative channel ontologies (*e.g.*, decomposition and recombination strategies).

EMBASSI system prototypes have been built for the application areas of consumer electronics & home control, car infotainment, and point-of-sales / point-of-information terminal access. The complete system has been on display at different conferences and fairs, such as the International Telecommunication Exhibition (IFA 2001) in Berlin.

6.2   Next Steps

Currently, we work on making SODA-POP available in a more conventional language (*i.e.*, Java). The goal is here to use SODA-POP in EMBASSI not only as research prototype

---

[6] Systems with a similar scope as EMBASSI are known to the authors that implement well above 100 interfaces, based on a single structuring mechanism.

[7] The source code of SODA-POP is included in [8].

for experimenting with self-organizing systems and as design paradigm, but also to use it as foundation for the next EMBASSI incarnation.

Also, work on SODA-POP is far from complete. Amongst others, the following aspects remain to be investigated in the future:

Temporal patterns. The definition of SODA-POP currently is more or less elaborate with respect to *decomposing* an event into a set of sub-events that is to be distributed to a set of receivers (spatial decomposition). However, there is currently no comparable mechanism for describing the *aggregation* of several events into one compound event – as is required for a simplified definition of transducers that are doing temporal aggregation. The concept of recombination strategies is just a first step in this direction[8]. Most notably, temporal aggregation could be described by such things as state machines, petri nets, or by parsers.

QoS guarantees. Currently, SODA-POP provides no mechanisms for specifying and verifying QoS properties such as:

Local QoS: *e.g.*, a reply with a certain minimum precision is guaranteed to arrive within a given time interval. Channels provide currently no mechanism for describing QoS guarrantees. The minimum would be that an answer – without a guarantee on its precision – is being made available after a given time. This could be achieved by incorporating strategies such as *successive refinement* into reply recombination.

Global QoS: *e.g.*, the current set of transducers and channels fulfills a certain data-flow topology (*i.e.*, for each required system function, at least one transducer is available). There is currently no mechanism defined for making global statements about a set of channels and transducers. These statements could contain both constraints on the topology of the channel / transducer network as well as constraints on their temporal behavior. Although technologies for specifying *and verifying* such properties exist (*e.g.*, temporal logic, petri nets, process calculi, . . .), it has not yet been investigated, which of these technologies suits best the needs of SODA-POP and how they can be integrated into an essentially *decentralized* system concept.

Concrete channel ontologies. Finally, the definition of concrete channel ontologies for the EMBASSI infrastructure is an important item of future work – after all, the need for transparent and self-organizing service arbitration in EMBASSI has been one of the main motivions for developing SODA-POP. The focus here is currently the $D - A$ channel: how do we automatically select between different A components that all claim to be able to solve a specific user goal detected by a D component?

Acknowledgements. The work underlying this project has been funded by the German Ministry of Education and Research under the grant signature 01 IL 904 G 0. The content of this publication is under sole responsibility of the authors.

---

[8] A recombination strategy exactly produces such a temporal aggregation.

References

1. Bass, L., Little, R., Pellegrino, R., Reed, S., Seacord, S., Sheppard, S., Szezur, M. The ARCH model: Seeheim revisitied. In *Papers presented at the User Interface Developers' Workshop*, Seeheim, Germany, 1991.
2. Clocksin, W., Mellish, S. *Programming in Prolog*. Springer, 1987.
3. Foley, J. D., Van Dam, A. *Fundamentals of interactive computer graphics*. Addison-Wesley, Reading, MA, 1982.
4. Gelernter, D. *Mirror Worlds*. Oxford University Press, New York, 1993.
5. HAVi, Inc. The HAVi Specification – Specification of the Home Audio/Video Interoperability (HAVi) Architecture – Version 1.1. www.havi.org, May 2001.
6. Herfet, T., Kirste, T. EMBASSI – Multimodal Assistance for Infotainment & Service Infrastructures. In *Proc. International Status Conference Lead Projects Human-Computer-Interaction*, pages 35–44, Saarbrücken, Germany, October 26–27 2001. BMBF.
7. Herfet, T., Kirste, T., Schnaider, M. EMBASSI: multimodal assistance for infotainment and service infrastructures. *Computers & Graphics*, 25(4):581–592, 2001.
8. Kirste, T. A communication model for data-flow based distributed agent systems. Technical Report 01i0011-FIGDR, Fraunhofer IGD Rostock, December 2001.
9. Kolski, C., Le Strugeon, E. A Review of Intelligent Human-Machine Interfaces in the Light of the ARCH Model. *International Journal of Human-Computer Interaction*, 10(3):193–231, 1998.
10. Martin, D. L., Cheyer, A. J., Moran, D. B. The Open Agent Architecture: a framework for building distributed software systems. *Applied Artificial Intelligence*, 13(1/2):91–128, 1999.
11. MITRE corporation. Galaxy communicator.
    http://communicator.sourceforge.net/, 2001.
12. Peyton Jones, S., Hughes, J. et al. Haskell 98: A Non-strict, Purely Functional Language. www.haskell.org, February 1999.
13. Schwartz, D. G. *Cooperating Heterogeneous Systems*. Kluwer Academic Publishers, Dordrecht, 1995.
14. Seneff, S., Hurley, E., Lau, R., Pao, C., Schmid, P., Zue, V. Galaxy-II: A Reference Architecture for Conversational System Development. In *ICSLP 98*, Sydney, Australia, November 1998.
15. Smith, D., Frank, J., Jonsson, A. Bridging the Gap Between Planning and Scheduling. *Knowledge Engineering Review*, 15(1), 2000.
16. SRI International AI Center. The Open Agent Architecture.
    http://www.ai.sri.com/~oaa/, 2000.
17. Sun Microsystems, Inc. Jini Technology Core Platform Specification – Version 1.1. www.jini.org, October 2000.
18. Turner, D. Miranda: a non-strict functional language with polymorphic types. In *Functional Programming Languages and Computer Architecture*, volume 201 of *Lecture Notes in Computer Science*, pages 1–16. Springer-Verlag, Nancy, France, September 1985.

Author Index

Lecture Notes in Computer Science

For information about Vols. 1–2465

please contact your bookseller or Springer-Verlag